An Introductory Guide to
POST-STRUCTURALISM
AND
POSTMODERNISM

Second edition

Madan Sarup

HARVESTER
WHEATSHEAF

New York   London   Toronto   Sydney   Tokyo   Singapore

First published 1993 by
Harvester Wheatsheaf
Campus 400, Maylands Avenue
Hemel Hempstead
Hertfordshire, HP2 7EZ
A division of
Simon & Schuster International Group

Typeset in 10/12pt Ehrhardt
by Hands Fotoset, Leicester

Printed and bound in Great Britain by
Biddles Ltd, Guildford and King's Lynn

British Library Cataloguing in Publication Data

A catalogue record for this book is available from
the British Library

ISBN 0-7450-1360-0

3   4   5   96   95   94

For Sita in reparation

□

Contents

□

Preface to the
second edition

I accept postmodernism as a useful term designating a profound mutation in recent thought and experience. If certain changes are taking place I want to know about them. I want to know what the symptoms are and what the consequences may be. You may feel the same. I hope that the second edition of this book will be helpful in understanding some of the more recent debates and controversies about postmodernism.

A book like this is never really finished. I have tried to improve it by making several major additions:

- I have added some feminist criticisms to my accounts of the work of Lacan and Foucault.
- There is also a new chapter on French feminist theory (Chapter 5) which focuses on the work of Hélène Cixous, Luce Irigaray and Julia Kristeva.
- The chapter on postmodernism (now Chapter 6) has been greatly expanded. There is a new introductory section which discusses the meaning of a cluster of concepts: moaernity, postmodernity, modernization, modernism and postmodernism.
- I have also enlarged the section on Lyotard so that there is a discussion of language games and of his use of the category 'sublime'.
- The chapter ends with a new section, a discussion of the relationship between feminism and postmodernism.
- A substantial chapter has been written on the work of Jean Baudrillard (Chapter 7), a cult figure on the current postmodernist scene whose ideas have attained a wide currency.
- Finally, there is a new section on some postmodern cultural practices: architecture, art, TV, video and film.

□

Acknowledgements

My students wanted a short, accessible account that made links between the many discourses – philosophy, psychoanalysis, literature, the social sciences, politics, art – that are usually taught in isolation. I would like to thank them for encouraging me to write this textbook. I have drawn on the work of many people – all writing is intertextual – and they are acknowledged in the Notes. For intellectual stimulus and emotional support I would like to thank Elza Adamowicz, John Colbeck, Peter Dunwoodie, Eileen Jebb, Anne Kampendonk, Paul Maltby, Tasneem Raja and many others. I am particularly grateful to Bernard Burgoyne and Peter Dews, from whom I have learnt so much.

□

Introduction

During the last thirty years or so the structuralists and post-structuralists have made some very important contributions to human understanding. Lévi-Strauss, Lacan, Derrida, Foucault, Deleuze, Lyotard have produced an impressive body of work. Though structuralism and post-structuralism are very different – the latter theory, for example, does not use structural linguistics in its work – there are some similarities: both approaches make critiques.

Firstly, there is a *critique of the human subject*. The term 'subject' refers to something quite different from the more familiar term 'individual'. The latter term dates from the Renaissance and presupposes that man is a free, intellectual agent and that thinking processes are not coerced by historical or cultural circumstances. This view of Reason is expressed in Descartes's philosophical work. Consider this phrase: 'I think, therefore I am.' Descartes's 'I' assumes itself to be fully conscious, and hence self-knowable. It is not only autonomous but coherent; the notion of another psychic territory, in contradiction to consciousness, is unimaginable. In his work Descartes offers us a narrator who imagines that he speaks without simultaneously being spoken.

Lévi-Strauss, a leading structuralist, called the human subject – the centre of being – the 'spoilt brat of philosophy'. He stated that the ultimate goal of the human sciences is not to constitute man but to dissolve him. This became the slogan of structuralism. The leading philosopher of the Left, Louis Althusser, reacting against Sartrean voluntarism, dissolved the subject by reinterpreting Marxism as a theoretical anti-humanism.[1]

The advance of structuralism, far from being deflected or halted by the new reading of Marxism, was accelerated by it. After the events of 1968 Althusser tried to adjust his theory but, on the whole, he did not develop his work. The consequence was the gradual effacement and dissolution of Althusserian Marxism by the mid-1970s.

Post-structuralists, like Foucault, want to deconstruct the conceptions by means of which we have so far understood the human. The term 'subject' helps us to conceive of human reality as a construction, as a product of signifying activities which are both culturally specific and generally unconscious. The category of the subject calls into question the notion of the self synonymous with consciousness; it 'decentres' consciousness.

The post-structuralists, then, also want to dissolve the subject; in a sense it could be said that Derrida and Foucault do not have a 'theory' of the subject. The exception is Lacan, who is committed to the subject because of his Hegelian philosophical formation and his commitment to psychoanalysis. What most of these theorists do not understand is that structure and subject are interdependent categories. The notion of a stable structure really depends on a subject distinct from it. One can see that a wholesale attack on the subject was in due course bound to subvert the notion of structure as well.

Secondly, both structuralism and post-structuralism make a *critique of historicism*. They have an antipathy to the notion that there is an overall pattern in history. A famous example is Lévi-Strauss's criticism of Sartre in *The Savage Mind*, in which he attacks Sartre's view of historical materialism and his assumption that present-day society is superior to past cultures.[2] He then goes on to say that Sartre's historicist view of history is not a valid cognitive enterprise. We will see in later discussions that Foucault writes about history without having the notion of progress, and that Derrida says there is no end point in history.

Thirdly, there is a *critique of meaning*. While philosophy in Britain was heavily influenced by theories of language during the early years of this century (I am thinking of the work of Wittgenstein, Ayer and others), this was not the case in France. It could be said that, in a way, structuralism is the delayed entry of language in French philosophy. It may be remembered that Saussure emphasized the distinction between the signifier and the signified. The sound image made by the word 'apple' is the signifier, and the *concept* of an apple is the signified. The structural relationship between the signifier and the signified constitutes a linguistic sign, and language is made up of these. The linguistic sign is arbitrary; this means that it stands for something by convention and common usage, not by necessity. Saussure also stressed the point that each signifier acquired its semantic value only by virtue of its differential position within the structure of language.[3] In this conception of the sign there is a precarious balance between signifier and signified.

In post-structuralism, broadly speaking, the signified is demoted and the signifier made dominant. This means there is no one-to-one correspondence between propositions and reality. Lacan, for example, writes of 'the incessant sliding of the signified under the signifier'.[4] The post-structuralist philosopher Derrida goes further; he believes in a system of floating signifiers pure and simple, with no determinable relation to any extra-linguistic referents at all.[5]

Fourthly, there is a *critique of philosophy*. In his early work Althusser wrote of 'theoretical' practice and argued that Marxist philosophy was a science.[6] He made a clear distinction between the young Marx, who wrote within a Hegelian, ideological problematic, and the older Marx who, with his understanding of economic concepts and processes, was a great scientist. It should be noted that when the structuralists moved language into the centre of French thought this was done in an anti-philosophical way – an approach similar to that taken earlier by Comte and Durkheim.

Having outlined some of the similarities, the continuities, between structuralism and post-structuralism, I want to mention some of the characteristic features of post-structuralism. While structuralism sees truth as being 'behind' or 'within' a text, post-structuralism stresses the interaction of reader and text as a productivity. In other words, reading has lost its status as a passive consumption of a product to become performance. Post-structuralism is highly critical of the unity of the stable sign (the Saussurian view). The new movement implies a shift from the signified to the signifier: and so there is a perpetual detour on the way to a truth that has lost any status or finality. Post-structuralists have produced critiques of the classical Cartesian conception of the unitary subject – the subject/author as originating consciousness, authority for meaning and truth. It is argued that the human subject does not have a unified consciousness but is structured by language. Post-structuralism, in short, involves a critique of metaphysics, of the concepts of causality, of identity, of the subject, and of truth. All this may seem difficult and abstract at the moment, but these issues will be clarified in the chapters that follow.

There is more continuity between structuralism and post-structuralism than between structuralism and phenomenology. But there are many

surprises and contradictions. Lacan, a Freudian psychoanalyst, has
studied Husserl and Heidegger deeply. Foucault's historical studies are
based on philosophical assumptions drawn from Nietzsche.

The first half of this text is an introduction to the differing theories,
the rival programmes, of the leading post-structuralists: Jacques Lacan,
Jacques Derrida and Michel Foucault. These thinkers share a
characteristic philosophical position which is incompatible with the
concept of structure but is also quite radically anti-scientific. They
question the status of science itself, and the possibility of the objectivity
of any language of description or analysis. They reject the assumptions
implicit in the Saussurian model of linguistics on which structuralism
was based. The topics explored in Chapters 1, 2 and 3 include:
psychoanalysis, the nature and role of language, the self and desire,
deconstruction, the rise of instrumental reason, the expansion of
apparatuses of social control, and the interconnections between
knowledge and power.

In Chapter 4 I examine the work of the 'younger generation' of post-
structuralists, such as Gilles Deleuze and Felix Guattari, Jean-François
Lyotard, and others (the 'new philosophers'), and argue that many of the
characteristic beliefs of post-structuralists have their roots in Nietzsche's
thought. Chapter 5 is an introduction to three French feminist thinkers,
Hélène Cixous, Luce Irigaray and Julia Kristeva. They have been
influenced, in different ways, by Lacanian psychoanalysis. They all have
important things to say about knowledge, subjectivity, language,
'feminine' writing, and the possibilities of social and subjective
transformation. Chapter 6 explores Lyotard's thesis concerning the
changing nature of knowledge in computerized societies – of what he
calls the 'postmodern condition'. Chapter 7 discusses the provocative
writings of Jean Baudrillard from his early Marxist writings to his
current postmodernist texts. It deals with topics such as consumption,
mass media, communications, and the main features of contemporary
culture. The chapter ends with a consideration of a number of cultural
practices: the role of postmodernist ideas in architecture, painting, TV,
video and film. The Conclusion consists of a discussion of the current
controversies about postmodernism and its critique of the Enlightenment project.

Chapter I

□

Lacan and psychoanalysis

Introduction

It could be said that the Marxist dialogue with psychoanalysis began in 1963 when Louis Althusser, the leading communist philosopher in France, invited Jacques Lacan to hold his seminars at the École Normale.[1] During this period there must have been considerable interdisciplinary activity; at any rate, a year later Althusser published the famous article 'Freud and Lacan'.[2] He argued that both Marx and Freud invented new sciences. Each discovered a new object of knowledge. They both defined a new way of knowing about the social, but, not surprisingly, they were weighed down by the cultural baggage of their time. Freud 'thought' his discovery in concepts borrowed from biology, mechanics and the psychology of his day. Marx thought his discovery using Hegelian notions of the subject. It is fascinating to read how Althusser sees Lacan as being involved in a similar project to his own. Just as he, Althusser, is trying to rethink Marxism without any reference to Hegel's absolute subject, he sees Lacan as trying to think psychoanalysis without any reference to a unified conception of self or ego.

A few years later, during the May '68 uprising, it was felt by many students and workers that a liberated politics could only emerge from liberated interpersonal relationships, and there was an explosion of interest in Lacanian psychoanalysis – a movement which seemed to reconcile existentialism and Marxism. A part of existentialism's popular appeal may have been that it provided a way to think through the issues of choice and individual responsibility. But as a theory of the self existentialism remained within Cartesianism. Its psychology tended to portray the individual as a rational, conscious actor who could understand the basis for his or her action. It remained firmly rooted in a philosophy of individual autonomy and rational choice.

At the time of the May '68 events people were very concerned with questions of self-expression, desire and sexuality, and Lacan's theory offered a way of thinking about the social and the linguistic construction of the self, of thinking through the problem of *the individual and society*. For Lacan there is no separation between self and society. Human beings become social with the appropriation of language; and it is language that constitutes us as a subject. Thus, we should not dichotomize the individual and society. Society inhabits each individual.

It is often said that Lacan wants to be understood only by those who want to make an effort. I think we should make the effort. Lacan's writing, which exemplifies his views about language, is very allusive. His language fuses the theoretical and the poetic. His associative style is intended to slow the reader down. His text is not there to convince, but to do something to you. He relies heavily on punning and word games, and he uses symbols, signs, etc., to express himself without referring to ordinary language. He wants to resist the over-simplification of much psychoanalytic writing. He also wants to subvert the normalization that everyday language imposes.

I believe that Lacan's unique achievement was that he fused phenomenology and structuralism. His early work coincided with the growth of French phenomenology and he was influenced by the thought of Hegel and Heidegger. Structuralism offered Lacan a way of talking about *systems* of interpretation. His work is fascinating in that it keeps sliding between phenomenology and structuralism. Phenomenology stresses the free self (the subject); structuralism emphasizes language determinism. Lacan uses structuralism but never rejects the subject.

Lacan also belongs, in part, to the hermeneutic tradition, which states that social phenomena always have meaning and that the task of the social sciences is not to explain (as traditional psychiatry seeks to do) but to understand. Psychoanalysis is a method of interpretation. However, Lacan is aware that in the act of interpretation we often impose our own assumptions.

His doctoral thesis 'On Paranoid Psychosis and its Relation to the Personality' is very interesting because he wrote it before Saussure's work on structuralist linguistics was available.[3] At that time he had not yet become a psychoanalyst; he was still a psychiatrist. What is revealing is the angle from which he approaches Freud and the way in which he repudiates physiological reductionism.

One of the main features of Lacan's work is that it is implacably anti-biological. The accepted view in the 1930s, for example, was that madness had organic causes. Lacan argues that organicist accounts cannot explain madness. Madness is a discourse, an attempt at communication, that must be interpreted. We have to understand rather than give causal explanations. He emphasizes that the personality is not 'the mind' but the whole being. We cannot separate a person's psychology from his or her personal history.

When Lacan became a psychoanalyst he made a few tentative criticisms of Freud. The main one was that Freud made a number of biologistic assumptions. Lacan's view is that biology is always interpreted by the human subject, refracted through language; that there is no such thing as 'the body' before language. It could be said that by shifting all descriptions from a biological-anatomic level to a symbolic one he shows how culture imposes meaning on anatomical parts.

Lacan denigrates not only behaviourist psychologists such as Pavlov and Skinner but also (American) ego psychologists such as Fromm and Horney. The latter stress the adaptation of the individual to the social environment. Lacan argues that they have watered down and sweetened Freud's ideas about the unconscious and infant sexuality.[4] Ego psychology asserts that 'self-improvement' is possible without calling society into question.

Lacan often asserts that he is returning to Freud, but this should not be taken too literally. He retains the main concepts but juggles with them to create a new system of thought. A subtle thinker, he offers us a rigorous reformulation of Freud. He is looking for objectivity, but not the objectivity of natural science. He is very interested in mathematical logic *and* poetry, and in his own writing tries to fuse them. His theory of language is such that he could not return to Freud: texts cannot have an unambiguous, pristine meaning. In his view, analysts must relate directly with the unconscious and this means that they must be practitioners of the language of the unconscious – that of poetry, puns, internal rhymes. In word play causal links dissolve and associations abound.

Overview

Lacan's psychoanalytic theory is partly based upon the discoveries of structural anthropology and linguistics. One of his main beliefs is that the unconscious is a hidden structure which resembles that of language. Knowledge of the world, of others and of self is determined by language. Language is the precondition for the act of becoming aware of oneself as a distinct entity. It is the I–Thou dialectic, defining the subjects by their mutual opposition, which founds subjectivity. But language is also the vehicle of a social given, a culture, prohibitions and laws. The young child is fashioned and will be indelibly marked by it without being aware of it. Let us look at some of the main stages in Lacan's theory.

In *Beyond the Pleasure Principle* Freud describes a child's game.[5] The child had a cotton reel with a piece of string tied to it. Holding the string he would throw the reel over the edge of his cot and utter sounds that Freud interpreted as being an attempt at the German '*fort*', meaning 'gone' or 'away'. He would then pull the reel back into his field of vision, greeting its reappearance with a joyful '*da*' ('there'). This game allowed the eighteen-month-old child to bear without protest the painful experience of his mother's absence, to cope with her disappearance and reappearance. It illustrates the birth of language in its autonomy from reality and allows a better understanding of how language distances us from the lived experience of the real. The distancing from the lived experience is effected in two stages: the child moves from the mother to the reel and finally to language.

The first articulation of the 'I' occurs in what Lacan calls the mirror stage. Lacan often refers to the mirror stage as it prefigures the whole dialectic between alienation and subjectivity.[6] Self-recognition in the mirror is effected (somewhere between the ages of six and eighteen months) in three successive stages. At first, the child who is together with an adult in front of a mirror confuses its own reflection with that of its adult companion. In the second phase the child acquires the notion of the image and understands that the reflection is not a real being. Finally, in the third stage, it realizes not only that the reflection is an image, but that the image is its own and is different from the image of the Other.

Lacan sees, in a way similar to Lévi-Strauss, the Oedipus complex as the pivot of humanization, as a transition from the natural register of life to a cultural register of group exchange and therefore of laws, language and organization. Lacan contends that at first the child does not merely desire contact with the mother and her care; it wishes, perhaps unconsciously, to be the complement of what is lacking in her: the phallus. At this stage the child is not a subject but a 'lack', a nothing.

In the second stage the father intervenes; he deprives the child of the object of its desire and he deprives the mother of the phallic object. The child encounters the Law of the father. The third stage is that of identification with the father. The father reinstates the phallus as the object of the mother's desire and no longer as the child-complement to what is lacking in her. There is, then, a symbolic castration: the father castrates the child by separating it from its mother. This is the debt which must be paid if one is to become completely one's self.

It needs to be stressed that the Oedipus complex for Lacan is not a stage like any other in genetic psychology: it is the moment in which the child humanizes itself by becoming aware of the self, the world and others. The resolution of the Oedipus complex liberates the subject by giving him, with his Name, a place in the family constellation, an original signifier of self and subjectivity. It promotes him in his realization of self through participation in the world of culture, language and civilization.[7]

As I mentioned earlier, Lacan has rethought Freud in the wider framework provided by linguistics and structural anthropology. In his view the unconscious shows itself in dreams, jokes, slips of the tongue, symptoms. The unconscious is comparable in structure to a language. In fact, Lacan argues that language is the condition for the unconscious, that it creates and gives rise to the unconscious. Like conscious discourse, the formations of the unconscious (dreams, etc.) are saying something quite different from what they appear to say. These formations are governed by the same mechanisms as language, namely metaphor and metonymy. At certain privileged points, such as in slips of the tongue and in some jokes, language seems to be torn apart. Conscious discourse is rather like those manuscripts where a first text has been rubbed out and covered by a second. In such manuscripts the first text can be glimpsed through the gaps in the second. The true speech – the unconscious – breaks through usually in a veiled and incomprehensible form.

Lacan suggests that, thanks to human beings' metaphoric ability, words convey multiple meanings and we use them to signify something quite different from their concrete meaning. This possibility of signifying something other than what is being said determines language's autonomy from meaning. Lacan insists on the autonomy of the signifier. He assimilates the metaphoric and metonymic processes of language to condensation and displacement respectively.[8] All the formations of the unconscious use these stylistic devices to outwit censorship.

Throughout his work Lacan strives to denounce the common illusion which identifies the ego with the self. In contrast to those who say

'I think, therefore I am' Lacan asserts: 'I think where I am not, therefore I am where I do not think.'[9] Or, 'I think where I cannot say that I am.'

Having provided a general introduction to Lacan's theory, I will now focus on some important aspects of his work: the relation between self and language; problems of self and identity; the main theoretical differences between Lacan and Freud; the influence on Lacan of Hegel; the meaning of need, demand and desire; the sense of loss.

Self and language

Lacan's theory cannot be presented coherently without a discussion of the function of language. He has a complete theory of language, which he links with subjectivity. He believes that there could not be a human subject without language but that the subject cannot be reduced to language. This is a circular (and not a reciprocal) relationship in which language has privilege. Lacan writes (in 'The Mirror Stage') that it is the ability to speak that distinguishes the subject. It is this feature that separates the social from the natural world. *There is no subject independent of language.* Lacan is highly critical of those encounter-therapy groups that tend to deny the role of verbal language and imply that the body and its gestures are more direct.

While Saussure implied that we can somehow stand outside language, Lacan insists that we are all immersed in everyday language and cannot get out of it. There is no such thing as metalanguage. We all have to represent ourselves in language. Indeed our only access to others is through language. (According to Lacan a psychotic person is someone who has not learnt what language is.)[10]

Saussure regarded the relationship between signifiers and signified as stable and predictable. He argued for the possibility of anchoring particular signifiers to particular signifieds in order to form linguistic signs. In Lacan's view, on the other hand, meaning emerges only through discourse, as a consequence of displacements along a signifying chain. Like Derrida, Lacan insists upon the commutability of the signified, upon the capacity of every signified to function in turn as a signifier. A consequence of the non-representational status of language is, of course, that the signified is always provisional.

In a Lacanian view of language a signifier always signifies another signifier; no word is free from metaphoricity (a metaphor is one signifier in the place of another). Lacan talks of *glissement* (slippage, slide) along the signifying chain, from signifier to signifier. Since any signifier can receive signification retrospectively, after the fact, no signification is ever closed, ever satisfied.[11] Each word is only definable in terms of other words. Moreover, each word uttered only makes complete sense when the sentence is finished; and it is perhaps only the very last word uttered which retrospectively establishes the full sense of each word that came before. From anything that is said it cannot be predicted what is going to be said. Any 'sentence' can always be added to. No sentence is ever completely saturated. There is no natural link between signifier and signified. In repression, for example, one signifier comes to substitute for another. The old signifier and what it signifies is 'pushed down' to the unconscious. In the course of a lifetime the individual builds up many chains of signification, always substituting new terms for old and always increasing the distance between the signifier that is accessible and visible and all those that are unconscious.

It is true that at the end of his life Lacan become interested in the possibility of expressing the laws of the unconscious in terms of mathematical statements called 'mathemes'; some people think that this was because he believed that through the process of formalization we might be able to find out what we *cannot* mathematize.

To illustrate that there is no unequivocal meaning, Lacan relates the following story:

> A train arrives at a station. A little boy and a little girl, brother and sister, are seated in a compartment face to face next to the window through which the buildings along the station platform can be seen passing as the train pulls to a stop. 'Look', says the brother, 'we're at Ladies!'; 'Idiot!' replies his sister, 'Can't you see we're at Gentlemen'.[12]

In this story each child is able to see only one of the rooms; each child sees a one-to-one correspondence between the word and the 'thing' – a way of understanding the relationship between signifier and signified that is totally inadequate. Note that it is the girl who sees 'Gentlemen' and the boy who sees 'Ladies', as if one could only see the sex one is not. Through the biological given of sitting on one side of the compartment or the other each sex is placed in a structure and as such is unable to see that structure. Lacan seems to be saying: we are all sitting on one side of the compartment or the other; we are all subject to the blindness imposed by our seats in the compartment; there is no other way of being on the train(chain).[13]

Self and identity

It should be stressed that Lacan uses the idea of a child before the mirror as a metaphor. The notion of reflection is a common one (especially in German Idealist philosophy), stemming from Hegel. In this philosophy there is a concern with questions such as: What is it to be conscious of oneself? How do we recognize the self? What is that 'something' that reflects consciousness back on to itself? In self-consciousness the subject and the object are identical; but can I reflect on the self and reflect on that reflection? Can the self that is self of consciousness grasp the self of consciousness? When we see ourselves we see only a look. We do not get nearer to what we are. This is called 'the infinity of reflection'.[14]

Another important Lacanian idea is 'the dialectic of recognition'. This refers to the idea that we get knowledge of what we are from how others respond to us. It is useful to compare D.W. Winnicott's discussion of the mirror role with Lacan's view. Winnicott suggests that the first mirror is the mother's face.[15] He argues that other people provide the stability of our self-identity. Some feminists have criticized him because he unquestioningly focuses only on the 'mother' role. (Moreover, what happens if the mother is ill or mentally disturbed and cannot send back an image?)

In contrast with Winnicott, Lacan says that we are never going to get a stable image. We try to interpret our relation to others but there is always the possibility of misinterpretation. There is always a gap, a mis-recognition. We can never be certain of the meaning of the other's response. We have an idea of our identity but it does not correspond with reality; the mirror image is back to front.

Our notion of the self as an isolated self is in some way connected with bourgeois individualism. (Lacan hints, however, that it may always be like this.) Lacan continually attacks the American psychologists (Erich Fromm and Karen Horney again) who keep stressing the ego. In his view the stable ego is illusory. We can shed the illusions of the ego only asymptotically (in geometry an asymptote is a curve approaching a straight line but never reaching it short of infinity).[16]

Lacan insists that we do not have a fixed set of characteristics. This is very much the view Sartre expressed in *Being and Nothingness*.[17] In Sartre's theory consciousness can never grasp itself. Reflection always turns the subject into an object. Sartre rejects the idea that drives determine consciousness. He suggests that as soon as we say, 'I'm like that – that's me', we have made ourselves into an object. We often build up a set of characteristics retrospectively. Sartre insists that we are more than a fixed set of categories. We should not think of ourselves as merely a set of characterizations. Nor should we go to the other extreme and conceive of ourselves as pure nothingness.

Lacan argues that we are never any one of our attributes. There is no truth if by truth is meant that an individual expresses an inherent characteristic. Sceptical of any 'underlying truth', he writes: 'If Freud had brought to man's knowledge nothing more than the truth that there is such a thing as the true, there would be no Freudian discovery. Freud would belong to a line of moralists . . . .'[18]

Lacan stresses the point that there is no subject except in representation, but that no representation captures us completely. I can neither be totally defined nor can I escape all definition. I am the quest for myself. Lacan believes that how we present ourselves is always subject to interpretation by others. On the other hand, any attempt to 'totalize' someone else, to grasp the other completely, is bound to fall short – no description does the other justice. Moreover, one can only see oneself as one *thinks* others see one.

There is an inherent tension, a feeling of threat, because one's identity depends on recognition by the other. This is the theme of Hegel's story of Master and Slave. I will give a detailed exposition of it later in the chapter. For the moment it is only necessary to say that Hegel argued that consciousness cannot grasp itself without recognition by others. The Master demands recognition from the Slave but this is a self-defeating process. He feels threatened because recognition of himself depends exclusively on the Slave. To generalize from the story, we would like to reduce others to an instrument – a mirror. There is a moment of aggression when we want to overcome our dependency. (We often hear people say: 'I've got to insist on my independence.')

But is there a possibility of mutual recognition? Lacan suggests that intersubjectivity can never be fully attained because we can never enter another person's consciousness completely. Full mutual recognition is not possible partly because of the ambiguity of signifiers. There is a gulf between saying and meaning. All this is reminiscent of Sartre, who says that when we love another we want that person's love – and this attitude instrumentalizes love. As soon as one person is the subject, the other is the object. Lacan belongs to the tradition that believes that the subject and the object are irreconcilably divided. Undoubtedly he has an ontology: we all have a need for wholeness, a longing for the state of unity, but the achievement of plenitude is a logical impossibility.

Freud and Lacan

There are many differences between Freud and Lacan and in this section I will discuss some of them. I will focus particularly on their different conceptualizations of the ego, the unconscious, the dream, and the Oedipus complex.

In Freud's early work the ego is connected with the reality principle, and the unconscious is related to the pleasure principle. Later Freud reformulated his theory: the ego is formed through an identification with parental figures. The important point to note is that Freud never says the ego is illusory.

Lacan's argument is the opposite of this. He believes that identification stabilizes the individual but at the same time takes us away from ourselves. He says that Freud starts from individuals' drives and their satisfactions and that he neglects social dimensions. For Lacan, however, the subject-to-subject relation, what we call intersubjectivity, is there right from the beginning.

Freud believed that the aim of analysis was to integrate a drive into 'the harmony of the ego'. Lacan, of course, would never use such a phrase. While for Freud the unconscious has a threatening aspect, in Lacan it is the locus of 'truth', of authenticity. And yet Lacan believes that the unconscious cannot be an object of knowledge; the ego projects itself and then fails to recognize itself. Self-knowledge, the notion that the self can reflect on itself, is not possible.

While Freud seems to have believed in the unconscious as a substantive concept, for Lacan 'the unconscious is not the real place of another discourse'. Lacan proclaims that the unconscious is neither primordial nor instinctual. The unconscious is implicit in everything we say and do. However, in trying to grasp the unconscious we lose it – like 'twice-lost Eurydice'. The unconscious is that which we can never know, but this does not mean that the effort is not worth while.

Two processes are of central importance in Freudian theory: the primary process, which is associated with the unconscious (irrational thought), and the secondary process, which is associated with the conscious (logical thought).[19] When the object of satisfaction is denied and life is difficult we often retreat from reality and overcome frustration by hallucinating. But after a certain time, in order for us to survive, the reality principle comes into play. The ego intervenes, separates things out and puts a stop to the hallucination. This secondary process is continually being interrupted by the unconscious. Human rationality is a thin, fragile 'façade' which the unconscious keeps bursting asunder. Again, Lacan rejects Freud's view. For him the unconscious is neither primordial nor instinctual; the secondary process is more like the primary process than Freud thought.

It is in the dream that we can see the operation of the primary process. As Freud said, it is the dream that is 'the royal road to the unconscious'. For Lacan a dream is not a pictorial representation; though it happens to be an image *a dream is really a text*:

> The dream is like the parlour-game in which one is supposed to get the spectators to guess some well-known saying or variant of it solely by dumb show. That the dream uses speech makes no difference since for the unconscious it is only one among several elements of the representation. It is precisely the fact that both the game and the dream run up against a lack of taxematic material for the representation of such logical articulations as causality, contradiction, hypothesis, etc. that proves they are a form of writing rather than of mime.[20]

It is in dreams that the processes of condensation and displacement take place. According to Lacan, in condensation there is a superimposition of the signifiers which metaphor takes as its field. A simple image can thus have different meanings. Displacement, another means used by the unconscious to foil censorship, is associated with metonymy.

Though Lacan believes that the desire of the dream is to communicate, he does not ever say to an analysand 'this is what you really want', or 'this is what your dream really means'. If he did, this would be another alienation. In his view the subject is a process and cannot be defined.

Freud was very interested in the relationship between nature and culture and emphasized the dominance of culture over nature. Lacan rejects the notion of an innate human nature. Nature, for Lacan, is the real which is out there but impossible to grasp in a pure state because it is always mediated through language. In Freud's work one is aware of a tragic element in the nature–culture dichotomy. In Lacan, tragedy lies in the fact that we have a perpetual lack of wholeness.

Freud and Lacan also have different views of the Oedipus complex. In Freud's theory the Oedipus complex must be understood in the context of his theory of psychosexuality. In the first stage of infant sexuality, the oral stage, there are fantasies of incorporating and devouring. The second stage, the anal/sadistic, is associated with submission and domination. In the third, the phallic stage, the boy wants the mother exclusively. He is threatened with castration and develops an impotence fear. There is an introjection of the father's threat which leads, finally, to a resolution of the complex.

Lacan tries to rationalize Freud's thesis by not taking the Oedipus complex literally. Whereas Freud's Oedipal Father might be taken for a real, biological father, Lacan's Name-of-the-Father operates in the register of language. The Name-of-the-Father is the Law. The legal assignation of a father's name to a child is meant to call a halt to uncertainty about the identity of the father.

Lacan does not abandon the idea of the focus on the oral, the anal and the phallic, but he says that these stages are intersubjective. Freud's theory refers to the physical and not the symbolic. In Freud the penis is a guarantee of a possible union with the mother. Lacan transforms all this to the level of the symbolic. This is why he writes not of the penis but of the phallus.[21]

Lacanians, separating the two notions 'penis' and 'phallus', argue that there is no phallus inequity; that is, neither sex can be or have the phallus. The penis is what men have and women do not, the phallus is the attribute of power which neither men nor women have. Lacan suggests that all our fantasies are symbolic representations of the desire for wholeness. We tend to think that if we were the phallus or had the other's phallus we would then, somehow, be whole. In other words, the phallus is the signifier of an original desire for a perfect union with the Other. The phallus refers to plenitude; it is the signifier of the wholeness that we lack.

There is another difference between Freud and Lacan. The former held that rational discourse was possible, even though it was often distorted by unconscious forces. For Lacan discourse *constitutes* the unconscious. Language and desire are related. In Lacan desire is ontological, a struggle for wholeness rather than a sexual force. 'Desire is the metonymy of the desire to want to be.'

While Freud talks of instincts and drives Lacan talks of desire – a concept which comes from Kojève's lectures on Hegel. These lectures are important, as Lacan, Sartre and others were highly influenced by them. Kojève describes the development of self-consciousness. Hegel insists that self-consciousness develops out of the biological self.

Self-consciousness would not be possible without an organic lack. A lack ('I feel hungry') makes us aware of ourselves as a being that needs something. Hegel continues that for a desire to develop in us we need to focus on a specific object. When we desire not a thing but another's desire we become human. Moreover, desire is mobile, not static; a desire can be continually negated, but it continues.

Hegel and Lacan

As what Lacan means by desire is drawn from Hegel, I want to retell in this section Hegel's metaphoric story of the Master and the Slave before I try to elucidate the Lacanian concepts of need, demand and desire.[22] What follows may seem a digression, but this 'detour' through Hegel is necessary because the Master/Slave theme, in both Marxist and Nietzschean versions, constantly reappears in contemporary social thought.

Hegel remarks that we all know that the person who attentively contemplates a thing is 'absorbed' by this thing and forgets himself. He may perhaps talk about the thing but he will never talk about himself; in his discourse the word 'I' will not occur.

For this word to appear, something other than purely passive contemplation must be present. And this other thing is, according to Hegel, Desire. Indeed, when man experiences a desire, when he is hungry, for example, and becomes aware of it he necessarily becomes aware of himself. Desire is always revealed to the individual as *his* desire, and to express desire he must use the word 'I'.[23]

Desire dis-quiets him and moves him to action. Action tends to satisfy desire but can do so only by the 'negation', the destruction or at least the transformation of the desired object: to satisfy hunger, for example, the food must be destroyed or in any case transformed. Thus, all action is 'negating'. The being that eats creates and preserves its own reality by overcoming a reality other than its own, by the 'transformation' of an alien reality into its own reality, by the 'assimilation', the 'internalization', of an 'external' reality. Generally speaking, the 'I' of Desire is an emptiness that receives a real positive content by a negating action that satisfies Desire in destroying, transforming and assimilating the desired non-I.

Desire, being the revelation of an emptiness, the presence of an absence, is something essentially different from the desired thing.

Desire is directed towards another Desire, another greedy emptiness, another 'I'. Desire is human only if one desires not the body but the Desire of the other; that is to say, if one wants to be 'desired' or, rather, 'recognized' in one's human value. All Desire is desire for a value. To desire the Desire of another is really to desire 'recognition'.

Master and Slave

If there is a multiplicity of desires seeking universal recognition, it is obvious that the action that is born of these desires can – at least in the beginning – be nothing but a life-and-death fight. It is assumed that the fight ends in such a way that both adversaries remain alive. Now, if this is to occur, one must suppose that one of the adversaries, preferring to live rather than die, gives in to the other and submits to him, recognizing him as the Master without being recognized by him. The Master, unable to recognize the other who recognizes him, finds himself in an impasse.

The Master makes the Slave work in order to satisfy his own desires. To satisfy the desires of the Master, the Slave has to repress his own instincts (for example, in the preparation of food that he will not eat), to negate or 'overcome' himself.[24] The Slave transcends himself by working, that is, he educates himself. In his work he transforms things and transforms himself at the same time. In becoming master of Nature by work, the Slave frees himself from Nature, from his own nature, and from the Master. It is because work is an auto-creative act that it can raise him from slavery to freedom. The future and history hence belong not to the warlike Master, but to the working Slave. The Slave changes himself by changing the world.

To summarize, according to Hegel it is a fight to the death for the sake of recognition that leads to a relation between a free man and a man who is enslaved to him. Hence man is necessarily either Master or Slave. But the difference between Master and Slave can be overcome in the course of time. Mastery and Slavery, then, are not given or innate characteristics. Man is not born slave or free but creates himself as one or the other through free or voluntary action. In short, the character of the Master/Slave opposition is the motive principle of the historical process. All of history is nothing but the progressive negation of Slavery by the Slave. Finally, the thesis of Mastery and the antithesis of Slavery are dialectically 'overcome'.

Identity and negativity

Thanks to identity every being remains the same being, eternally identical to itself and different from the others. But thanks to negativity an identical being can negate or overcome its identity with itself and become other than it is, even its own opposite. Identity and negativity do not exist in an isolated state. Just like totality itself they are only complementary aspects of one and the same real being.[25]

The thesis describes the given material to which the action is going to be applied, the antithesis reveals this action itself as well as the thought which animates it ('the project'), while the synthesis shows the result of that action, that is, the completed and objectively real product. The new product is also given and can provoke other negating actions. Human beings are always negating the given. Negativity is the negation of identity. Human beings are truly free or really human only in and by effective negation of the given real. Negativity, then, is nothing other than human freedom. The freedom which is realized and manifested as dialectical or negating action is thereby essentially a creation. What is involved is not replacing one given by another given, but overcoming the given in favour of what does not (yet) exist. In short, man is neither identity nor negativity alone but totality or synthesis; that is, he 'overcomes' himself while preserving and sublimating himself.

In my view this discussion has a direct bearing on education. All education implies a long series of auto-negations effected by the child. As Kojève remarks,

> it is only because of these auto-negations ('repressions') that every 'educated' child is not only a trained animal (which is 'identical' to itself and in itself) but a truly human or 'complex' being; although in most cases, he is human only to a very small extent, since 'education' (that is, auto-negations) generally stops too soon.[26]

Particularity and universality

Particularity refers to the individual agent. Every man, to the extent that he is human, would like – on the one hand – to be different from all others. But on the other hand he would like to be recognized, in his unique particularity itself, as a positive value; and he would like this recognition to be shown by as many people as possible. Universality refers to the social aspect of man's existence. It is only in and by the universal recognition of human particularity that individuality realizes and manifests itself.

Individuality is a synthesis of the particular and the universal, the universal being the negation or the antithesis of the particular, which is the thetical given, identical to itself. In other words, individuality is a totality and the being which is individual is, by the very fact, dialectical. Man is and exists only to the extent that he overcomes himself dialectically (i.e. while preserving and sublimating himself). The opposition of particularity and universality is fundamental for Hegel. In his view history will develop by the formation of a society, of a state, in which the strictly particular, personal, individual value of each is recognized as such, in its very particularity, by all. The synthesis of particularity and universality is possible only after the 'overcoming' of the opposition between the Master and the Slave, since the synthesis of the particular and the universal is also the synthesis of Mastery and Slavery.[27]

The desire for desire

What use does Lacan make of these Hegelian insights? We all have physical needs to satisfy. The child in the oral phase, for example, wants the mother's breast. It makes an appeal to its mother to have its needs met. This is the transformation from need to demand, but there is also the desire for love, for recognition. Needs, then, are biological. In demand the biological is mediated; a demand is always specific. Desire is what cannot be specified by demand.[28] A child cries. The mother gives a bar of chocolate; but the child can never know whether this action was performed for the satisfaction of its need or as an act of love. Lacan believes that such a response is inherently ambiguous. And because the response is ambiguous the demand is repeated, repeated . . . *ad infinitum*.

Need, demand, desire – how are these three categories interconnected? A child cries. It can use physical hunger as a vehicle for a communication. Sometimes the food satisfies a physical need but it can also become symbolically freighted. There can be a split between need and desire. In an account of anorexia Lacan states how a young woman is given food but wants love. The meaning of demand is not intrinsic but is partly determined by the response by the other to the demand. Though our demand is specific we can never be certain of other people's responses to ourselves. After all, how do you give love?

People can continually be making a demand but they need not to be conscious of it. A demand is the means of revealing desire, but it is oblique. Desire is desire for the Other but it has to be interpreted. Lacan says that need is cancelled by demand which re-emerges on the other side of desire. We often want an object that could be given only to *us*, but there is no such object. A demand is for a response, but that response is never particular enough. We can never be certain that others love us for our unique particularity.

It could be said that some people are too confident that they are loved. Lacan suggests that their identities may become rather rigid. And there are other people who lack confidence. Desire emerges when satisfaction of need is not enough, when there is a doubt or gap which cannot be closed. Desire arises out of the lack of satisfaction and it pushes you to another demand. In other words, it is the disappointment of demand that is the basis of the growth of desire.

The sense of loss

In this section I will retell Lacan's story and will focus specifically on the sense of loss or lack that the subject undergoes. You will have noticed that Lacan's theory of the subject reads like a classic narrative; it begins with birth and then moves in turn through the territorialization of the body, the mirror stage, access to language and the Oedipus complex. Each of the stages of this narrative is conceived in terms of some kind of self-loss or lack.

Lacan situates the first loss in the history of the subject at the moment of birth. To be more precise, he dates it from the moment of sexual differentiation within the womb; but it is not realized until the separation of the child from the mother at birth. This lack is sexual in definition and has to do with the impossibility of being physiologically both male and female. The notion of an original androgynous whole is central to Lacan's argument. The subject is defined as lacking because it is believed to be a fragment of something larger and primordial.

Let me clarify this briefly. Lacan often makes references to a fable on the subject of love in Plato's *Symposium*.[29] Aristophanes speaks of beings that, 'once upon a time', were globular in shape, with rounded back and sides, four arms and legs and two faces. Strong, energetic and arrogant, they tried to scale the heights of heaven and set upon the gods. Zeus retaliated by cutting them all in half so that each one would be only half as strong.

Now, when the work of bisection was complete it left each half with a desperate yearning for the other and they ran together and flung their arms around each other's necks and asked for nothing better than to be rolled into one. So much so that they began to die. Zeus felt so sorry for them that he devised another scheme. He moved their genitals round to the front and made them propagate among themselves. So you see how far back we can trace our innate love for one another, and how this love is always trying to reintegrate our former nature, to make two into one and to bridge the gulf between one human being and another.

The second loss suffered by the subject occurs after birth but prior to the acquisition of language. The loss in question is inflicted by what might be called the 'pre-Oedipal territorialization' of the subject's body. For a time after its birth the child does not differentiate between itself and the mother upon whose nurture it relies. Then the child's body undergoes a process of differentiation; erotogenic zones are inscribed and the libido is encouraged to follow certain established routes. By indicating the channels through which that libido can move the mother or nurse assists in the conversion of incoherent energy into coherent drives which can later be culturally regulated. The drives possess a coherence which needs do not have, because they are attached to particular corporal zones. As a result of this attachment the drives provide only an indirect expression of the original libidinal flow. Thus very early in its history the subject loses unmediated contact with its own libidinal flows and succumbs to the domination of its culture's genital economy.

'Imaginary' is the term used by Lacan to designate that order of the subject's experience which is dominated by identification and duality. Within the Lacanian scheme it not only precedes the symbolic order, which introduces the subject to language and Oedipal triangulation, but continues to coexist with it afterwards. The imaginary order is best exemplified by the mirror stage.

Lacan tells us that somewhere between the ages of six and eighteen months the subject arrives at an apprehension of both its self and the Other – indeed of itself as Other. This discovery is assisted by the child seeing, for the first time, its own reflection in a mirror. That reflection has a coherence which the subject itself lacks. But this self-recognition is, Lacan insists, a mis-recognition. The mirror stage is a moment of alienation, since to know oneself through an external image is to be defined through self-alienation. The subject, then, has a profoundly ambivalent relationship to that reflection. It loves the coherent identity which the mirror provides. However, because the image remains external to it, it also hates that image. The subject experiences many radical oscillations between contrary emotions.

Lacan believes that once the subject has entered the symbolic order (language) its organic needs pass through the 'defiles' or narrow network of signification and are transformed in a way which makes them thereafter impossible to satisfy. The drives offer only a partial and indirect expression of those needs, but language severs the relationship altogether.

The *fort/da* game can be seen as the child's first signifying chain and hence its entry into language. It should be noted that whereas Freud describes the child's actions in the *fort/da* game as an attempt to diminish the unpleasure caused by his mother's absences, Lacan stresses instead the self-alienation which those actions dramatize. Lacan identifies the toy reel with which the child plays as an *objet petit autre* – that thing the loss of which has resulted in a sense of deficiency or lack. The breast, for example, certainly represents that part of himself that the individual loses at birth and which may serve to symbolize the most profound lost object. (Other objects which enjoy the same privileged status as the breast include the gaze and voice of the mother.) Lacan thus interprets the story as being more about the disappearance of the self than that of the mother. Like Freud Lacan reads the *fort/da* episode as an allegory about the linguistic mastery of the drives. Lacan describes this complete rupture with the drives as the 'fading' of the subject's being, as 'aphanisis'. Not only is the subject thereby split off or partitioned from its own drives, but it is subordinated to a symbolic order which will henceforth determine its identity and desires.

The formation of the unconscious, the emergence of the subject into the symbolic order and the inauguration of desire are all closely connected events. Desire is directed towards ideal representations which remain forever beyond the subject's reach. Since others will be loved only if they are believed to be capable of completing the subject, desire must be understood as fundamentally narcissistic. Object love is nothing more than the continued search for the lost complement.

Lacan conceptualizes the Oedipus complex as a linguistic transaction. He supports this claim by pointing out that the incest taboo can only be articulated through the differentiation of certain cultural members from others by means of linguistic categories like 'father' and 'mother'. Lacan defines the paternal signifier, what he calls the 'Name-of-the-Father', as the all-important one in both the history of the subject and the organization of the larger symbolic field.

This means that Lacan gives us a very different account of sexual difference from that provided by Freud, one in which the privileged term is no longer 'penis' but 'phallus'. The word 'phallus' is used by Lacan to refer to all of those values which are opposed to lack. He is at pains to emphasize its discursive (rather than its anatomical) status, but it seems to have two radically different meanings. On the one hand, the phallus is a signifier for those things which have been partitioned off from the subject during the various stages of its constitution and which will never be restored to it. The phallus is a signifier for the organic reality or needs which the subject relinquishes in order to achieve meaning, in order to gain access to the symbolic register. It signifies that thing whose loss inaugurates desire. On the other hand, the phallus is a signifier for the cultural privileges and positive values which define male subjectivity within patriarchal society but from which the female subject remains isolated. The phallus, in other words, is a signifier both for those things which are lost during the male subject's entry into culture and for those things which are gained.

Lacan believes that the discourse within which the subject finds its identity is always the discourse of the Other – of a symbolic order which transcends the subject and which orchestrates its entire history. An important part is played by sexual difference within that order, and this has made us aware of the phallocentricity of our current practices.

One Lacanian tenet is that subjectivity is entirely relational; it only comes into play through the principle of difference, by the opposition of the 'other' or the 'you' to the 'I'. In other words, subjectivity is not an essence but a set of relationships. It can only be induced by the activation of a signifying system which exists before the individual and which determines his or her cultural identity. Discourse, then, is the agency whereby the subject is produced and the existing order sustained.

The imaginary, the symbolic and the real

I will now try to bring some of the threads together by briefly stating what Lacan means by the imaginary, the symbolic and the real. This will also enable me to recapitulate some of the key points of this chapter. It is clear that the imaginary – a kind of pre-verbal register whose logic is essentially visual – precedes the symbolic as a stage in the development of the psyche. Its moment of formation has been named the 'mirror stage'. At this stage there does not yet exist that ego formation which would permit a child to distinguish its own form from that of others. The child who hits says it has been hit, the child who sees another child fall begins to cry. (It is from Melanie Klein's pioneering psychoanalysis of children that the basic features of the Lacanian imaginary are drawn.)

The imaginary order is pre-Oedipal. The self yearns to fuse with what is perceived as Other. The child confuses others with its own mirror reflections; and since the self is formed from a composite of intro-jections based on such mis-recognitions, it can hardly constitute a unified personality. In other words, we experience a profoundly divided self.

Lacan suggests that the infant's first desire for the mother signifies the wish to be what the mother desires. (*Désir de la mère* refers to the desire for the mother *and* to the mother's desire.) The infant wants to complete the mother, to be what she lacks – the phallus. The child's relationship with the mother is fusional, dual and immediate. Later, the child's desire to be its mother's desire gives way to an identification with the father.

The child's asocial, dual and fusional relationship with its mother is forsworn for the world of symbolic discourse. The father becomes the third term and we enter the symbolic order by accepting his name and interdictions. In the symbolic there is no longer a one-to-one correspondence between things and what they are called – a symbol evokes an open-ended system of meaning. Symbolic signification is social, not narcissistic. It is the Oedipal crisis which marks the child's entrance into the world of the symbolic. The laws of language and society come to dwell within the child as he accepts the father's name and the father's 'no'.

I said earlier that Lacan understands the Oedipus story in terms of language, not in terms of the body, and that there is no such thing as the body before language. Biology is always interpreted by the human subject. But not only biology, all experience is symbolically mediated and has to be interpreted (in the context of social convention).

The Lacanian notion of *the symbolic order* is an attempt to create mediations between libidinal analysis and the linguistic categories, to provide, in other words, a transcoding scheme which allows us to speak of both within a common conceptual framework. The Oedipus complex is transliterated by Lacan into a linguistic phenomenon which he designates as the discovery by the subject of the Name-of-the-Father. Lacan feels that the apprenticeship of language is an alienation for the psyche but he realizes that it is impossible to return to an archaic, pre-verbal stage of the psyche itself.

I have underlined the point that Lacan places great emphasis on the linguistic development of the child. He argues that the acquisition of a name results in a thoroughgoing transformation of the position of the subject in his object world. There is a determination of the subject by language. The Freudian unconscious is seen in terms of language: 'The unconscious is the discourse of the Other' – a notion that tends to surprise those who associate language with thinking and consciousness.

Lacan's theory has attracted a good deal of interest among feminists because the emphasis on the production of gendered subjectivity via signification (the processes whereby meaning is produced at the same time as subjects are fabricated and positioned in social relations) implies that it is possible to escape the subordination of women inherent in Freud's recourse to biological difference. However, it could be argued that, in privileging the phallus as the sign of difference as opposed to the penis, Lacan's analysis is not any less deterministic than Freud's.[30] This is because Lacan relies heavily on Lévi-Strauss's structural analysis of the incest taboo which, it is said, underlies all human societies. The use of Lévi-Strauss's thesis means that the terms of the debate are fixed around the 'Law of the Father'. Because Lévi-Strauss's theory is a universalist one Lacan's account tends to collapse into an account of a universal subject who is not situated historically.

The third order is the real. The reality which we can never know is the real – it lies beyond language . . . the reality we must assume although we can never know it. This is the most problematic of the three orders or registers since it can never be experienced immediately, but only by way of the mediation of the other two: 'the Real, or what is perceived as such, is what resists symbolization absolutely'. Fredric Jameson, however, thinks that it is not terribly difficult to say what is meant by the real in Lacan: 'It is simply History itself.'[31]

Some criticisms of Lacan

To conclude the chapter, let me now turn to some criticisms of Lacan. It is often said that he intellectualizes everything and does not consider the emotions. He is highly critical, for example, of the Reichian approach which asserts that we can get to the emotions directly.[32] For Lacan an emotion is a signifier; it means something but what it means is an open question. Secondly, as his writings lack clinical material it is difficult to learn from his procedures or to test their validity. He seems to be more interested in developing theory in the university than in clinical practice. (On the other hand, it could be argued that though Lacan fails to provide case studies one way out of the problem is to examine the work of his followers, for example child psychologists such as Françoise Dolto and Maud Mannoni.) As he believes that in analysis nothing should be routine or predictable his sessions are sometimes only ten minutes long! He argues that psychoanalysis is not a psychology. If it was a psychology it would be like ethology (the study of animal behaviour); but the salient difference is that we cannot predict human behaviour. Moreover, Lacan holds that only an analyst can authorize himself or herself as an analyst. But, surely, self-authorization leads to problems about standards? Is it enough to be told that becoming an analyst is like becoming a poet, one who has a new, intimate relationship with language?

Feminist criticisms of Lacan

Lacan continues to be one of the most controversial figures within contemporary feminist theory. Many feminists use his work to challenge phallocentric knowledges; others are extremely hostile to it, seeing it as élitist, male-dominated and itself as phallocentric. Three key areas of Lacan's work are of deep interest to feminists: the interlocking domains of subjectivity, sexuality and language. His decentring of the rational, conscious subject (identified with the ego), his undermining of common assumptions about the intentionality or purposiveness of the speaking subject's 'rational' discourses and his problematizations of the idea of a 'natural' sexuality have helped to free feminist theory of the constraints of humanism.

It seems that feminist relations to psychoanalysis fall into two broad categories: those committed to Lacan's work, seeing it as a means of describing patriarchal power relations, and those who reject it from a pre- or non-psychoanalytic position. In the first category can be included Juliet Mitchell, Ellie Ragland-Sullivan, Julia Kristeva, Monique Plaza and Catherine Clément. In the second category are Germaine Greer, Dale Spender and others.

There are, however, feminists who occupy neither category. Here can be included feminists who have an impressive familiarity with Lacan's work while maintaining a critical distance from it: Jane Gallop, Jacqueline Rose, Sara Kofman, Luce Irigaray.

On behalf of Lacan it could be argued that, firstly, his work is a necessary counterbalance to the humanism so common in theories of human subjectivity. Secondly, his sharp distance from ego-psychology and object-relations accounts of psychoanalysis makes Freud's work more useful to feminism. And, thirdly, his intermingling of language-like processes with Freud's notion of sexuality and the unconscious have been useful to feminists in a wide variety of disciplines in which questions of subjectivity and desire are usually ignored.

On the other hand, many feminists have criticized Lacan and he is often censured for his conception of woman as lack, as other, as castrated. Secondly, Lacan is accused of privileging masculinity and participating in, and perhaps developing, Freud's phallocentrism. A fierce critic of Lacan, Luce Irigaray, has suggested that what Lacan's work does is to renew the familiar theme of the female as support or substratum of the male subject.

One of Irigaray's objections is the way in which Lacan takes a particular discursive organization to be unchangeable. The Lacanian conceptual system offers little possibility for radical social change. It implies a deep social conservatism as far as the situation of women is concerned. The conservatism is embedded in the Lacanian concept of the symbolic order. Since this order is phallocentric, structured according to the law of the father, it represses the truly feminine, defining femininity in patriarchal terms as a consequence of lack.

Irigaray argues that Western systems of representation privilege *seeing*; what can be seen (presence) is privileged over what cannot be seen (absence) and guarantees Being. Nothing to be seen is equivalent to having nothing. No being and no truth. As a result, within discourse, the feminine finds itself defined as lack, deficiency, or as imitation and negative image of the subject.[33].

Irigaray has examined the role of the mirror in the construction of subjectivity. Taking Lacan's mirror as an image of representation, she asks why he used a flat mirror, 'in that the flat mirror reflects the greater part of women's sexual organs only as a hole'.[34] To put it in another way, the flat mirror does not reflect the sexual specificity of the woman. For the exploration of woman's sexual specificity, a different sort of mirror would be needed – for example, a speculum, the concave mirror which gynaecologists use to inspect the 'cavities' of the female body. I will be discussing Irigaray's work in Chapter 5.

In defending Lacan, Juliet Mitchell has made some important points. She claims that feminists have not adequately understood Lacan's position and she suggests that he provides an accurate *description* of patriarchal power relations. Moreover, she argues that feminists have not fully understood the psychoanalytic explanation of patriarchy as not simply relations between men and women, but the relation *both* have to the phallus.

Other writers, like Ellie Ragland-Sullivan, also defend Lacan and emphasize his achievement in ridding Freudian theory of biologism. She argues that some critics of Lacan, like Irigaray, read him substantively rather than structurally and thus see him as prescriptive instead of descriptive and analytic. In her view, Irigaray's assessment of Lacan as a phallocrat is wrong; she does not fully understand the symbolic nature of the Lacanian phallic signifier which is neutral in its own right.

Elizabeth Grosz believes that Lacan's defenders are correct on two counts.[35] One, Lacan does shift the ground of our understanding of patriarchal power relations and their social reproduction. That is to say, it is not men *per se* who cause women's oppression, but rather the socio-economic and linguistic structure. Yet in his formulation of this structure as an inevitable law, patriarchal dominance is not so much challenged as displaced, from biology to the equally unchangeable socio-linguistic law of the father. Two, although he himself does not acknowledge the structure of patriarchal oppression, Lacan does provide some crucial elements for a description and explanation of the psychic components of women's oppression.

Further reading

B. Benvenuto and R. Kennedy, *The Works of Jacques Lacan: An Introduction*, London: Free Association Books, 1986.
This clear and helpful book discusses Lacan's major texts from the early works, 1926–33, to the works of the mid-1970s in chronological order. An excellent introduction.

M. Bowie, *Lacan*, London: Fontana Press, 1991.
In the Fontana Modern Masters Series, this book is a coherent and comprehensive outline of Lacan's theory.

M. Bowie, *Freud, Proust and Lacan: Theory as Fiction*, Cambridge: Cambridge University Press, 1987.
Three interconnected case studies of the theoretical imagination at work. A very interesting book which contains an analysis of Freud's self-images as archaeologist and *conquistador*. Bowie argues that Freud's

desire-laden fantasies are the fertile psychical soil from which Freud's working fictions and conceptual models sprang. After a consideration of the similarities between Freud and Proust, there is a concise introduction to Lacan's work.

C. Clément, *The Lives and Legends of Jacques Lacan*, New York: Columbia University Press, 1983.
One of the most accessible accounts that I know. A very readable introduction that explains many aspects of Lacan's work.

J. Gallop, *Reading Lacan*, Ithaca: Cornell University Press, 1985.
An accessible and helpful book. Most of the chapters focus on the famous texts in Lacan's *Écrits*.

E. Grosz, *Jacques Lacan: A Feminist Introduction*, London: Routledge, 1990.
A sympathetic overview from a feminist perspective. The topics covered include: the ego, the Oedipus complex, language and the unconscious. The chapters on sexual relations and feminism are particularly useful.

A. Lemaire, *Jacques Lacan*, London: Routledge, 1977.
An informative and useful guide to the 'structuralist' (post-1955) Lacan, whose debts to Heidegger, Kojève, Bataille and others are not mentioned. Lacan's work is presented as a system; and Lemaire reads it in purely synchronic terms.

D. Macey, *Lacan in Contexts*, London: Verso, 1988.
The title is accurate. The book is a clear introduction to the social-historical context of Lacan's work. It contains chapters on his early writings, the influence of Surrealism, his relationship with philosophers like Hegel, Heidegger and Sartre, linguistics, and the nature of femininity. There is also a useful overview of the major events in Lacan's life from 1901–81.

J. Mitchell and J. Rose (eds), *Feminine Sexuality: Jacques Lacan and the École Freudienne*, London: Macmillan, 1982.
An indispensable collection of seven articles written by Lacan between 1964 and 1981. The aim of the editors, especially in the lucid Introduction, is to show the importance of Lacan for psychoanalysts, and of psychoanalysis for feminism.

S. Schneiderman, *Jacques Lacan: The Death of an Intellectual Hero*, Cambridge, Mass.: Harvard University Press, 1983.
Is it true that Lacan spent so much of his time on theory that he lost

touch with clinical practice? And is the theory so intellectual that it neglects emotion and affect? I found this book a valuable account of this and other matters. He writes sensitively about death and its symbolization, the relation of the dead and the living, and the importance of Sophocles's *Antigone* for an understanding of ethical conduct. The author describes the organization of the École Freudienne and the short session.

S. Turkle, *Psychoanalytic Politics: Jacques Lacan and Freud's French Revolution*, London: Burnett Books, 1979.
A clear introduction to the post-1968 growth of psychoanalysis in France. Part One is most useful as it places Lacan's thought in a post-war social and political context.

E. Wright, *Psychoanalytic Criticism: Theory in Practice*, London: Methuen, 1984.
The key theme is the relationship between different psychoanalytic theories and theories of art and literature. It is an excellent introduction to Freud, Klein and Lacan.

Chapter 2

□

Derrida and deconstruction

Introduction

Deconstruction, which has attained widespread recognition as one of the most important avant-garde intellectual movements in France and America, is essentially post-phenomenological and post-structuralist. In the history of contemporary deconstruction the leading figure is Jacques Derrida, who published three influential books in 1967: *Of Grammatology, Speech and Phenomena* and *Writing and Difference.*[1] Among other things these texts contain powerful critiques of phenomenology (Husserl), linguistics (Saussure), Lacanian psychoanalysis, and structuralism (Lévi-Strauss).

In this chapter I give an exposition of Derrida's thought. Beginning with an outline of his view of language I give an explanation of what he means by phonocentrism and logocentrism. I then present his arguments against the work of Jean-Jacques Rousseau, Claude Lévi-Strauss and Jacques Lacan. There are also sections on his 'predecessors' Freud and Nietzsche and an account of how they have influenced Derrida's thinking on reading texts and the nature of metaphor. After that I examine some metaphors in common use. Finally, after situating metaphor in the context of political and ideological struggle, I discuss the relationship between deconstruction and Marxism.

The instability of language

In trying to understand Derrida's work one of the most important concepts to grasp is the idea of '*sous rature*', a term usually translated as 'under erasure'. To put a term '*sous rature*' is to write a word, cross it out, and then print both word and deletion. The idea is this: since the word is inaccurate, or, rather, inadequate, it is crossed out. Since it is necessary it remains legible. This strategically important device which Derrida uses derives from Martin Heidegger, who often crossed out the word Being (like this:~~Being~~) and let both deletion and word stand because the word was *inadequate yet necessary*. Heidegger felt that Being cannot be contained by, is always prior to, indeed transcends, signification. Being is the final signified to which all signifiers refer, the 'transcendental signified'.

In Derrida's view of language the signifier is not directly related to the signified. There is no one-to-one set of corrrespondences between them. In Saussurean thought a sign is seen as a unity, but in Derrida's view word and thing or thought never in fact become one. He sees the sign as a structure of difference: half of it is always 'not there' and the other half is always 'not that'. Signifiers and signified are continually breaking apart and reattaching in new combinations, thus revealing the inadequacy of Saussure's model of the sign, according to which the signifier and signified relate as if they were two sides of the same sheet of paper. Indeed, there is no fixed distinction between signifiers and signified. If one answers a child's question or consults a dictionary, one soon finds that one sign leads to another and so on, indefinitely. Signifiers keep transforming into signifieds, and vice versa, and you never arrive at a final signified which is not a signifier in itself.

In other words, Derrida argues that when we read a sign, meaning is not immediately clear to us. Signs refer to what is absent, so in a sense meanings are absent, too. Meaning is continually moving along on a chain of signifiers, and we cannot be precise about its exact 'location', because it is never tied to one particular sign.

Now, for Derrida the structure of the sign is determined by the trace (the French meaning carries strong implications of track, footprint, imprint) of that other which is forever absent. This other is, of course, never to be found in its full being. Rather like the answer to a child's question or a definition in a dictionary, one sign leads to another and so on indefinitely . . .

What is the implication of this? That the projected 'end' of knowledge could ever coincide with its 'means' is an impossible dream of plenitude. No one can make the 'means' (the sign) and the 'end' (meaning) become identical. Sign will always lead to sign, one substituting the other as signifier and signified in turn. For Derrida the sign cannot be taken as a homogeneous unit bridging an origin (referent) and an end (meaning), as semiology, the study of signs, would have it. The sign must be studied 'under erasure', always already inhabited by the trace of another sign which never appears as such.   ⟶ 'secular' (worldly).

In addition, language is a temporal process. When I read a sentence its meaning often does not emerge until the end of the sentence; and even then the meaning can be modified by later signifiers. In each sign there are traces of other words which that sign has excluded in order to be itself. And words contain the trace of the ones which have gone before. All words/signs contain traces. They are like reminders of what has gone before. Every word in a sentence, every sign in a chain of meaning, has these traces in an inexhaustible complexity.

Meaning is never identical with itself; because a sign appears in different contexts it is never absolutely the same. Meaning will never stay quite the same from context to context; the signified will be altered by the various chains of signifiers in which it is entangled.

The implication of this is that language is a much less stable affair than was thought by structuralists such as Lévi-Strauss. None of the elements is absolutely definable; everything is caught up and traced through by everything else. Eagleton explains: 'Nothing is ever fully present in signs. It is an illusion for me to believe that I can ever be fully present to you in what I say or write, because to use signs at all entails my meaning being always somehow dispersed, divided and never quite at one with itself. Not only my meaning, indeed, but I myself: since language is something I am made out of, rather than a convenient tool I use, the whole idea that I am a stable, unified entity must also be a fiction.'[2]

Phonocentrism–logocentrism

Derrida is mainly concerned with the role and function of language and is famous for having developed a procedure called deconstruction. This is a method of reading a text so closely that the author's conceptual distinctions on which the text relies are shown to fail on account of the inconsistent and paradoxical use made of these very concepts within the text as a whole. In other words, the text is seen to fail by its own criteria; the standards or definitions which the text sets up are used reflexively to unsettle and shatter the original distinctions. Derrida has used this technique against Husserl, Rousseau, Saussure, Plato, Freud and others; but the method can be applied to any text.

The method of deconstruction is connected with what Derrida calls the 'metaphysics of presence'. It is Derrida's contention that Husserl, along with almost all other philosophers, relies on the assumption of an immediately available area of certainty. The origin and foundation of most philosophers' theories is presence. In Husserl's case the search for the form of pure expression is at the same time a search for that which is immediately present; thus implicitly, by being present in an unmediated way and present to itself, it is undeniably certain.

Derrida, however, denies the possibility of this presence and in so doing removes the ground from which philosophers have in general proceeded. By denying presence, Derrida is denying that there is a present in the sense of a single definable moment which is 'now'. For most people the present is the province of the known. We may be unsure of what took place in the past, of what may take place in the future, or of what is taking place elsewhere, but we rely on our knowledge of the present, the here and now – the present perceptual world as we are experiencing it. By challenging access to the present Derrida poses a threat to both positivism and phenomenology.

Husserl made an important distinction in *The Logical Investigations* between expression and indication. The expression, linked to the intention of the speaker, is what we might call the pure meaning of the sign, and as such is distinguished from indication, which has a pointing function and could occur without any intentional meaning. Now, Derrida has argued that pure expression will always involve an indicative element. Indication can never be successfully excluded from expression. Signs cannot refer to something totally other than themselves. There is no signified which is independent of the signifier. There is no realm of meaning which can be isolated from the marks which are used to point to it.

Having argued that a realm of the independent signified does not exist, Derrida concludes, first, that no particular sign can be regarded as referring to any particular signified and, second, that we are unable to escape the system of signifiers. In combination these conclusions imply that there can be no unqualified presence.

Now, it is because of the assumption of presence that a priority has been given to speech over writing. Derrida calls this phonocentrism. Speech has been regarded as prior because it is closer to the possibility of presence. It is closer because speech implies immediacy. In speech meaning is apparently immanent, above all when, using the inner voice of consciousness, we speak to ourselves. In the moment of speech we appear to grasp its meaning and are thereby able to capture presence, as if the meaning was decided once and for all. Thus, unlike writing, which is hopelessly mediated, speech is linked to the apparent moment and place of presence and for this reason has had priority over writing. For Derrida, therefore, phonocentrism is one of the effects of presence. Derrida's attempt to deconstruct the opposition betwen speech and writing is linked to the uncovering of the metaphysics of presence as a whole.

Derrida has also criticized Saussure for prescribing that linguistics should be a study of speech alone rather than of speech and writing. This is an emphasis shared by Jakobson, by Lévi-Strauss, indeed by all semiological structuralists. Derrida suggests in *Of Grammatology* that this rejection of writing as an appendage, a mere technique and yet a menace built into speech – in effect, a scapegoat – is a symptom of a much broader tendency. He relates this phonocentrism to logocentrism, the belief that the first and last thing is the Logos, the Word, the Divine Mind, the *self-presence of full self-consciousness.*

Derrida suggests that Husserl found evidence for self-presence in the voice (*phone*) – not the 'real' voice, but the principle of the voice in our interior soliloquy: 'When I speak I hear myself. I hear and understand at the same time that I speak.' Husserl's model of meaningful speech is the silent conversation of consciousness with itself in solitary mental life.

Speech is thought of as remaining closer to psychic interiority than writing which symbolizes interiority only at one remove. When I speak, I seem to be truly myself. My spoken words seem to come from me, my true, or real being. Writing does not seem to be so direct, so natural or sincere. Compared with speech writing seems mechanical, second-hand, a transcript of speech. Writing can be seen as deriving from speech because it is thought of as purely phonetic transcription. Derrida argues that from Plato to Heidegger and Lévi-Strauss, the Western philosophical tradition has downgraded writing as if it were artificial and alienated compared with the immediacy and vivacity of the human voice. (This will be discussed in the next section when we consider Derrida's examination of specific texts by Rousseau and Lévi-Strauss.) Behind this bias is a particular view of human beings; it is assumed that they can spontaneously express themselves and that they can use language as if it were a transparent medium for an inner truth about their being. What this theory fails to see is that speaking could be just as much said to be a second-hand form of writing as writing is said to be an inferior form of speaking.

One of Derrida's main concerns has been this privileging of voice as the medium of meaning and the consequent dismissal of writing as a derivative form of expression. Western philosophy has focused on speech, it has emphasized the voice. In this tradition the phenomenological structure of the voice is regarded as the most immediate evidence of self-presence. Besides being 'phonocentric', Western philosophy is also 'logocentric'. Derrida uses the term 'logocentric' as a substitute for metaphysics in order to foreground that which has determined metaphysical systems of thought: their dependence on a *logos*. Western philosophy assumes that there is an essence, or truth which acts as the foundation of all our beliefs; hence there seems to be a disposition, a longing, for a 'transcendental signifier' which would directly relate, correspond, to a secure stable 'transcendental signified' (i.e. a *logos*). Examples of such signs include: Idea, Matter, the World Spirit, God, etc. Each of these concepts acts as the foundation of a system of thought and forms an axis around which all other signs circulate. Derrida argues that any such transcendental meaning is a fiction.

There are certain signifieds or meanings attached to such signifiers as Authority, Freedom, Order which are highly valued in society. Sometimes we think of these meanings as if they were the origin of all the others. But it could be argued that for these meanings to have been possible, other signs must already have been in existence in the first place. Whenever we think of an origin we often want to go back to an even earlier starting point. But these meanings are not always seen in terms of origin, they are often seen in terms of goals, towards which all other meanings are advancing. Conceiving of things in terms of their orientation towards a *telos* or end point – teleology – is a way of organizing meanings in a hierarchy of significance.

Derrida calls 'metaphysical' any thought-system which depends on a foundation, a ground, or a first principle. First principles are often defined by what they exclude, by a sort of 'binary opposition' to other concepts. These principles and their implied 'binary opposites' can always be deconstructed.

Derrida argues that all the conceptual oppositions of metaphysics have for ultimate reference the presence of a present. (He often uses the word 'metaphysics' as shorthand for 'being as presence'.) For Derrida the binary oppositions of metaphysics include: signifier/signified, sensible/intelligible, speech/writing, speech (*parole*)/language (*langue*), diachrony/synchrony, space/time, passivity/activity. One of his criticisms of the structuralists, as we shall see, is that they have not put these concepts 'under erasure', that they have not put these binary oppositions into question.

What are binary oppositions? They are a way of seeing, rather like ideologies. We know that ideologies draw sharp distinctions between conceptual opposites such as truth and falsity, meaning and nonsense, centre and periphery. Derrida suggests that we should try to break down the oppositions by which we are accustomed to think and which ensure the survival of metaphysics in our thinking: matter/spirit, subject/object, veil/truth, body/soul, text/meaning, interior/exterior, representation/presence, appearance/essence, etc. Derrida's importance is that he has suggested a method whereby we can subvert these oppositions and show that one term relies on and inheres within the other.

Derrida argues that phonocentrism–logocentrism relates to centrism itself – the human desire to posit a 'central' presence at beginning and end. He states that it is this longing for a centre, an authorizing pressure, that spawns hierarchized oppositions. The superior term in these oppositions belongs to presence and the logos, the inferior serves to define its status and mark a fall. The oppositions between intelligible and sensible, soul and body, seem to have lasted out 'the history of Western philosophy', bequeathing their burden to modern linguistics with its opposition between meaning and word. The opposition between speech and writing takes its place within this pattern.

Rousseau and Lévi-Strauss

Derrida writes that many philosophers throughout history use the opposition nature/culture. It is often stated that archaic man, living in an innocent state of nature, comes upon a danger or insufficiency of one sort or another bringing about a need or desire for community. In the evolution of human beings from nature to society the latter stage of existence is pictured as an addition to the original happy stage of nature. In other words, culture supplements nature. Before long culture comes to take the place of nature. Culture, then, functions as a supplement in two ways: it adds and it substitutes. At the same time it is potentially both detrimental and beneficial. The structure of the nature/culture opposition repeats itself in other traditional polarities: for example, health/disease, purity/contamination, good/evil, speech/writing. The first term in each opposition traditionally constitutes the privileged entity, the better state.

Derrida argues that when Rousseau describes an event or phenomenon he invariably ends up relying on the supplement. Although nature is declared to be self-sufficient it needs culture. (In a similar way education for Rousseau aids the insufficiencies of the untrained intellect.) It is suggested by Derrida that there is no original, unsupplemented nature but that ~~nature~~ is always already a supplemented entity. This device, *sous rature*, indicates the equivocal status of the term erased, warning, as I suggested earlier, the reader not to accept the word at face value. The marks of erasure acknowledge both the inadequacy of the terms employed – their highly provisional status – and the fact that thought simply cannot manage without them. Similarly, Derrida has a mistrust of metaphysical language but accepts the necessity to work within that language.

Rousseau believed that speech was the originary, the healthiest and the most natural condition of language; writing was merely derivative and somehow debilitating. What Derrida does (by a close analysis of Rousseau's texts, particularly the *Essay on the Origin of Languages*) is to show that Rousseau contradicts himself, so that, far from proving speech to be the origin of language – and writing merely a parasitic growth – his essay confirms the priority of writing. In other words, Rousseau's text confesses what he is at such pains to deny; his text cannot mean what it says or literally say what it means.

The theme of lost innocence is also to be found in the work of Lévi-Strauss, to which I now turn. However before I outline Derrida's criticism of Lévi-Strauss, it may be useful to go over the main features of the latter's structuralist approach. Structuralism, an attempt to isolate the general structures of human activity, found its main analogies in linguistics. It is well known that structural linguistics performs four *basic* operations: it shifts from the study of conscious linguistic phenomena to the study of their unconscious infrastructure; second, it does not treat terms as independent entities, taking instead as its basis of analysis the relations between terms; third, it introduces the concept of system; finally, it aims at discovering general laws.

What are Derrida's criticisms of structuralism? Firstly, he doubts the possibility of general laws. Secondly, he questions the opposition of the subject and the object, upon which the possibility of objective descriptions rests. In his view the description of the object is contaminated by the patterns of the subject's desire. Thirdly, he questions the structure of binary oppositions. He invites us to undo the need for balanced equations, to see if each term in an opposition is not, after all, an accomplice of the other.

The structuralism of Lévi-Strauss can be characterized as a search for invariant structures or formal universals which reflect the nature of human intelligence. This approach lends support to the traditional idea of the text as a bearer of stable meanings and the critic as a faithful seeker after truth in the text. Derrida suggests that when Lévi-Strauss describes the life of the Nambikwara and their transition to civilization he takes upon himself the burden of guilt produced by this encounter between civilization and the 'innocent' culture it ceaselessly exploits.[3] Lévi-Strauss gives expression, like Rousseau, to an eloquent longing for the lost primordial unity of speech before writing. Writing for Lévi-Strauss is an instrument of oppression, means of colonizing the primitive mind. In Derrida's view there is no pure 'authenticity' as Lévi-Strauss imagines; the theme of lost innocence is a romantic illusion.

Derrida's critique of Lévi-Strauss follows much the same path as his deconstructive readings of Saussure and Rousseau.[4] Once again it is a matter of taking a repressed theme, pursuing its textual ramifications and showing how these subvert the very order that strives to hold them in check. The 'nature' which Rousseau identifies with a pure, unmediated speech, and Lévi-Strauss with the dawn of tribal awareness, expresses nostalgia for lost innocence, an illusory meta- physics of presence which ignores the self-alienating character of all social existence.

Derrida situates the project of Lévi-Strauss (like those of Saussure and Lacan) in logocentrism. One of the central problems of anthropology is the passage from nature to culture. Derrida argues that Lévi-Strauss regularly and symptomatically ends up privileging the state of nature over culture. He appears sentimental and nostalgic, trapped in a Rousseauistic dream of innocent and natural primitive societies. Beneath the guilt and nostalgia, endemic to the field of anthropology, lies a Western ethnocentrism masking itself as liberal and humane anti-ethnocentrism.

As for writing, Lévi-Strauss conceptualizes it as a late cultural arrival, a supplement to speech, an external instrument. Speech is endowed with all the metaphorical attributes of life and healthy vitality, writing with dark connotations of violence and death.[5]

Derrida has made similar comments on Saussure. He has criticized Saussure's *Course in General Linguistics* for the sharp distinction which it maintains between the signifier and the signified, a distinction which is congruent with the traditional opposition of matter and spirit, or substance and thought. (Traditionally, this opposition has always been elaborated in ways which privilege spirit and/or thought as something that precedes matter or substance.) Derrida suggests that the distinction between signifier and signified can only be maintained if one term is believed to be final, incapable of referring beyond itself to any other term. If there is no such term, then every signified functions in turn as a signifier, in an endless play of signification.

Derrida, in short, is critical of Saussure's notion of the sign and argues that the traditional concept of signifier and signified rests firmly within the phonocentric–logocentric *episteme.* One of the characteristics of the logocentric epoch is that there is a general debasement of writing and a preference for phonetic writing (writing as imitated speech). There is, then, a rooted Western prejudice which tries to reduce writing to a stable meaning equated with the character of speech. It is widely held that in spoken language meaning is 'present' to the speaker through an act of inward self-surveillance which assures a perfect, intuitive 'fit' between intention and utterance.

Derrida demonstrates that in Saussurian linguistics privilege is granted to speech as opposed to written language. Voice becomes a metaphor of truth and authenticity, a source of self-present 'living' speech as opposed to the secondary, lifeless emanations of writing. Writing is systematically degraded and is seen as a threat to the traditional view that associates truth with self-presence. This repression of writing lies deep in Saussure's proposed methodology and shows in his refusal to consider any form of linguistic notation outside the phonetic-alphabetical script of Western culture. Against this view Derrida argues that writing is, in fact, the precondition of language and must be conceived as prior to speech. Writing is the 'free play' or element of undecidability within every system of communication.

It should be pointed out that for Derrida 'writing' does not refer to the empirical concept of writing (which denotes an intelligible system of notations on a material substance); writing is the name of the structure always already inhabited by the trace. This broadening of the term, Derrida argues, was made possible by Sigmund Freud.

Freud and Lacan

Derrida argues that it is no accident that when Freud tried to describe the workings of the psyche he had recourse to metaphorical models which are borrowed not from spoken language but from *writing*.[6] (This, of course, raises the question of what a text is and what the psyche must be like if it can be represented by a text.)

At first, from about the time of 'Project for a Scientific Psychology' (1895), Freud used mechanical models, but these were soon discarded. As Freud moved from neurological to psychical modes of explanation he began increasingly to refer to metaphors of optical mechanisms. Then, in *The Interpretation of Dreams* (1900), Freud thought it more appropriate to compare dreams with a system of writing than with spoken language. In order to suggest the strangeness of the logico-temporal relations in dreams Freud constantly referred to alphabetic writing as well as non-phonetic writing (pictographs, rebuses, hieroglyphics) in general. Dream symbols, he wrote, frequently have more than one or even several meanings and, as with Chinese script, the correct interpretation can only be arrived at on each occasion from the context.

Later, in 'Note on the Mystic Writing Pad' (1925), Freud used a writing apparatus as a metaphor for the working of the psyche. A child's toy had come on the market under the name of the Mystic Writing Pad. You may have come across a modern version of it. Basically, it consisted of a celluloid covering-sheet which rested upon a wax slab. One could write on it with a pointed stylus and the writing could be erased by raising the double covering sheet by a little pull, starting from the free lower end. The pad, cleared of writing, is thus ready to receive fresh messages. Freud argued that its construction was very much like that of the perceptual apparatus. It had an ever-ready receptive surface and could retain permanent traces of the inscriptions made on it; the wax slab, in fact, represented the unconscious.

In short, Freud found in the Mystic Writing Pad a model that would contain the problematics of the psyche – a virgin surface that still retained permanent traces. The Freudian argument is that the establishment of permanent traces in the psychic apparatus precludes the possibility of immediate perception. In other words, we have 'memory-traces', marks which are not a part of conscious memory, which may be energized into consciousness long afterwards and so affect us.

Derrida's chief interest in Freudian psychoanalysis lies in the fact that it teaches and uses a certain method of deciphering texts. Freud lists the four techniques used by the 'dream-work' of the psychic apparatus to distort or refract the 'forbidden' dream-thoughts, to produce the pictographic script of the dream: condensation, displacement, considerations of representability and secondary revision. Condensation and displacement may be rhetorically translated as metaphor and metonymy. The third item on the list refers to the technique which distorts an idea so that it can be presented as an image. Secondary revision is a psychic force that smooths over contradictions and creates an apparent connectedness.

Freud suggested that the verbal text is constituted by concealment as much as by revelation. Freud suggests that where the subject is not in control of the text, where the text looks very smooth or very clumsy, is where readers should fix their gaze. Derrida develops this further; he suggests that we should fasten upon a small but tell-tale moment in the text which harbours the author's sleight of hand and which cannot be dismissed simply as contradiction. We should examine that passage where we can provisionally locate the moment when the text · transgresses the laws it apparently sets up for itself, and thus unravel – deconstruct – the very text.

Freud's greatest contemporary interpreter is Jacques Lacan. Let me briefly remind you of the key features of Lacan's thought before outlining Derrida's critique of it. Like Freud, Lacan denies that there is a difference in kind between 'the normal' and 'the abnormal'. Moreover, he rejects the work of those American psychologists who stress that the ego is the primary determinant of the psyche. In his view 'the subject' can never be a total personality and is forever divided from the object of its desire. Lacan goes on to define the unconscious in terms of the structure of a language. This extends Freud in a direction that Derrida would endorse, but, nevertheless, the relationship between these thinkers is an uneasy one.

It would seem to an outside observer that Lacan and Derrida have a lot in common: they are both deeply concerned with anti-positivist theories of language and are highly aware of language's metaphoricity. Secondly, both thinkers have been influenced by Freud's theories of the unconscious and the dream as a text. This means that they are interested in (ways of) 'reading' and (styles of) 'writing'. Thirdly, they both draw attention, as did Freud, to the relationship between nature and culture.

And so, why is there an uneasy relationship between them? Derrida argues that the goal of Lacanian analysis is to draw out and establish 'the truth' of the subject, and it appears to him that in spite of giving to the unconscious the structure of a language Lacan has entrenched some of Freud's (metaphysical) suggestions by making the unconscious the source of 'truth'. Derrida believes that Lacan sees himself as unveiling 'the true' Freud and is sceptical of Lacan's notions of 'truth' and 'authenticity', seeing them as remnants of a post-war existentialist ethic, the unacknowledged debts to Hegelian phenomenology.

Derrida believes that Lacan simplifies Freud's text. In Lacanian analysis the truth (logos) systematically shines forth as spoken or voiced. Psychoanalysis remains 'the talking cure' founded on spoken truth.[7] Derrida cautions us that when we learn to reject the notion of the primacy of the signified (of meaning over word) we should not satisfy our longing for transcendence by giving primacy to the signifier (word over meaning). He feels that Lacan has done precisely this.

I stated earlier that Derrida is attempting to subvert the logocentric theory of the sign. Traditionally, the signifier refers to the signified, that is, an acoustic image signifies an ideal concept, both of which are present to consciousness. The signifier 'dog' indicates the idea 'dog'; the real dog, the referent, is not present. In Derrida's view *the sign marks an absent presence*. Rather than present the object we employ the sign; however, the meaning of the sign is always postponed or deferred.

Derrida has developed a concept which he calls 'différance' and which refers to 'to differ' – to be unlike or dissimilar in nature, quality or form – and to 'to defer' – to delay, to postpone (the French verb *différer* · has both these meanings). Spoken French makes no phonetic distinction between the endings '-ance' and '-ence'; the word registers as *différence*. This undetected difference shows up only in writing.

The advent of the concept of writing, then, is a challenge to the very idea of structure; for a structure always presumes a centre, a fixed principle, a hierarchy of meaning and a solid foundation; and it is just these notions which the endless differing and deferring of writing throws into question.

As we have seen, Derrida's analysis of Husserl led him to portray language as an endless play of signifiers. Once an independent signified was abandoned signifiers referred to other signifiers which yet again referred to signifiers. Language is thus the play of differences which are generated by signifiers which are themselves the product of those differences. Derrida incorporates into the meaning of *différance* the sense of deferring. *Différance* is itself endlessly deferred.

Nietzsche and metaphor

Derrida's acknowledged 'precursors' were Nietzsche, Freud and Heidegger. They all felt a need for the strategy of *'sous rature'*. Heidegger put 'Being' under erasure, Freud 'the psyche', and Nietzsche 'knowing'.[8] It seems that post-structuralists such as Derrida have not so much followed in Nietzsche's footsteps as rediscovered his philosophical stance, a stance that owes its character to an all-pervasive reflexivity.

The current emphasis on reflexivity (a form of self-awareness, a turning back on oneself) is in part due to a critical shift of focus from the individual subject to the text. Thus from Nietzsche to Derrida we see the human subject – traditionally the focus of philosophical thought as the place of experience, morality, choice and will – gradually abandoned.

Derrida suggests that the main characteristics of Nietzsche's work are a systematic mistrust of metaphysics and a suspicion of the values of 'truth' and 'meaning'. Many cultural relativists believe that, although we may interpret the world differently according to our social context, there is a single world which we are all interpreting. For Nietzsche, however, there is no single physical reality beyond our interpretations. There are only perspectives.

Rooted in Nietzsche's philosophy is the implicit stance that there are no final conclusions; the text can never be fixed and as a result it can never be deciphered either. Nietzsche believes that we are unable to escape the constraints of language and thus have no alternative but to operate within language. He is aware of the reflexive problem: if we say 'we are trapped within language and its concepts', that claim is in itself, of course, part of language. We wish to express our 'trappedness' but we are unable to do so other than in the very concepts which trap us. The original thought therefore eludes us, for if we could express it, we would not, after all, be trapped.[9]

Nietzsche, then, was deeply aware of the problem that one is bound by one's perspective. One of his ways of coping with this was by the strategy of intersubstituting opposites. If one is always bound by one's perspective, one can at least deliberately reverse perspectives as often as possible, in the process undoing opposed perspectives, showing that the two terms of an opposition are merely accomplices of each other. In this way Nietzsche problematized, for example, the opposition between 'metaphor' and 'concept', 'body' and 'mind'. I mention this because

Nietzsche's undoing of opposites is rather like Derrida's undoing of them as a part of deconstructive practice.

For Nietzsche there is no possibility of a literal, true, self-identical meaning. (Derrida, too, is deeply committed to the view that philosophical discourse is something to be deciphered.) Nietzsche described the figurative drive as the impulse towards the formation of metaphors. Every idea, he said, originates through an equating of the unequal. Metaphor is the establishing of an identity between dissimilar things:

> What, therefore, is truth? A mobile army of metaphors, metonymies, anthropomorphisms; truths are illusions of which one has forgotten that they are illusions ... coins which have their obverse effaced and now are no longer of account as coins but merely as metal.[10]

In his later work Nietzsche gave this figurative drive the name 'will to power'. Our so-called will to truth is the will to power because the so-called drive for knowledge can be traced back to a drive to appropriate and conquer. Sometimes Nietzsche places this abstract will to power, an incessant figuration, not under the control of any knowing subject but rather in the unconscious. Indeed, for Nietzsche the important main activity is unconscious, that is, it takes place in that vast arena of the mind of which the so-called 'subject' knows nothing. Derrida has remarked that both Nietzsche and Freud questioned, often in a very similar way, the self-assured certitude of consciousness.

In many ways, then, Nietzsche anticipates both the style and the strategy of Derrida's writing. Nietzsche held that philosophy from Plato to the present had suppressed the fact that language is radically metaphorical in character. Philosophy utilized metaphors but disguised this fact. All philosophies, whatever their claim to logic or reason, rested on a shifting texture of figurative language, the signs of which were systematically repressed. In Nietzsche's view the Sophists, a school of rhetorician-philosophers in ancient Greece, came closer to wisdom by implicitly acknowledging what Socrates has to deny: that thinking is always and inseparably bound to the rhetorical devices that support it.

Following Nietzsche, Derrida makes the point that all language is ineradicably metaphorical, working by tropes and figures. It is a mistake to believe that any language is literally literal. Literary works are in a sense less deluded than other forms of discourse, because they implicitly acknowledge their own rhetorical status. Other forms of writing are just as figurative and ambiguous but pass themselves off as unquestionable truth.

One of the implications of this view is that literature can no longer be seen as a kind of poor relation to philosophy. There is no clear division between literature and philosophy, nor between 'criticism' and 'creation'. Since metaphors are essentially 'groundless', mere substitutions of one set of signs for another, language tends to betray its own fictive and arbitrary nature at just those points where it is offering to be most intensively persuasive. In short, philosophy, law and political theory work by metaphor just as poems do, and so are just as fictional.

Understanding metaphor

The study of metaphor is becoming important as it is being realized that language does not simply reflect reality but helps to constitute it. Attention is now being increasingly given to how rhetorical devices shape our experience and our judgements, how language serves to promote the possibilities of certain kinds of action and exclude the practicability of others.

In the past, metaphor was often studied as an aspect of the expressive function of language, but it is actually one of the essential conditions of speech. Language works by means of transference from one kind of reality to another and is thus essentially metaphorical. Some people have urged that technical and scientific language should be purged of metaphor but, as we have seen, metaphorical expressions are rooted in language itself. For example, we habitually think of organizations spatially, in terms of up and down. We tend to think of theories as though they were buildings, and so we talk of foundations, frameworks, etc. 'Base' and 'superstructure' are fundamental concepts in Marxism. As Derrida has shown, even philosophy is permeated with metaphor without knowing it.

Meaning shifts around, and metaphor is the name of the process by which it does so. It is a threat to orderly language and allows for the proliferation of meaning. First, there is no limit to the number of metaphors for any given idea. Second, metaphor is a sort of rhetorical double-bind, which states one thing but requires you to understand something different. (I found it interesting to learn that many schizophrenics cling to the literal and avoid metaphors because these are ultimately undecidable.) Metaphors evoke relationships and the making of the relationships is very much the task of the hearer or reader. Indeed, understanding a metaphor is as much a creative endeavour as making a metaphor, and as little guided by rules. Metaphor is ubiquitous and ineradicable.

I want to stress the point that metaphors are not just the concern of the poet or the literary critic, not just figures of speech; they represent one of the ways in which many kinds of discourse are structured and powerfully influence how we conceive things. I would like you to consider for a moment the metaphor 'time is money'. In our culture time is money in many ways; we calculate telephone calls, hourly wages, interests on loans. But not only do we *act* as if time is a valuable commodity, we also *conceive* of time that way. 'I don't have the time to give you.' 'How do you spend your time these days?' Thus we understand and experience time as the kind of thing that can be spent, wasted, budgeted, invested wisely or foolishly, saved or squandered. 'Time is money', 'time is a limited resource' and 'time is a valuable commodity' are all metaphorical concepts. They are metaphorical since we are using our everyday experiences with money, limited resources and valuable commodities to conceptualize time. But this is not the only way in which human beings may conceptualize time; it is tied to our culture. There are cultures where time is none of these things.

Let us consider another example: the organizing metaphors surrounding work and leisure. One does a full day's work; one is in or out of work. Leisure time, on the other hand, is to be filled; holiday weekends are breaks between work. We associate the metaphor of work with plenitude, with something of importance, and that of leisure with emptiness, with a vacuum. The metaphors reinforce the idea of life as first and foremost the life of work, while activities outside of it belong to the frivolous and not to the main business of life. Metaphors like these are particularly insidious since they are so interwoven into our speech that their flavour of metaphor is lost upon speakers and hearers.

The politics of metaphor

Our ordinary language is saturated with metaphor. For example, in our society argument is in part structured, understood, performed and talked about in terms of war. There is a position to be established and defended, you can win or lose, you have an opponent whose position you attack and try to destroy and whose argument you try to shoot down. The language of argument is, basically, the language of physical combat. That 'argument is war' is built into the conceptual system of the culture in which we live. Lakoff and Johnson have pointed out that it need not be so; that one can easily imagine societies in which argument is conceived differently – for example as theatrical performance.[11] In such a society both argument itself and the criteria for success or failure in argument would be quite unlike our own.

Some metaphors, in certain historical periods, have been liberating. The historian Christopher Hill has described how in the seventeenth century nature came to be thought of as a machine to be understood, controlled and improved upon by knowledge.[12] Nature as a machine was (at that time) a tremendously exciting, liberating idea. Human beings were freed from Providence or divine will and could not only understand the world better but could begin to change it.

I think that the creative or imaginative aspect of sociological theories often lies in their use of metaphor. Parsons likens society to a biological organism; Marx uses the metaphor of a building, the base and superstructure; Goffman uses the metaphor of a stage 'performance'. Metaphors serve to draw attention not only to similarities but to differences. As the theory develops and becomes more precise, concepts emerge that sometimes have little to do with the original metaphor.

An influential post-structuralist thinker, the late Michel Foucault (whose work on the social sciences and the relations between power and knowledge will be discussed in the next chapter), was particularly fond of using 'geographical' metaphors such as territory, domain, soil, horizon, archipelago, geopolitics, region, landscape. He also makes profuse use of spatial metaphors – position, displacement, site, field. Althusser, too, in *Reading Capital* uses many spatial metaphors (terrain, space, site, etc.). Foucault suggests that, since Bergson perhaps, there has been a devaluation of space. Space has been treated as the dead, the fixed, the undialectical, the immobile; time, on the contrary, was richness, fecundity, life, dialectic. But to talk in terms of space does not mean that one is hostile to time. Althusser believed that the use of spatial metaphors in his work was necessary but at the same time regressive, non-rigorous. Foucault, on the other hand, was more positive. He said that *it is through these spatial obsessions that he came to what he was looking for*: the relations that are possible between power and knowledge. 'Once knowledge can be analysed in terms of region, domain, implantation, displacement, transposition, one is able to capture the process by which knowledge functions as a form of power and disseminates the effects of power.'[13]

I believe that metaphors determine to a large extent what we can think in any field. Metaphors are not idle flourishes – they shape what we do. They can help to make, and defend, a world view. It is important that the implications of the metaphors we employ or accept are made explicit and that the ways in which they structure our thought and even our action are better understood. I also want to stress that metaphors can be productive of new insights and fresh illuminations. They can promote unexpected or subtle parallels or analogies. Metaphors can encapsulate and put forward proposals for another way of looking at things. Through metaphor we can have an increased awareness of alternative possible worlds.

Deconstruction and Marxism

The metaphor most often used by deconstructionists is that of the palimpsest; reading texts resembles the X-raying of pictures which discovers, under the epidermis of the last painting, another hidden picture. Deconstructive criticism takes the 'metaphoric' structure of a text seriously. Since metaphors are not reducible to truth, their own structures 'as such' are part of the text. The deconstructive procedure is to spot the point where a text covers up its grammatical structure. Gayatri Spivak puts it like this:

> If in the process of deciphering a text in the traditional way we come across a word that seems to harbour an unresolvable contradiction, and by virtue of being one word is made sometimes to work in one way and sometimes in another and thus is made to point away from the absence of a unified meaning, we shall catch at that word. If a metaphor seems to suppress its implications, we shall catch at that metaphor. We shall follow its adventures through the text coming undone as a structure of concealment, revealing its self-transgression, its undecidability.[14]

Derrida has provided a method of 'close-reading' a 'text' very similar to psychoanalytic approaches to neurotic symptoms. Deconstructive 'close-reading', having 'interrogated' the text, breaks through its defences and shows that a set of binary oppositions can be found 'inscribed' within it. In each of the pairs, private/public, masculine/feminine, same/other, rational/irrational, true/false, central/peripheral, etc., the first term is privileged. Deconstructors show that the 'privileged' term depends for its identity on its excluding the other and demonstrate that primacy really belongs to the subordinate term instead.

Derrida's procedure is to examine the minute particulars of an undecidable moment, nearly imperceptible displacements, that might otherwise escape the reader's eye. He tries to locate not a moment of ambiguity or irony ultimately incorporated into the text's system of unified meaning but rather a moment that genuinely threatens to collapse that system. Derrida's method is not that of Hegel. Hegel's idealist method consists in resolving by sublation the contradictions between the binary oppositions.

Derrida stresses the point that it is not enough simply to neutralize the binary oppositions of metaphysics. Deconstruction involves reversal and displacement. Within the familiar philosophical oppositions there is always a violent hierarchy. One of the two terms controls the other, holds the superior position. The first move in deconstructing the opposition is to overthrow the hierarchy. In the next phase this reversal must be displaced, the winning term put 'under erasure'. Deconstruction, then, is the attempt

> to locate the promising marginal text, to disclose the undecidable moment, to pry it loose with the positive lever of the signifier, to reverse the resident hierarchy, only to displace it; to dismantle in order to reconstitute what is always already inscribed.[15]

Before making some critical remarks, let me try to sum up. Derrida has made a close study of many philosophers: Nietzsche, Rousseau, Husserl, Heidegger and others. He argues that they have been able to impose their various systems of thought only by ignoring or suppressing the disruptive effects of language. One of the ruling illusions of Western metaphysics is that reason can somehow grasp the world without a close attention to language and arrive at a pure, self-authenticating truth or method. Derrida's work draws attention to the ways in which language deflects the philosopher's project. He does this by focusing on metaphors and other figurative devices at work in the texts of philosophy. In this way Derrida underlines the rhetorical nature of philosophical arguments.

Deconstruction stresses the irreducibility of metaphor, the difference at play within the very constitution of literal meaning. It should be remembered that deconstruction is not simply a strategic reversal of categories which otherwise remain distinct and unaffected. It is an activity of reading in which texts must be read in a radically new way. There must be an awareness of ambivalence, of the discrepancy between meaning and the author's assertion. Derrida discovers a set of paradoxical themes at odds with their manifest argument. His method consists of showing how the privileged term is held in place by the force of a dominant metaphor and not, as it might seem, by any conclusive logic.[16] Metaphors often disrupt the logic of an argument.

Derrida writes that we have a metaphysical desire to make the end coincide with the means, create an enclosure, make the definition coincide with the defined, the 'father' with the 'son'; within the logic of identity to balance the equation, close the circle. In short, he is asking us' to change certain habits of mind; he is telling us that the authority of the text is provisional, the origin is a trace. Contradicting logic, we must learn to use and erase our language at the same time. Derrida wants us to 'erase' all oppositions, undoing yet preserving them.

Deconstructionists tend to say that if a text seems to refer beyond itself, that reference can finally be only to another text. Just as signs refer only to other signs, texts can refer only to other texts, generating an intersecting and indefinitely expandable web called *intertextuality*. There is a proliferation of interpretations, and no interpretation can claim to be the final one. Now, Derrida is sometimes taken to be denying the possibility of truth. This is not so. It is more plausible to think of him as trying to avoid assertions about the nature of truth.

The usual superficial criticism of Derrida is that he questions the value of 'truth' and 'logic' and yet uses logic to demonstrate the truth of his own arguments. The point is that the overt concern of Derrida's writing is the predicament of having to use the resources of the heritage that he questions.

Derrida's work confronts us with many problems. Having argued that there cannot be a realm of the signified independent of the signifier, he opens up the vista of an endless play of signifiers that refer not to signifieds but to other signifiers, so that meaning is always ultimately undecidable. Derrida gives as an example of undecidability Plato's frequent presentation of writing as a drug, *pharmakon*. This Greek word can mean either 'poison' or 'cure' and, as with a drug, which way it is taken (translated) makes a lot of difference. Consider another important case of undecidability: an isolated note found among Nietzsche's unpublished manuscripts, a single sentence in quotation marks: 'I have forgotten my umbrella.' In a sense, we all know what this phrase means, and yet we have no idea of what its meaning is in this instance. Is it a jotting to himself, a citation, or a phrase overheard and noted for further use? Perhaps the umbrella is seen as some sort of defence, a protection from the weather? Nietzsche, on the verge of breakdown, has left his defences behind; caught in a rainstorm, he has forgotten his umbrella. Of course, it could also be analysed in Freudian terms, as psychoanalysis often focuses on the significance of forgetting and phallic objects. 'I have forgotten my umbrella': the phrase is undecidable. This illustration could be a metaphor for the whole of Derrida's text.

As we saw with Derrida's work on Saussure and Lévi-Strauss, deconstruction questions the self-identity of signifier and signified and the self-presence of the speaking subject and the voiced sign. There is an abandonment of all reference to a centre, to a fixed subject, to a privileged reference, to an origin, to an absolute founding and controlling first principle.

Deconstruction disarticulates traditional conceptions of the author and the work and undermines conventional notions of reading and history. Instead of mimetic, expressive and didactic theories of 'literature' it offers textuality (*écriture*). It kills the author, turns history and tradition into intertextuality and celebrates the reader.[17]

One of the main features of post-structuralist theory is the deconstruction of the self. In place of a unified and stable being or consciousness we get a multifaceted and disintegrating play of selves. The reader, like the text, is unstable. With deconstruction the categories 'criticism', 'philosophy' and 'literature' collapse, borders are overrun. The work, now called 'text', explodes beyond stable meaning and truth towards the radical and ceaseless play of infinite meanings. Critical writing, formerly analytical and coherent, becomes playfully fragmented.

Is this a result of Derrida's view of language? It has been suggested by Terry Eagleton that

> meaning may well be ultimately undecidable if we view language contemplatively, as a chain of signifiers on a page; it becomes 'decidable' and words like 'truth', 'reality', 'knowledge', and 'certainty' have something of their force restored to them when we think of language rather as something we *do*, as indissociably interwoven with our practical forms of life.[18]

The deconstructor's method often consists of deliberately inverting traditional oppositions and marking the play of hitherto invisible concepts that reside unnamed in the gap between opposing terms. In the move from hermeneutics and semiotics to deconstruction there is a shift of focus from identities to differences, unities to fragmentations, ontology to philosophy of language, epistemology to rhetoric, presence to absence. According to one recent commentator 'deconstruction celebrates dissemination over truth, explosion and fragmentation over unity and coherence, undecidable spaces over prudent closures, playfulness and hysteria over care and rationality'.[19]

It is said that every boundary, limit, division, frame or margin instals a line separating one entity or concept from another. That is to say, every border marks a difference. The question of the border is a question of difference. Derrida writes, 'No border is guaranteed, inside or out.' Applied to texts, this finding becomes 'no meaning can be fixed or decided upon'. According to deconstructionists there is nothing other than interpretation.[20] As there is neither an undifferentiated nor a literal bottom or ground, the activity of interpretation is endless. It is also a fact that every text tends itself to deconstruction and to further deconstruction, with nowhere any end in sight. Finally, no escape outside the logocentric enclosure is possible since the interpreter must use the concepts and figures of the Western metaphysical tradition. The term used to describe the impasse of interpretation ('there is no way out') is *aporia*. 'The supreme irony of what Derrida has called logocentrism is that its critique, deconstruction, is as insistent, as monotonous and as inadvertently systematizing as logocentrism itself.'[21]

Having given a few criticisms of Derrida and deconstruction, I now want to ask, 'Are his methods allied or opposed to Marxism?' When faced with new approaches such as deconstruction it is very hard to try to work out whether they are useful aids in building a new socialist order or are just other forms of bourgeois recuperation and domination. I think I am right in saying that deconstruction is, for Derrida, ultimately a political practice, an attempt to dismantle the logic by which a particular system of thought and, behind that, a whole system of political structures and social institutions maintains its force. But in practice it cannot be denied that his work has been grossly unhistorical and politically evasive.[22] One post-structuralist, Michel Foucault, argued that Derrida's own decision to avoid questions about the extent to which the text arises out of and reflects underlying social practices itself reflects a social practice. He said that by deliberately restricting himself to textual analysis the question of evaluating textual analysis as a social and political practice cannot be raised. In so far as textual undecidability precludes raising questions about truth it perpetuates the status quo.

On the other hand, some commentators have suggested that deconstruction, by unsettling the theories with which we have surrounded ourselves, serves to indicate that our account of the world *could* be different but that it cannot tell us how it would be different. Derrida seems to believe that deconstruction is able gradually to shift the structures within which we operate 'little by little to modify the terrain of our work, and thereby produce new figurations'. Is this enough? Is Derrida playing among the webs of language, 'parodying himself, and then parodying the parody'?[23]

Derrida has himself observed that certain American uses of deconstruction work to ensure 'an institutional closure' which serves the dominant political and economic interests of American society. He has also said that Marxist texts are shot through with metaphors disguised as concepts, themes that carry along with them a whole unrecognized baggage of presuppositions. But on the whole Derrida has been silent about Marx – a silence that can be construed as a prolonged postponement, a refusal as yet to engage with Marxist thought.

There are some critics, like Fredric Jameson, who feel that the claims of synchronic thought must somehow be reconciled with those of historical understanding, that there must be a *rapprochement* between rhetoric and Marxist dialetic.[24] But other critics have suggested that the Marxist model of representation, however refined in theory, is caught up in a rhetoric of tropes and images that entirely controls its logic. Christopher Norris, for example, has argued that deconstruction is inimical to Marxist thought. In his view the insights of deconstruction are inevitably couched in a rhetoric which itself lies open to further deconstructive reading: 'Once criticism enters the labyrinth of deconstruction it is committed to a sceptical epistemology that leads back to Nietzsche, rather than Marx.'[25]

Some of the most trenchant criticisms of deconstruction have been made by the English Marxist critic Terry Eagleton. According to' Eagleton the main characteristics of deconstruction are that it rejects any notion of totality and that it is against the privileging of the unitary subject. Deconstructionism asserts that literary texts do not have relations to something other than themselves. It follows that deconstruction is not concerned with blaming anybody for the exploitation that exists, since this would entail some kind of vantage point from which definite judgements could be delivered. Eagleton, in 1981, wrote that

> many of the vauntedly novel themes of deconstruction do little more than reproduce some of the most commonplace topics of bourgeois liberalism. The modest disownment of theory, method and system; the revulsion from

the dominative, totalising and unequivocally denotative; the privileging of plurality and heterogeneity; the recurrent gestures of hesitation and indeterminacy; the devotion to gliding and process, slippage and movement; the distaste for the definitive – it is not difficult to see why such an idiom should become so quickly absorbed within the Anglo-Saxon academies.[26]

It is suggested by Eagleton that deconstruction is not only reformist but ultra-leftist too. On the one hand, deconstruction is a sort of patient, probing reformism of the text. Because it can only imagine contradiction as the external warring of two monistic essences, it fails to comprehend class dialectics. On the other hand, deconstruction is ultra-left in that it is 'a problematic that sees meaning itself as terroristic'. Both left reformism (social democracy) and ultra-leftism are among other things antithetical responses to the failure or absence of a mass revolutionary movement.

In a recent book the leading exponent of Derrida's thought in Britain, Christopher Norris, reminds us that Derrida wants to stress the non-availability of any such thing as a direct unmediated knowledge of the world. Derrida wants to emphasize the culturally produced (as opposed to the natural) character of thought and perception. In his polemic against Jean Baudrillard and others, Norris argues that deconstruction has nothing in common with those forms of extreme anti-cognitivist doctrine that would claim to have come out 'beyond' all distinctions between truth and falsehood, reason and rhetoric, fact and fiction. In Norris's view, Derrida has been at some pains to dissociate his project from the kind of irrationalist or nihilist outlook which takes it for granted that truth and reason are obsolete values. He has a continuing critical engagement with the truth-claims and ethical values of Enlightenment thought.[27] Derridean deconstruction supports the Enlightenment critique even while subjecting that tradition to a radical reassessment.

Further reading

D. Hoy, 'Jacques Derrida', in Q. Skinner (ed.), *The Return of Grand Theory in the Human Sciences*, Cambridge: Cambridge University Press, 1985.
A useful discussion of Derridean deconstruction and the Derrida–Foucault dispute.

C. Norris, *Deconstruction: Theory and Practice*, London: Methuen, 1982.
A good introduction to the subject. Two excellent chapters on Derrida
are followed by others that discuss the implications of Nietzsche's
writings, the relation between deconstruction and Marxist thought, and
the work of contemporary American literary critics.

C. Norris, *Derrida*, London: Fontana Press, 1987.
An excellent book; besides introducing Derrida's writings on Plato,
Hegel, Saussure, Rousseau, Kant, it explains the significance of his
work, and discusses recent philosophical controversies. It contains a
useful bibliography.

D. Wood, 'An Introduction to Derrida', in R. Edgley and R. Osborne
(eds), *Radical Philosophy Reader*, London: Verso, 1985.
A lucid exposition.

D. Wood, 'Beyond Deconstruction?', in A. Phillips Griffiths (ed.),
Contemporary French Philosophy, Cambridge: Cambridge University
Press, 1987.
A clear and useful defence of Derrida's deconstruction from the
accusation of nihilism, empty reversalism and textual idealism.

Chapter 3

□

Foucault and the social sciences

Introduction: Foucault's view of history

Foucault is against any form of global theorizing. He wants to avoid totalizing forms of analysis and is critical of systematicity. Though his works do not constitute a system, nevertheless there is an underlying coherence which stems from the fact that Foucault's works are based on a vision of history derived from Nietzsche. Indeed, he expressed his indebtedness to Nietzsche for having outlined a conception of history called genealogy.[1]

Nietzsche's book *On the Genealogy of Morals* was an effort to delegitimize the present by separating it from the past. This is what Foucault tries to do. Unlike the historian who traces a line of inevitability, Foucault breaks off the past from the present and, by demonstrating the foreignness of the past, relativizes and undercuts the legitimacy of the present.

Foucault rejects the Hegelian teleological model, in which one mode of production flows dialectically out of another, in favour of a Nietzschean tactic of critique through the presentation of *difference*. The Nietzschean historian begins with the present and goes backward in time until a difference is located. Then s/he proceeds forward again, tracing the transformation and taking care to preserve the discontinuities as well as the connections. This is the method used by Foucault. The alien discourses/practices are explored in such a way that their negativity in relation to the present explodes the 'rationality' of phenomena that are taken for granted. When the technology of power of the past is elaborated in detail, present-day assumptions which posit the past as 'irrational' are undermined.

The gap between the past and the present underlines the principle of difference at the heart of Foucault's historiography. He allows the discontinuity to remain unexplained. The role of cause or explanation is severely reduced in most post-structuralist texts, since it leads to evolutionist conclusions and works against the purposes of the genealogy of difference.

Genealogical analysis, then, differs from traditional forms of historical analysis in several ways. Whereas traditional or 'total' history inserts events into grand explanatory systems and linear processes, celebrates great moments and individuals and seeks to document a point of origin, genealogical analysis attempts to establish and preserve the singularity of events, turns away from the spectacular in favour of the discredited, the neglected and a whole range of phenomena which have been denied a history. According to Foucault there has been an insurrection of subjugated knowledges, of a whole set of knowledges that have been disqualified as inadequate – naïve knowledges located low down on the hierarchy, beneath the required level of scientificity. Foucault often uses the term genealogy to refer to the union of erudite knowledge and local memories which allows us to establish a historical knowledge of struggles and to make use of this knowledge tactically today. Genealogies focus on local, discontinuous, disqualified, illegitimate knowledges against the claims of a unitary body of theory which would filter, hierarchize and order them in the name of some true knowledge.

Genealogy, I repeat, is a form of critique. It rejects the pursuit of the origin in favour of a conception of historical beginnings as lowly, complex and contingent. It attempts to reveal the multiplicity of factors behind an event and the fragility of historical forms. In this view of history, which Foucault's writings exemplify, there can be no constants, no essences, no immobile forms of uninterrupted continuities structuring the past.

Reason and unreason

Foucault's early work is mainly concerned with the growth of those disciplines which are collectively known as the social or human sciences. His books are an answer to the question of how the human sciences are historically possible and what the consequences of their existence are. His studies repeatedly centre on the eighteenth century – the period in which the human sciences in their modern forms were constituted and certain new 'technologies' elaborated. Both of these developments were linked to a new philosophical conception of Man as a simultaneous subject and object of knowledge.

Throughout his life Foucault was interested in that which reason excludes: madness, chance, discontinuity. He believed that the literary text allows 'otherness' to speak. In philosophy and law this otherness is silent, whereas in madness it is not listened to. Foucault valued the literature of transgression – it attempts to subvert the constraints of all other forms of discourse by its difference. And so he admired the literary tradition that includes writers such as de Sade, Nerval, Artaud and Nietzsche.

In his first well-known book, *Madness and Civilization*, Foucault describes how madness, along with poverty, unemployment and the inability to work, comes in the seventeenth century to be perceived as a 'social problem' which falls within the ambit of responsibility of the state.[2] There is a new conception of the state as preserver and augmenter of the general welfare. In the book there is an important discussion of the emergence of 'humanitarian' attitudes towards the insane at the end of the eighteenth century. The opening of Tuke's Retreat at York and Pinel's liberation of the insane at Bicêtre are portrayed as leading to a 'gigantic moral imprisonment', more oppressive than the former practices of brutal incarceration since they operate on the mind rather than merely on the body.

The great confinement

At the end of the Middle Ages leprosy disappeared from the Western world. Foucault suggests a connection between this and some of the attitudes then taken towards madness. As leprosy vanished a void was created and the moral values had to find another scapegoat. He shows how in the 'classical period' (1500–1800) madness attracted that stigma.

During the Renaissance madmen led an easy, wandering existence. The towns drove them outside their limits and they were allowed to wander in the open countryside. One common way of dealing with the mad was to put them on a ship and entrust them to mariners, because folly, water and sea, as everyone then 'knew', had an affinity with each other. These 'Ships of Fools' were to be found criss-crossing the seas and canals of Europe. Many texts and paintings, for example the works of Breughel, Bosch and Dürer, refer to the theme of madness. These works of art express an enormous anxiety about the relationships between the real and the imaginary. Then, within the space of a hundred years, the 'madship' was replaced by the 'madhouse'; instead of embarkation there was *confinement*. Men did not wait until the seventeenth century to 'shut up' the mad, but it was in this period that they began to 'confine' them.

Why was this? Foucault argues that during the second half of the seventeenth century social sensibility, common to European culture, began to manifest itself; a 'sensibility to poverty and to the duties of assistance, new forms of reaction to the problems of unemployment and idleness, a new ethic of work'.[3] And so, enormous houses of confinement (sometimes called 'houses of correction') were created throughout Europe. To these places a (strangely) mixed group of people, poor vagabonds, the unemployed, the sick, the criminals and the insane were sent. No differentiation was made between them.

Confinement was a massive phenomenon, a 'police' matter whose task was to supress beggary and idleness as a source of disorder.

> The unemployed person was no longer driven away or punished; he was taken in charge, at the expense of the nation but at the cost of his individual liberty. Between him and society an implicit system of obligation was established: he had the right to be fed, but he must accept the physical and moral constraint of confinement.[4]

The repressive function of the houses of confinement was combined with a new use: the internees were made to work. In the Middle Ages the great sin had been pride, in the seventeenth century it was sloth. Since sloth had become the absolute form of rebellion, the idle were forced to work. Labour was instituted as an exercise in moral reform. Confinement played a double role: it absorbed the unemployed in order to mask their poverty and it also avoided the social or political disadvantages of agitation.

In the Renaissance madness had been present everywhere, but the houses of confinement hid it away. Confinement marked a decisive event: 'The new meanings assigned to poverty, the importance given to the obligation to work, and all the ethical values that are linked to labour, ultimately determined the experience of madness and inflected its course.'[5] Most of Foucault's book is a detailed description of how madness was thought about in the seventeenth and eighteenth centuries: he writes about mania and melancholia, hysteria and hypochondria; how it was thought that the savage danger of madness was related to the danger of the passions, and how madness was conceived as a form of animality to be mastered only by discipline.

Gradually in the eighteenth century confinement came to be seen as a gross error; it began to be said that charity was a cause of impoverishment and that vagabonds should seek employment. Moreover, legislators were beginning to be embarrassed because they no longer knew where to place mad people – in prison, hospital or the family. Measured by their functional value alone, the houses of confinement were a failure: when the unemployed were herded into forced-labour shops, there was less work available in neighbouring regions and so unemployment increased. Thus the houses of confinement, a social precaution clumsily formulatd by a nascent industrialization, disappeared throughout Europe at the beginning of the nineteenth century.

The birth of the asylum

The legislation passed to segregate criminals and poor people from fools was prompted, as often as not, by a desire to protect the poor and the criminal from the frightening bestiality of the madman. A hallowed tradition has associated Tuke in England and Pinel in France with the liberation of the insane and the abolition of constraint. But, Foucault argues, we must be sceptical of this claim. In fact, Tuke created an asylum where the partial abolition of physical constraint was part of a system whose essential element was the constitution of a self-restraint. 'He substituted for the free terror of madness the stifling anguish of responsibility . . . The asylum no longer punished the madman's guilt, it is true, it did more, it organized that guilt.'[6]

The Quaker Samuel Tuke organized his Retreat so that it had a religious ethos. In it work was imposed as a moral rule, a submission to order. Instead of repression there was surveillance and judgement by 'authority'. Everything at the asylum was arranged so that the insane were transformed into minors and given rewards and punishments like children. A new system of education was applied; first the inmates were to be subjugated, then encouraged, then applied to work: 'The asylum would keep the insane in the imperative fiction of the family; the madman remains a minor, and for a long time reason will retain for him the aspect of the Father.'[7]

During the 'classical period' poverty, laziness, vice and madness mingled in an equal guilt within unreason. Madness during the nineteenth century began to be categorized as social failure. The doctor gained a new social status and increasingly the patient surrendered to the medical profession. In short, the asylum of the age of positivism was not a free realm of observation, diagnosis and therapeutics. In the hands of Tuke and Pinel it became a juridical space where one was accused, judged and condemned – an instrument of moral uniformity. Invoking the names of those who have gone mad, such as Artaud, Hölderlin, Nerval, Nietzsche and Van Gogh, Foucault reminds us that we are in the habit of calling this gigantic moral imprisonment the 'liberation' of the insane.

Foucault's book has a sense of great loss. It states that during the Middle Ages mad people were not locked up; indeed they possessed a certain freedom. There was a notion of the 'wise fool' – like the character in *King Lear*. Even in the eighteenth century madness had still not lost its power; but in the nineteenth century the dialogue between reason and unreason was broken. There is now only the monologue of reason *on* madness. Foucault suggests that there are dimensions that are missing in reason or, to put it in another way, there may be a wisdom in madness.

Human beings have been released from the physical chains, but these have been replaced by mental ones. One of the main themes of the book is how external violence has been replaced by internalization. The birth of the asylum can be seen as an allegory on the constitution of subjectivity. It is an indictment of modern consciousness. *Madness and Civilization* is as much concerned with the plight of everyday consciousness in the modern world as with the specific fate of those labelled insane. Foucault implies that modern forms of public provision and welfare are inseparable from ever tighter forms of social and psychological control. From the beginning, intervention and administrative control have defined the modern state.

According to Foucault madness can never be captured; madness is not exhausted by the concepts we use to describe it. His work contains the Nietzschean idea that there is more to madness than scientific categorization; but in associating freedom with madness he seems to me to romanticize madness. For Foucault, to be free would be *not* to be a rational, conscious being. Though Foucault's position is a relativist one, he actually had deep-seated preferences. Critics of Foucault asked, 'How could Foucault capture the spirit of madness when he was so obviously writing from the viewpoint of reason?'[8] Shouldn't he, logically, have given up writing altogether?

Most of Foucault's books are really analyses of *the process of modernization*. One of the characteristics of his work is the tendency to condense a general historical argument into a tracing of the emergence of specific institutions. His second main work, *The Birth of the Clinic*, is subtitled 'An Archaeology of Medical Perception'.[9] This perception or 'gaze' is formed by the new, untrammelled type of observation made possible for the doctor at the bedside of the hospitalized patient intersecting with a system of monitoring the state of health of the nation through the new teaching hospital.

Foucault's subsequent books, *The Order of Things* and *The Archaeology of Knowledge*, deal largely with the structure of scientific discourses.[10] (Discourses are perhaps best understood as practices that systematically form the objects of which they speak.) Foucault is concerned with the question, what set of rules permit certain statements to be made?

In *The Order of Things* Foucault argues that in certain empirical forms of knowledge such as biology, psychiatry, medicine, etc., the rhythms of transformation do not follow the continuist schemas of development which are normally accepted. In medicine, for example, within a period of about twenty-five years there arose a completely new way of speaking and seeing. How is it that at certain moments and in certain knowledges there are these sudden transformations? There seem to be changes in the rules of formation of statements which are accepted as scientifically true. There is a whole new 'regime' of discourse which makes possible the separation not of the true from the false but of what may be characterized as scientific from what may not be characterized as scientific.

Unlike most of Foucault's other work, *The Order of Things* and *The Archaeology of Knowledge* are not concerned with the emergence of modern forms of administration. One reason for this may be that the structuralists during the 1960s veered away from any form of political analysis and that he was influenced by them.

Looking back on his early work, Foucault conceded that what was missing was a consideration of the effects of power:

> When I think back now, I ask myself what else it was that I was talking about, in *Madness and Civilization* or *The Birth of the Clinic*, but power? Yet I'm perfectly aware that I scarcely ever used the word and never had such a field of analysis at my disposal.[11]

In his later work, where Foucault is concerned with power and knowledge, he is much more inclined to talk about 'apparatuses'. An apparatus is a structure of heterogeneous elements such as discourses, laws, institutions, in short, the said as much as the unsaid. The apparatus contains strategies of relations of forces supporting, and supported by, types of knowledge.

A struggle over meaning

Foucault returned to some of the topics discussed in *Madness and Civilization* in a book which he edited twelve years later called *I, Pierre Rivière . . . A Case of Parricide in the 19th Century*.[12] One of the main themes of this 'dossier' is the problematic division between the innocence of unreason and the guilt of crime. This work is truly interdisciplinary in that one can approach it from the point of view of history, politics, literature, psychiatry, or the law.

It raises many important questions about these forms of knowledge and their interrelationship. The case of Pierre Rivière marked the border where many types of discourse, institutions and powers confronted one another. To anyone wishing to read a case study of a struggle over meaning or wanting to understand what Foucault means by a 'battle among discourses through discourses' I would recommend this book.

Pierre Rivière was, in two different ways but in virtually a single deed, an 'author'. In 1835 the twenty-year-old peasant killed his mother, his sister and his brother. While he was detained he wrote a memoir giving particulars and an explanation of the crime. Though he had received only a village education he produced a text that has beauty and eloquence. The memoir is of interest to historians and others because it raises so many questions. Frightful crimes were being committed in the countryside at that time, but what were those acts saying and why did they speak such a terrifying language? Why was parricide equated with regicide?

The life story of this obscure peasant (who resembles Julien Sorel) has considerable literary value; and as there are so many interpretations it raises the question, 'How do we read a text?' What is fascinating is that the book shows how two conflicting arguments (that advanced by the doctors and that put forward by the lawyers) could be constructed from two different accounts of Rivière's life, both of them based on the *same* sources of information. Of course, the frontier between rationality and madness is hard to establish, but can they coexist in the form of a partial delusion and the lucid interval? While some people saw in Rivière's memoir a proof of rationality and therefore wanted to condemn him to the guillotine, other people saw in the memoir a sign of madness and hence wanted to isolate him in an asylum.

Some said that the same signs of madness could be found alike in the fact of premeditated murder and in the particulars of what was narrated; others said that the same signs of lucidity could be found both in the *preparation and circumstances* of the murder and in the fact that Rivière had written it down. In other words, the fact of killing and the fact of writing, the deeds done and the things narrated, coincided since they were elements of a like nature.

While the doctors presented Rivière as always having been mad, the lawyers claimed that he was always sane. The doctors stressed his 'bizarre behaviour' as a sign of his madness; lawyers, by stressing Rivière's intelligence, ascribed to him full responsibility for his crime. What was really happening in this competition between the medical and the penal authorities was an attempt to pathologize a sector of criminality. Emergent psychiatry was attempting to gain a space for its intervention and create a new apparatus. There is an interesting section in the book on how the development of the theory of limited responsibility, the existence of extenuating circumstances, opened the way in introducing not merely psychiatry but all the social and human sciences, psychology, sociology, genetics and so on, into judicial procedure.

This book, then, gives us an idea of how a particular kind of knowledge such as medicine or psychiatry is formed. Foucault tells us that the documents in the book give us a key to the relations of power, domination and conflict within which discourses emerge and function, and hence provide material for a potential analysis of discourse which may be both tactical and political and therefore strategic. In short, the book exemplifies one of Foucault's main preoccupations: the attempt to rediscover the interaction of discourses as weapons of attack and defence in the relations of power and knowledge.

Disciplinary power

I have mentioned several times that Foucault's work owes much to Nietzsche. Many of the themes that have reappeared in post-structuralism, such as relativism and the relationship between knowledge and power, can be found in Nietzsche's work. Foucault inverts, following Nietzsche, the common-sense view of the relation between power and knowledge. Whereas we might normally regard knowledge as providing us with power to do things that without it we could not do, Foucault argues that knowledge is a power over others, the power to define others. In his view knowledge ceases to be a liberation and becomes a mode of surveillance, regulation, discipline.

Foucault's masterpiece, *Discipline and Punish*, focuses on the moment when it became understood that it was more efficient and profitable to place people under surveillance than to subject them to some exemplary penalty. This transition in the eighteenth century corresponds to the formation of a new mode of exercise of power.[13] The book begins with a horrifying description of a regicide's torture and public execution. The author then describes how within eighty years vast changes occurred: torture disappeared, there was regulation of prisoners, and the new mechanisms of surveillance began to be applied in barracks, hospitals, prisons and schools.

Foucault suggests that under a feudal and monarchical system individualization is greatest at the summit of society. Power is visibly embodied in the person of the king, who has unlimited power over an anonymous body of subjects. Under this type of regime the notion of crime is still not fully distinguished from that of sacrilege, so that punishment takes the form of a ritual intended not to 'reform' the offender but to express and restore the sanctity of the law which has been broken. In general, power in feudal societies tends to be haphazard and imprecise, whereas in modern societies the agencies of punishment become part of a pervasive, impersonal system of surveillance and correction which pays an ever-increasing attention to the psychology of the individual. Intention rather than transgression now becomes the central criterion of culpability.

Let me restate Foucault's argument. In feudal societies, under *monarchical power*, the judiciary only arrested a very small proportion of criminals and it was argued that punishment must be spectacular so as to frighten the others. The new theorists of the eighteenth century objected to this: such a form of power was too costly in proportion to its results. In contrast to monarchical power, there is *disciplinary power*, a system of surveillance which is interiorized to the point that each person is his or her own overseer. Power is thus exercised continuously at a minimal cost.

Once you suppress the idea of vengeance, which previously was the act of a sovereign threatened in his very sovereignty by the crime, punishment can only have a meaning within a technology of reform. Foucault's hypothesis is that the prison was linked from its beginning to a project for the transformation of individuals. The failure of the project was immediate and this was realized virtually from the start. People knew that prisons did not reform but on the contrary manufactured criminals and criminality. It was soon discovered that criminals could be put to good use as informers, pimps, policemen. Foucault writes that at the end of the eighteenth century people dreamed of a society without crime. And then the dream evaporated. Crime was too useful to dream of anything as dangerous as a society without crime. 'No crime means no police. What makes the presence and control of the police tolerable for the population, if not fear of the criminal?'[14] In short, supervised illegality was directly useful. It provided a justification and a means for the general surveillance, the policing of the entire population.

The transformation of Western societies from monarchical (or sovereign) power to disciplinary power is epitomized in Foucault's description of the Panopticon, an architectural device advocated by Jeremy Bentham towards the end of the eighteenth century. In this circular building of cells no prisoner can be certain of not being observed from the central watch-tower, and so the prisoners gradually begin to police their own behaviour.

This new mode of power, which we can call panopticism, was used first of all in schools, barracks and hospitals. People learned how to establish dossiers, systems of marking and classifying. Then there was the permanent surveillance of a group of pupils or patients; and at a certain moment in time these methods began to be generalized.

If you have already read *Discipline and Punish* you will have noticed the likeness between the Panopticon (the 'all-seeing') and the Christian God's infinite knowledge. It is also similar to Freud's concept of the super-ego as the internal monitor of unconscious wishes. Another parallel is between the Panopticon and the computer monitoring of individuals in advanced capitalism. Foucault hints that the new techniques of power were needed to grapple with the increase in population: to undertake its administration and control because of newly-arising problems of public health, hygiene, housing conditions, longevity, fertility, sex. As we shall see in a moment, sex is politically significant because it is located at the point of intersection of the discipline of the body and the control of the population.

At times *Discipline and Punish* regresses to a totalizing logic in which the Panopticon becomes the model for all forms of domination. Moreover, though Foucault makes a powerful case against the modern prison system, he offers nothing as a constructive alternative to it. One point that puzzles me is that, according to Foucault, the Panopticon is a machine in which everyone is caught and which no one knows. What, then, is the origin of this strategy, how do these tactics arise? Foucault does not give a clear answer; he merely states that all these tactics were invented and organized from the starting points of local conditions and particular needs, that they took shape in piecemeal fashion, prior to any class strategy.

Technical rationality

What was the problem that really worried Foucault? Bourgeois thought stresses the idea of the conscious subject who calculates means and ends. The subject is rational, autonomous and capable of initiating action. But the more autonomous one becomes the more important the criterion of means and ends becomes. Now, the work of Foucault has often been compared with that of Max Weber, one of whose central themes was rationalization. Weber held that action could be rational in its ends or its means. Bureaucracies stressed efficiency of means. In impersonal, bureaucratic organizations reason was shaped into scientific rationality. The objective of scientific rationality is to gain mastery over the physical and the social environment. Weber, following Nietzsche, argued that scientific rationality focused on means but not on ends. Instrumental reason cannot tell us anything about how to live our lives. In a sense Foucault reiterates the fears of (Nietzsche and) Weber: science uncovers the mythology in the world; but science itself is a myth which has to be superseded. Scientific knowledge has brought about a disenchantment of the world. Means can be calculated with efficiency – this is what is called technical rationality – but ends, values, become increasingly problematic to determine. One effect of the rise of technical or instrumental rationality is the process of reification which has produced disenchantment.

This analysis is in some ways close to the one made by the 'critical theorists' of the Frankfurt School. Theodor Adorno and Max Horkheimer, much influenced by Weber, analysed the capitalist economy as merely one form of the autonomous dynamic of a means–end rationality. This makes possible not only an unprecedented increase in the forces of production, and therefore in the domination of external nature, but also in the domination of human beings who are adapted to the system of production through social engineering and psychological manipulation. According to Adorno and Horkheimer the calculating instrumental rationality required of the subject in its struggle to gain independence from the overwhelming powers of external nature requires a corresponding repression of the spontaneity of inner nature.[15] For Weber and the Frankfurt School the social forms engendered by (technical or) instrumental rationality represent a profounder threat to human freedom than class oppression. Adorno and Horkheimer believed that even the space for individual responsibility and initiative, which was opened during the early phases of capitalism, is now closed by the administered society.

Foucault, too, was worried about the productivity and efficiency of those instrumental–rational forms of organization which Weber detected in modern bureaucracies and in the capitalist organization of the labour process. Foucault's view that power cannot be considered a possession of groups or individuals should be understood in the light of Weber's account of the transition from 'traditional' to 'legal–rational' forms of domination. That is to say, power in modern societies does not depend upon the prowess and prestige of individuals but is exercised through an impersonal administrative machinery operating in accordance with abstract rules.

Sexuality and power

Foucault is generally known as the historian who stresses discontinuities. But in fact, when he writes about other thinkers he often emphasizes the continuities in their work. For example, at the time Althusser was emphasizing the epistemological break in Marx's work (separating the early 'ideological' texts from the later anti-humanist, economic work) Foucault argued that Marx's concepts were only a development of those of David Ricardo and, what is more, that Marxism fitted into nineteenth-century thought like a fish in water; that is, it was unable to breathe anywhere else. Similarly, Freud's work does not represent a radical break; psychoanalysis is, in fact, an episode in the machinery of the confession. (By confession Foucault means all those procedures by which subjects are incited to produce a discourse of truth about their sexuality which is capable of having effects on the subjects themselves.) In the usual histories one reads that sexuality was ignored by medicine and psychiatry and that at last Freud discovered the sexual origin of neuroses. Now everyone knows, says Foucault, that that is not true; the problem of sexuality was massively inscribed in the medicine and psychiatry of the nineteenth century.

Psychoanalysis was established in opposition to a certain kind of psychiatry, the psychiatry of degeneracy, eugenics and heredity. In relation to that psychiatry psychoanalysis played a liberating role; some of its activities, however, have the function of control and normalization. In Foucault's view psychoanalysis grew out of the institutionalization of confessional procedures which has been so characteristic of our civilization. Viewed over a shorter span of time, it forms part of that medicalization of sexuality which is another phenomenon of the West.

These are some of the views expressed in *The History of Sexuality; Volume One: An Introduction.*[16] One of the main points of the book is that sexuality is far more a positive product of power than power was ever repression of sexuality. Foucault states that we have only had sexuality since the eighteenth century, and sex since the nineteenth. What we had before that was, no doubt, the flesh.

Foucault argues that at one time the Christian confession was the locus of sexuality. In the Middle Ages the priest was concerned with what people did; the faithful were asked in detail about their sexual activities. In that period sexuality, in the understanding of society, concerned only the body. With the Reformation and the Counter-Reformation the discourse on sexuality takes another form. In the confession the priest begins to inquire not only about actions but also about intentions. Sexuality begins to be defined in terms of the mind as well as the body. This is similar to the pattern of change discovered by Foucault in his history of crime and punishment; there also, discourse intensifies from a concern with action and the body to a concern with the mind and its intentions.

Foucault's work shows how in the eighteenth century processes of training and regulation of human bodies emerged in a wide range of specific institutional locations: in factories, prisons and schools. The overall outcome of these disciplinary practices were bodies that were useful and docile, productive and subjected. And then, at the beginning of the twentieth century, the discourse on sex became a matter of science. Foucault's main example of a modern discourse on sexuality, a new scientific confessional, is psychoanalysis. He says that by positing a sexual instinct Freud opened up a new realm for the domination of science over sexuality.

Foucault draws attention to the dissolution of the forms of group identity characteristic of traditional societies, and their replacement by a form of identity which depends increasingly upon the capacity of the individual to reflect upon and articulate the domain of private experience. It is an attack on what he calls 'the repressive hypothesis', the assumption that the asceticism and work discipline of bourgeois society demanded a repression of sexuality. The sexual-repression hypothesis is associated with Wilhelm Reich and the Frankfurt School. Reich's story, to put it simply, is that with the onset of capitalism there was an increasing repression and confinement of (natural) human sexuality. The authoritarian bourgeois father, devoted obsessively to accumulating capital, hoarded his energies for the market place and the factory. Foucault's *The History of Sexuality* opens with an attack on this Freudo-Marxist position. He claims that it was precisely during this period that there was 'a veritable explosion' of discourses about sexuality in, for example, medical, psychiatric and educational theories and the practices that were both informed and presupposed by these discourses.

Foucault's main objection to the repressive hypothesis is its reliance upon a negative conception of power as prohibition or limitation. Against this he maintains that since the eighteenth century power has become increasingly positive or productive, involving the careful construction of new capacities rather than the repression or removal of pre-existing ones. The fundamental thesis of the book is that sexuality is not a natural reality but the product of a system of discourses and practices which form part of the intensifying surveillance and control of the individual. Foucault suggests that liberation is a form of servitude, since our apparently 'natural' sexuality is in fact a product of power.

Foucault's primary objective is to provide a critique of the way modern societies control and discipline their populations by sanctioning the knowledge claims and practices of the human sciences: medicine, psychiatry, psychology, criminology and sociology. The human sciences have established certain norms and these are reproduced and legitimized through the practices of teachers, social workers, doctors, judges, policemen and administrators. The human sciences have made man a subject of study and a subject of the state. There has been an unrelenting expansion of rationalized systems of administration and social control. It is time to examine Foucault's theory of power.

Power and knowledge

In structuralism all relations were seen as linguistic, symbolic, discursive. After a while such a linguistic model was seen to be limited and some theorists became increasingly interested in power. Foucault's writings are an example of this trend. His work in the 1960s focused on language and the constitution of the subject in discourse. The individual subject was an empty entity, an intersection of discourses. In his later work Foucault shifted from linguistic determination to the view that individuals are constituted by power relations, power being the ultimate principle of social reality.

Foucault remarked that Nietzsche's contemporary presence is increasingly important. It was Nietzsche who specified the power relation as the general focus, whereas for Marx it was the production relation. Nietzsche is the philosopher of power, a philosopher who managed to think of power without having to confine himself within a political theory in order to do so. Historians have studied those who held power and there have been many anecdotal histories of kings and generals; contrasted with this there has been the history of economic processes. Again distinct from this we have histories of institutions. But power in its strategies and its mechanisms has never been studied. What has been studied even less is the relation between power and knowledge. It is, of course, the interdependence of power and knowledge (*pouvoir–savoir*) that constitutes the strategic fulcrum of Foucault's later work.

Traditionally, power has often been thought of in negative terms and been seen as an essentially judicial mechanism: as that which lays down the law, which limits, obstructs, refuses, prohibits and censors. It presupposes a sovereign whose role is to forbid: to have power is to say no. And the challenging of power thus conceived can appear only as transgression.

This is the view that Foucault accepted in his early work; but by around 1971–2 he realized that the question of power needed to be reformulated. He replaced a judicial, negative conception of power with a technical and strategic one. This positive view can be seen in *Discipline and Punish* and *The History of Sexuality*. Modern power operates through the construction of 'new' capacities and modes of activity rather than through the limitation of pre-existing ones.

Foucault argues that power is not a possession or a capacity.[17] It is not something subordinate to or in the service of the economy. He insists that relations of power do not emanate from a sovereign or a state; nor should power be conceptualized as the property of an individual or class. Power is not simply a commodity which may be acquired or seized. Rather it has the character of a network; its threads extend everywhere. Foucault suggests that an analysis of power should concentrate not on the level of conscious intention but on the point of application of power. In other words, he wants to shift attention from questions such as 'Who has power?' or 'What intentions or aims do power holders have?' to the processes by which subjects are constituted as effects of power.

He rejects analyses which locate the source of origin of power within a structure or an institution at a centre or summit. Foucault's view calls into question the Marxist notion of conflict between a ruling class and a subordinate class. Foucault states that the mechanisms, techniques and procedures of power were not invented by the bourgeoisie, were not the creation of a class seeking to exercise effective forms of domination; rather they were deployed from the moment that they revealed their political and economic utility for the bourgeoisie.

For Foucault, then, conceiving of power as repression, constraint or prohibition is inadequate: power 'produces reality'; it 'produces domains of objects and rituals of truth'. Foucault remarks that we often hear the cliché 'power makes mad', but we should consider the fact that the exercise of power itself creates and causes to emerge new objects of knowledge. Conversely, knowledge induces effects of power. It is not possible for power to be exercised without knowledge, it is impossible for knowledge not to engender power.

I now want to say something about Foucault's views on power and the role of intellectuals. Foucault's constant emphasis on power and on discourse provides a unifying core to his work. As I implied above, Foucault argues that power no longer operates through a straight-forward 'top-down' mechanism where those in authority exert various forms of coercive restraint upon the mass of more or less compliant subjects. In his view complex differential power relationships extend to every aspect of our social, cultural and political lives, involving all manner of (often contradictory) 'subject-positions', and securing our assent not so much by the threat of punitive sanctions as by persuading us to internalize the norms and values that prevail within the social order.

Foucault asserts that we should not view the subject as the knowing, willing, autonomous, self-critical or 'transcendental' subject of Kantian discourse. We should now understand the subject as a locus of multiple, dispersed or decentred discourses. The death of the 'transcendental subject' removed the very ground of truth-telling moral authority that Noam Chomsky and Jean-Paul Sartre occupied.

Foucault is highly critical of those 'universal' intellectuals (like Sartre) who know a lot about a specialized topic and then exploit their position in order to pose as the intellectual conscience of their age. In contrast, he believes in 'specific intellectuals', those who work in particular, well-defined areas of local expertise. This seems to go with his belief in the micro-politics of localized struggles and specific power relations. Specific intellectuals do not have universalist aspirations.

In Foucault's view, intellectuals now have to acknowledge that the Enlightenment was one particular historically dated and culture-specific discourse whose truth-claims and values amounted to no more than a transient episode in the modern history of ideas. History is often used to describe a homogenizing approach to the past and is often associated with a master narrative. In contrast, Foucault adopts a Nietzschean or genealogical perspective which treats all truth-claims as products of the ubiquitous will-to-power within language, discourse or representation.

Foucault and Althusser

Foucault's thesis that subjects are constituted by power derives from Nietzsche (who remarked that an internalized moral control of behaviour can only be inculcated through threats and violence).[18] Like Nietzsche Foucault analyses the transition from a state of overt violence and brutality to a condition of internalized restraint. As I said earlier, Foucault argues that the physical confinement and repression that occurred in the sixteenth, seventeenth and eighteenth centuries left a greater power and freedom to madness than modern methods of treatment, which aim at transforming the consciousness of the insane. Where formerly there had been the 'free terror of madness' there now reigns the 'stifling anguish of responsibility'. This regime of incessant observation and judgement forms the conditions for the internalization of morality. As Peter Dews has observed, what Foucault is really talking about here is not the specific regime of the modern asylum but the makings of modern subjectivity.[19]

Foucault is against the philosophical tradition which takes for granted that human subjects are responsible and autonomous. He is critical of the notion of the subject throughout his work. You will remember that in

Discipline and Punish Foucault wrote that the Panopticon creates subjects responsible for their own subjection. Self-enslavement is the moment of horror. The book can be read as a parable about human subjectivity. At one time the ruler was individualized and the mass was anonymous. Now the bureaucracy is anonymous and the subject is individualized. Foucault is ambiguous about whether the Panopticon is power or an apparatus of power. He believes, like Althusser, that ideology will not end in the future, that there will never be a transparent society.

It could be argued that Foucault's notion of the Panopticon is in some ways rather like Althusser's account of ideology. In Althusser there are many small subjects in subordinate positions in relation to the absolute subject.[20] Similarly, in Foucault there are many separate, individual prisoners who are subject to 'the look', the gaze. The inmates in the circular building do not know when they are being observed from the central tower, and so they tend to behave as if they were always under surveillance.

I think this may be a good place to consider some of the similarities – and the differences – between Foucault and Althusser that are often overlooked but which are really quite important. One of the most obvious similarities is their *anti-humanist* approach. You may remember that Althusser attempted to make a distinction between ideology and science and argued that humanism has an ideological character. Let me quickly distinguish some of the characteristic features of humanism. There is, firstly, the Cartesian notion of the subject: 'I think, therefore I am. I have intentions, purposes, goals, therefore I am the sole source and free agent of my actions.' Humanism is also associated with 'methodological individualism' (the idea that societies consist only of individuals). Humanism is sometimes accompanied by the belief that social relations in a socialist society will be transparent. Anti-humanists argue that unconditional emancipation is a fantasy – and that fantasies are dangerous. Althusser and Foucault regard humanism as an error; and yet there is the irony that, in a sense, we are all humanists. We experience the world as humanists, but this is not necessarily the way we theorize.

Another similarity between Althusser and Foucault is that they both emphasize the necessity of applying certain anti-humanist theories to the reading of texts. It must be said, however, that just as there is no clear way of deciding what is idealist and what is materialist, there is no simple way of deciding what is humanist and what is anti-humanist.[21] Thirdly, both Althusser and Foucault produced work that raises problems rather than provides solutions. Althusser's books *For Marx* and *Reading Capital* are good examples of this.[22] Many of Foucault's writings are polemical and his concepts are unstable because of their provisional character.

Indeed, Foucault is often depicted as some sort of freewheeling relativist in contrast to Althusser, the guardian of Marxist truth; but it has been argued by Mark Cousins and Athar Hussain that both Foucault and Althusser are against a rigid notion of truth and falsity.[23] One of Althusser's main points is that science produces its own objects and that it is itself the product of social practices. Foucault argues that the character of the knowledge of the human sciences is different from that of the natural sciences. In the human sciences (what Foucault calls) Man is both subject and object.

There are also many *differences* between Foucault and Althusser which must be remembered. Althusser is committed by his espousal of Marxist materialism both to a strong view of the mind-independent reality of the objects of scientific knowledge *and* to a positive valuation of the cognitive authority of science. Ted Benton has perceptively suggested that many of the inner tensions and oscillations in Althusser's work stem from his difficulties in synthesizing the French epistemological tradition, which stresses that knowledge is culturally produced, with Marxist materialism with its stress on the existence of a mind-independent reality.[24]

Althusser makes a sharp distinction between ideology and science. He believes that, historically, ideology precedes the science that is produced when there is an 'epistemological break', but that it survives alongside science as an essential element of every social formation. Foucault, however, rejects the concept of ideology. What he tries to do is to talk about the social function of ideology but without an epistemological dimension; it is as if he did not want to get trapped in the interminable debates about reality and illusion.

What are Foucault's objections to the concept of ideology? In Marxist thought ideology is usually conceived as a form of mystification; it does not have the status of scientific knowledge. From Foucault's Nietzschean viewpoint, however, all discourses are merely perspectives. I think Foucault's objection to the concept of ideology derives from his anti-humanism. The humanist notion of ideology places the sources of ideas in subjects, but Foucault's project is not to study Man but the mechanisms of the human sciences. He believes that by taking a point of view other than that of the subject one can decipher the mechanisms through which the human sciences come to dominate, not liberate, the subject. Furthermore, Foucault is opposed to the central feature of historical materialism upon which the concept of ideology rests: the distinction between base and superstructure. He believes that ideas are not reducible to the mode of production. In his view discourses are already powers and do not need to find their material force somewhere else, as in the mode of production. Let us look in more detail at Foucault's criticisms of Marxism.

Foucault's critique of Marxism

Foucault is very concerned about the inhibiting effect of global, totalitarian theories (Marxism and psychoanalysis) and argues that the attempt to think in terms of a totality has in fact proved a hindrance to research. As I mentioned earlier, Foucault believes that Marx's analysis of the formation of capital is for a large part governed by the concepts he derives from the framework of Ricardian economics. In short, Marx did not escape from the epistemological space established by Ricardo.[25]

What are Foucault's criticisms of the Marxist conception of the state and of the revolutionary movement? Firstly, in order to be able to fight a state which is more than just a government, the revolutionary movement must possess equivalent politico-military forces and hence must constitute itself as a party, organized internally in the same way as a state apparatus with the same mechanisms of hierarchies and structures of power. This consequence is heavy with significance. Secondly, during the period of the dictatorship of the proletariat the state apparatuses must be kept sufficiently intact for them to be employed against the class enemy. In order to operate these state apparatuses which have been taken over but not destroyed it is necessary to use specialists from the bourgeoisie. (This is what happened in the USSR.) But, Foucault argues, power is not localized in the state apparatuses and nothing in society will be changed if the mechanisms of power that function outside, below and alongside the state apparatuses on a much more minute and everyday level are not also changed.

Power is not located in the state apparatus; it passes through much finer channels and is much more ambiguous, since each individual has at his or her disposal at least some power. Moreover, it should be remembered that the reproduction of the relations of production is not the only function served by power. The systems of domination and the circuits of exploitation certainly interact, intersect and support each other, but they do not coincide. Excessive insistence on the state playing an exclusive role leads to the risk of overlooking all the mechanisms and effects of power which do not pass directly via the state apparatus, yet often sustain the state more effectively than its own institutions. In fact, the state can only function on the basis of other already existing power networks such as the family, kinship, knowledge and so forth. Of course, the critics of Foucault argue against this position because in their opinion he neglects the state and focuses only on the micro-powers that are exercised at the level of daily life.

Foucault is deeply antagonistic to the Marxist concept of ideology; he says that it is difficult to make use of it for three reasons. Firstly, it always stands in virtual opposition to something else which is supposed to count as truth. What interests him, of course, is how effects of truth are produced within discourses which in themselves are neither true nor false. Secondly, analyses which prioritize ideology trouble him because they always presuppose a human subject on the lines of the model provided by classical philosophy. Foucault wants to dispense with the constituent subject. Thirdly, ideology stands in a secondary position relative to something which functions as its base, as its material economic determinant. Perhaps I should add here that Foucault is also highly critical of the concept 'repression', which he regards as negative, psychological and insufficiently analytical. What makes power accepted is that it not only weighs on us as a force that says no, but it produces things: it induces pleasure, forms of knowledge, produces discourse.

Foucault has little to say about class consciousness, class ideology, class interest or class struggle for the simple reason that he does not believe in class. He writes, 'one should not assume a massive and primal condition of domination, a binary structure with "dominators" on one side and "dominated" on the other, but rather a multiform production of relations of domination . . .'[26]

Foucault therefore stresses the importance of *local, specific struggles* and believes that they can have effects and implications which are not simply professional or sectoral. In his view the universal intellectual (usually a writer), the bearer of values in which all can recognize themselves, has become outmoded. Intellectuals now tend to work within specific sectors such as housing, the hospital, the asylum, the laboratory, the university, family and sexual relations. He refers to these people as 'specific' intellectuals. They do not formulate the global systematic theory which holds everything in place, but analyse the specificity of mechanisms of power. He writes: 'The project, tactics, and goals to be adopted are a matter for those who do the fighting. What the intellectual can do is to provide instruments of analysis, and at present this is the historian's essential role.'[27]

Foucault thinks that many people are obsessed with a determination to make a science out of Marxism. He is particularly critical of those Marxists who say, 'Marxism, as the science of sciences, can provide the theory of science and draw the boundary between science and ideology.'[28] Those who are trying to establish the scientificity of Marxism he asks, 'What types of knowledge do you want to disqualify in the very instant of your demand: "Is it a science?" '[29] In his view the method of genealogy involves a painstaking rediscovery of struggles, an attack on the tyranny of what he calls 'totalizing discourses' and a rediscovery of fragmented, subjugated, local and specific knowledge. It is directed against great truths and grand theories. But he provides no grounds for distinguishing between different struggles and does not seem to be able to commit himself to a conception of the human good.[30]

Some criticisms of Foucault's work

Having outlined some of Foucault's arguments against Marxism, I now want to make some criticisms of his work. The first criticism is this: Foucault refuses to be committed to a general ontology of history, society or the human subject, or to advance any general theory of power. Many commentators, however, believe that this is precisely his strength; his value lies in *particular* analyses (of the clinic, the asylum, the prison). While there is much that is valuable and insightful in these studies, it must be admitted that Foucault's refusal to deal with epistemological questions means that it is difficult to evaluate them. As he does not present his own methodological protocols we do not know what standards should be used to assess his work.[31] What are the procedures by which one archaeologist of knowledge can confirm or question the analyses of another? If we are to engage seriously with Foucault's writings, considerable theoretical work on his epistemological and ontological protocols will have to be done. .

In his writings Foucault often describes a coherent rational strategy, but it is not possible to identify a person who conceived it. It seems to be *a strategy without a subject*. In an interview Foucault was asked who or what it is that co-ordinates the activities of agents. His reply, in my opinion, does not answer the question:

> Take the example of philanthropy in the early nineteenth century: people appear who make it their business to involve themselves in other people's lives, health, nutrition, housing; then, out of this confused set of functions there emerge certain personages, institutions, forms of knowledge: public hygiene, inspectors, social workers, psychologists. And we are now seeing a whole proliferation of different categories of social work.[32]

Consider another example: the strategy for the moralization of the working class. Foucault insists that one cannot say that the bourgeois class (on the level of its ideology or its economic project) invented and forcibly imposed this strategy on the working class.[33] The objective existed and the strategy was developed with ever-growing coherence but without it being necessary to attribute to it a subject.

The Panopticon is Foucault's apt metaphor for the anonymous centralization of power. But what is the principle, force or entity which power crushes or subdues? In other words, what does this modern power operate against? How would a situation change if an operation of power was cancelled? Foucault is vague in his replies to these questions. He has difficulty in defining what this power operates against. It seems that power is almost a metaphysical principle. Power is everywhere: it filters up from below, it is produced at every moment. Now, though he remarks that wherever there is power there is resistance, he offers no grounds for encouraging resistance or struggle. This is partly because he believes that there is no constant human subject in history. History does not reveal the gradual triumph of human rationality, nor does it fulfil an ultimate goal. History is uncontrolled and directionless.

In an interview Foucault was asked: 'Given that there are relations of forces and struggles, the question inevitably arises of who is doing the struggling and against whom?' He replied: 'This is preoccupying me. I'm not sure what the answer is.' The interviewer persisted: 'So who ultimately are the subjects who oppose each other?' Foucault answered:

> This is just a hypothesis, but I would say it's all against all. There aren't immediately given subjects of the struggle, one the proletariat, the other the bourgeoisie. Who fights against whom? We all fight each other. And there is always within each of us something that fights something else.[34]

Underlying Foucault's work there seem to be the following presuppositions: One, social power is omnipotent with respect to the psychic formation of the individual. Two, human individuals exist merely as an embodied nexus to be transformed by the deployment of external causal powers. This ontology is immediately qualified by Foucault. Power, he says, always produces resistance. But the question is, why should it? If power cannot be identified with repression (Foucault insists that it is both productive and regulative), what is the mechanism that generates resistance? Why do people resist? Why do they obey? People obey laws because of external reasons (physical force) or because of internal reasons (ideology). Foucault says that people obey or resist for *many* reasons. This may not seem very helpful, but perhaps his work reminds us that we should avoid easy answers.

When Foucault was pressed to explain resistance he was forced back to saying that there is 'something in the social body, in classes, groups, and individuals themselves which in some sense escapes relations of power . . . an inverse energy, a discharge . . . a plebeian quality or aspect'.[35] It is not surprising that Nicos Poulantzas scorned this attempt to ground resistance in an essentialized, absolutized, externalized spirit of refusal. In short, though the phrase 'wherever there is power there is resistance' is an appealing one, there is no doubt that 'resistance' is really a residual category in Foucault's work. It remains unanalysed.

One useful way of thinking about Foucault has been provided by Poulantzas, who found Foucault helpful *as a theorist of specific techniques of power* and of aspects of the state, but who carefully rejected his more general theoretical project. Poulantzas conceded that Foucault's analysis of normalization and the state's role in shaping corporality was superior to his own. Indeed, there are several interesting parallels between the work of Poulantzas and Foucault.[36] The latter considered that power is immanent in all social relations; Poulantzas also argued that all social relations are relations of power. Both theorists adopt a relational approach to power and explore the links between power and strategies. They also agree that power is productive rather than simply repressive and negative. Another similarity is their interest in 'micro-revolts'. Foucault emphasized that there is a multiplicity of dispersed micro-power relations. Poulantzas, too, was interested in the autonomous role of new social movements but he focused more on the question of how such micro-diversity culminates into the macro-necessity of bourgeois domination.

In spite of these similar interests Poulantzas goes on to make some trenchant criticisms. In his view Foucault neglects to study the modern form of the state and how it is derived from capitalist relations of production. He does not see that all social phenomena always occur in relation to the state and class division. To put this in another way, Foucault disregards the fact that domination has its basis in the relations of production and exploitation and in the organization of the state.

Foucault exaggerates the importance of disciplinary techniques in the modern state and thus neglects the continued importance of violence, legal coercion and law in general. Poulantzas argues that law and the state are each characterized equally by negative and positive features. The law is not only involved in organizing repression but is also essential for reproducing consent. Likewise the state is not only involved in repression and police measures, it is also active in constituting social relations and winning mass support.

According to Poulantzas Foucault emphasizes only the repressive, prohibitive side of law and the positive productive side of (state) power. In emphasizing the internalized repression achieved through disciplinary normalization, Foucault ignores the direct role coercion plays in sustaining the web of disciplinary and ideological mechanisms as well as the continued importance of overt violence in the state's activities. On the other hand, some commentators have remarked that the tacit social theory of *Discipline and Punish* describes all social relations in terms of power, domination and subordination and that Foucault neglects aspects of human sociability, in the family and in civil society generally, which are based on co-operation and reciprocity.[37]

Let me now try to summarize the main points. Foucault's historical analyses of specific institutions focus on the themes of centralization, increasing efficiency (technical rationality), and the replacement of overt violence by moralization. Power in modern societies is essentially orientated towards the production of regimented, isolated and self-policing subjects. According to Foucault power is everywhere. The idea that 'power' is located at, or emanates from, a given point seems to him to be based on a misguided analysis. In his view power is not always exercised from above in a negative or repressive way but is an open cluster of relations. Power is not an institution, a structure, or a certain force with which certain people are endowed; it is a name given to a complex strategic relation in a given society. All social relations are power relations. But if all social relations are power relations, how do we choose between one society and another?

When Foucault had to answer a question such as this he became evasive. Theoretically he had put himself in a situation where he could not use terms like equality, freedom, justice. These concepts are merely tokens in a game, in an interplay of forces. This is a viewpoint very much like that of Nietzsche (who wrote 'when the oppressed want justice it is just a pretext for the fact that they want power for themselves'). History, according to this view, is an endless play of domination.

I said earlier that Foucault does not conceptualize power in terms of the state or the intentionality of an agent, as a property or a possession, or as purely repressive. His analyses of power employ a conception of power as positive, productive and relational. It has been said that Foucault is trapped within a logical 'impasse'. Given his conception of power, there can be no escape, no locus of opposition or resistance, because *power itself has no specific basis or ground.*[38]

According to Foucault the existence of power relations presupposes forms of resistance. Just as power is present everywhere in the social network, so is resistance; there are a multiplicity of resistances which are constantly shifting and regrouping. Foucault does not say more than this. *The concept of resistance remains undeveloped.*

Additionally, *an analysis of the state is absent from his work.* Foucauldians like Donzelot have deliberately decentred the question of the state. They do not believe that the state is the locus or prime operator of power. To put it in another way, they have suspended assumptions concerning the unity, functionality and importance of the state.

Moreover, Foucault believes that it is no longer feasible to conceptualize relations of power simply in terms of the state, class struggle, relations of production and capitalist exploitation. And so it is not surprising that Foucault *underestimates the significance of social class and class struggle* and *neglects the role of law and physical repression.* He is so concerned with the anonymity of modern forms of administration that he neglects class domination.

Foucault's philosophy is embedded in the historical analyses that have been described. It is rooted in story-telling. Foucault neither claims nor seeks scientific status for his analyses. I refer to the fact that he said that his histories – which seek to forge connections, establish relationships and transgress the established – were fictions:

> I am well aware that I have never written anything but fictions. I do not mean to say, however, that truth is therefore absent. It seems to me that the possibility exists for fiction to function in truth, for a fictional discourse to induce effects of truth . . . [39]

There are different systems or 'regimes' of truth; truth is conventional. Foucault wants to avoid questions of epistemology and so in his work truth plays no part in the transformation of knowledges. Instead he celebrates, like Nietzsche, the perspectivity of knowledge.

Foucault is acutely aware that there are different sorts of knowledge; there is disqualified knowledge, knowledge not only from above but from below. His claim that truth is always relative is not easy to accept. It is because of this position that he cannot say that one historical period or society or theory is better than another. This, of course, raises the question: from what position is Foucault able to write his own descriptions? What is the status of his own theory?

A feminist criticism

Some perceptive criticisms of Foucault's work have been made by Rosi Braidotti from a feminist perspective.[40] She contrasts the work of Foucault with that of Irigaray. She writes that Foucault elaborates a critique that remains within the confines of sexual sameness, whereas Irigaray is arguing for sexual difference, otherness, as a strategy for the assertion of feminine subjectivity.

Braidotti begins by reminding us that over a century ago Nietzsche stated that all decadent, diseased and corrupted cultures acquired a taste for 'the feminine'. She says that the feminine is often used as the sign, the metaphor or the symptom of illness, discontent or crisis, and that this habit must be questioned. There is a kind of (male) philosophical thought at the present time that has a fascination for 'the feminine' but it neglects the dynamic impact of the women's movement. There seems to be a collision between patriarchal assumptions about the feminine and the existential reality of women's lives and thought. Let us now consider Foucault's blindness to sexual difference. Foucault's central theme is the critical, historical analysis of the modes of constitution of the subject: the ways in which, in our culture, human beings are made into subjects.[41] He outlines three main modes of objectification, which transform human beings into subjects. These correspond to different stages of his work.

In the first phase (*The Order of Things*, *The Archaeology of Knowledge*) Foucault analyses the type of discourse which claims the status of science, especially in the field of the human sciences. His work leads him to the critique of the role that the 'knowing subject' plays in the history of Western philosophy.

The second phase of Foucault's work (*Madness and Civilization, Birth of the Clinic*, to *Discipline and Punish*) deals with the constitution of the subject through what he calls 'the dividing practices': exclusion, separation and domination within oneself as well as towards the others. Foucault states that the modes in which human beings are made into subjects in our culture rest on a complex network of power relations, which he defines in terms of 'the microphysics of power'. In his view the body is the privileged target of the mechanisms of power relations; it must be made docile, submissive, erotic, usable and productive.[42]

In the third phase of Foucault's work (*The History of Sexuality*) he concentrates on the ways in which a human being turns him/herself into a subject: the internal modes of submission and domination by the subject.

Braidotti argues that in his early texts Foucault's androcentric bias is manifest; he uses the term 'man' as a universal form, thus betraying his blindness to sexual difference. In his later works, however, he is conscious of the fact that the system of control of sexuality which he is analysing rests on a profound dissymmetry between the sexes. In short, he is aware of the *disqualification* of women as ethical agents and consequently as subjects.

Arguing that governing oneself, managing one's estate and participating in the administration of the city were three practices of the same kind, Foucault emphasizes the key value of 'ethical virility' as the ideal on which the system as a whole rests. In turn this implies perfect coincidence between one's anatomical sex – male – and the imaginary construction of masculine sexuality. Moreover, he stresses the accordance of both to the ruling representations of what ought to be the universal ethical standard: symbolic virility. Thus the male body is all at one with the body politic.

Braidotti remarks that it is a world for and about men. In her view the whole history of philosophy we have come to inherit has been conjugated in the male, masculine and virile mode. Foucault is a male philosopher who is bringing out the highly sexed rules governing philosophical discourse. Far from being universal, philosophy rests on the most gender-specific premises: those which posit the primacy of masculine sexuality as a site of social and political power. In Foucault's last work phallologocentric discourse is a specific political and libidinal economy – one which assigns the sexes to precise roles, and functions, to the detriment of the feminine.

In Braidotti's view Foucault elaborates a critique which emphasizes sexual sameness. What ultimately interests Foucault is the attempt to try to elaborate a modern ethics, one suited to the here and now of our place of enunciation. Foucault declares that we are historically condemned to rethink the basis of our relationship to the values that we have inherited, especially from the nineteenth century.

In contrast, Irigaray stresses sexual difference as a way of asserting female subjectivity. (Her work will be fully discussed in Chapter 5 on French feminist theory.) She believes that conceptual thinking is not neutral but very gender-specific. Irigaray's project, in short, concerns the question: how can we learn to think differently about human subjectivity and alterity?

Conclusion

In this chapter I have tried to show that Foucault was especially concerned with how knowledge is enmeshed in disciplinary power. He rejected the traditional liberal view that power interferes with the free formation of truth. For Foucault power is necessary for the production of knowledge and is an inherent feature of all social relationships. I want particularly to stress the fact that Foucault believed that Marxism was authoritarian and outmoded: 'one must try to think of struggle and its forms, objectives, means and processes in terms of a logic free of the sterilising constraints of the dialectic'.[43] His many followers, both in France and internationally, have propagated this view. Nietzsche's thought influenced Foucault so deeply that it is not surprising that he rejected Marx's view of economics, history, politics and method. In the next chapter I will consider the influence of Nietzsche's thought on some of the 'younger generation' of post-structuralist thinkers.

Further reading

H. Dreyfus and P. Rabinow, *Michel Foucault: Beyond Structuralism and Hermeneutics*, Brighton: Harvester Press, 1982.
An excellent book; it is an accessible and comprehensive exposition and discussion of the main works. The authors are particularly interested in Foucault's effort to develop a new method. It also contains an important Afterword by Foucault, 'The Subject and Power'.

C. Gordon, 'Birth of the Subject – Foucault' in R. Edgley and R. Osborne (eds), *Radical Philosophy Reader*, London: Verso, 1985.

A useful discussion of the main themes in *Discipline and Punish* and *The History of Sexuality*.

D. Hoy (ed.), *Foucault: A Critical Reader*, Oxford: Basil Blackwell, 1986.
An important collection of thirteen essays which are critical discussions of Foucault's archaeology, epistemology, ethics, politics, his views on power and the Enlightenment by writers such as Ian Hacking, Richard Rorty, Jürgen Habermas, Edward Said, Barry Smart, Martin Jay, Mark Poster and others. For more advanced work.

L. Martin, H. Gutman and P. Hulton (eds), *Technologies of the Self: A Seminar with Michel Foucault*, London: Tavistock, 1988.
This interesting and readable book contains an interview with Foucault, two lectures by him on the differing ways in which self is formulated and becomes an object of knowledge, and five essays on this topic by other contributors.

J. G. Merquior, *Foucault*, London: Fontana Press, 1985.
There is a discussion of all the main texts in this lively critical assessment. It contains many cogent criticisms of Foucault's work, especially in the last chapter, 'Portrait of the Neo-Anarchist'.

M. Poster, *Foucault, Marxism, and History: Mode of Production versus Mode of Information*, Cambridge: Polity Press, 1984.
An interesting and accessible book. After a critique of Marxism and the dialectic, the author introduces Nietzsche's view of history (genealogy). There is then a clear discussion of two works – *Discipline and Punish* and *The History of Sexuality* – which exemplify a Nietzschean approach to history.

A. Sheridan, *Michel Foucault: The Will to Truth*, London: Tavistock, 1980.
Still one of the best – and most readable – introductions to the whole of Foucault's work.

B. Smart, *Foucault, Marxism and Critique*, London: Routledge & Kegan Paul, 1983.
The first half of this book emphasizes the limits and limitations of Marxism. Smart sees the necessity of deploying other modes of analysis. The second half is a commentary on the work of Foucault, his views on power, the state, discipline. I found the comparison of the work of Max Weber with that of Foucault useful.

The following books discuss Foucault from a feminist point of view:

J. Butler, *Gender Trouble: Feminism and the Subversion of Identity*, London: Routledge, 1990.

N. Fraser, *Unruly Practices: Power, Discourse and Gender in Contemporary Social Theory*, Cambridge: Polity Press, 1989.

L. McNay, *Foucault and Feminism: Power, Gender and the Self*, Cambridge: Polity Press, 1992.

Chapter 4

□

Some currents within
post-structuralism

Nietzsche contra Hegel

Many post-structuralist thinkers have been greatly influenced by the philosophy of Nietzsche, with its denunciation of the 'illusion' of truth and static notions of meaning, its belief in the will to power, its affirmation of the Dionysian way of life, and its hostility to egalitarianism. To give only a few examples, Michel Foucault was influenced by Nietzsche's thought in the late 1950s, and he began to be critical of historicism and humanism. Another writer, Jean-François Lyotard, who had been a left-wing militant for a long time, denounced the Soviet Union and turned to Nietzsche's ideas. Jacques Derrida constantly invokes Nietzsche in his writing. Gilles Deleuze, too, has been deeply swayed by Nietzsche. Many writers suggest that Marx sublates Hegel by appropriating the radical form (the dialectical method) and dispensing with the conservative content. Deleuze rejects completely both the form and content of Hegel's philosophy and claims that Nietzsche was the first real critic of Hegel and dialectical thought.

Let us try to see how certain features of Nietzsche's philosophy are being used in the polemic against Hegel and Marx. Nietzsche is often misunderstood; he often speaks of 'war' even when he is evidently thinking of 'strife', of 'power' rather than 'self-perfection', and of the 'Dionysian' rather than the 'classical'. I can see that there is much that is appealing in his thought. In Nietzsche's philosophy, for example, there is a sustained celebration of creativity – all genuine creation is a creation of new values and norms. I think that perhaps we should make a distinction between Nietzsche and Nietzscheanism. To be a Nietzschean is in a sense a contradiction in terms; to be a Nietzschean one must not be Nietzschean.

Nietzsche opposed both the idolatry of the state and political liberalism because he was basically anti-political. He loathed the idea of belonging to any 'party' whatever. Nietzsche objects to the state because it appears to him as the power that intimidates men and women into conformity. However, Nietzsche opposes not only the state but any overestimation of the political. In short, the leitmotiv of his life and thought is *the anti-political individual who seeks self-perfection* far from the modern world. He thus thinks that the Goethean man embodies the great contemplative type who is essentially unrevolutionary, even anti-revolutionary.

Nietzsche had strong philosophical reasons for not having a system. He held that a system is reducible to a set of premises which cannot be questioned within the framework of the system: 'The will to a system is a lack of integrity.' All assumptions have to be questioned. No one system reveals the entire truth; at best each adopts one point of view or perspective. We must consider many perspectives and not imprison our thought in one system. Nietzsche held that the coherence of a finite system could never be a guarantee of its truth. His entire attack on systems is based on his objection to the irrationality which he finds in the failure to question premises. For him science is not a finished and impersonal system but a passionate quest for knowledge, an unceasing series of small, courageous experiments. He has in mind the 'gay science' of fearless experiment and the goodwill to accept new evidence and to abandon previous positions if necessary.

There are many important differences between the philosophies of Hegel and Nietzsche. In Hegel's dialectic, concepts are inadequate and contradictions lead to a more adequate concept at a higher level. This process continually repeats itself as the dialectic moves towards the Absolute. In Nietzsche, however, the dialectic undercuts, undermines itself. Hegel always stressed the result of the process, the synthesis, and the larger unit, while Nietzsche concerned himself with the negative and the individual. A consequence of Nietzsche's emphasis on the negative may be seen in the tremendous importance he attached to suffering and cruelty – the negative aspect of self-overcoming. Nietzsche was much concerned with the individual and his/her attempts at self-realization. He was, unlike Hegel, more of a psychologist than a historian. In the end, Nietzsche's emphasis on individuality led him to the conception of a vast plurality of individual wills to power. He asserted that not all people are equally capable of being good and creating the beautiful. It seems that some people are more favoured by nature than others. This is the basis of his opposition to socialism and democracy.

I turn now to a crucial point in Nietzsche's philosophy of history and theory of values. One of his hypotheses was the doctrine of the eternal recurrence. It refers to the unconditional and infinitely repeated circular course of all things. This conception depends on Nietzsche's denial of definite progress, of a plan or goal to give meaning to history or life. He deprecated any faith that pins its hopes on the future. Empirical facts do not seem to him to warrant the belief that history is a story of progress: 'The goal of humanity cannot lie at the end of time but only in its highest specimens' (*Thoughts out of Season*).

In contrast to this view Hegel believed that there was an Absolute Spirit that was working itself through all the concrete manifestations of the world. He held that reality unfolded itself through its contradictions and rose to ever higher levels until Spirit at last became conscious of itself. For all its philosophical idealism this view compels one to see human culture and history as a part of a total process. This is why political institutions, works of art and social customs so often appear as the varied expression of a single inner essence.

Marx abolished the idealism of Hegel's system and stressed the material laws of historical development. He replaced Spirit with Economy; in his view economic forces determined the particular system of social relations that characterizes each stage of historical development. Class struggle became the central principle of historical development.

One of the reasons why I have given the above outline is that many thinkers are opposed to this sort of 'teleological' Marxism. The French right-wing 'new philosophers' assert that Marxism of this sort transforms Marx into the teller of a salvational story rather than a scientific theorist of historical laws. But they say more than this – they contend that there is a direct line from Hegel to the Gulag. The stages are these: first of all there is Hegel's invention of the notion of Absolute Spirit with its teleology of history. Then Marx relocates this teleology within history conceived in materialist terms. Finally, the annulment of contradiction at the end of the teleological process becomes (with Stalinism) an abolition of differences through sheer force. The Absolute Spirit becomes the knock at the door, in the name of history, of the secret police.

Deleuze and Guattari: the return to the imaginary

One source of the ideas mentioned above is the book *Anti-Oedipus: Capitalism and Schizophrenia.*[1] Its authors, Gilles Deleuze and Félix Guattari, have combined the three concepts 'desire', 'production' and 'machine' from Freud and Marx into a new idea: we are desiring machines. They call the outward, linguistic manifestation of desire *délire*. *Délire* is an effect produced by the machinery of desire. *Anti-Oedipus* stresses the collective nature of *délire* (even if it is produced by an individual) and its social character. At the present time the dominant tendency is to privatize *délire*. Against this trend Deleuze and Guattari have implicitly adopted one of the slogans of the French Left of the 1970s: the personal is the political. There is no separation between the personal and the social, the individual and the collective. Both the political and the psychological field are permeated by the same form of energy, libido, which has effects both political (the class struggle) and individual (*délire*). Libido and politics interpenetrate.

Deleuze and Guattari distinguish two types of desire, the paranoid and the schizophrenic, corresponding to two main forms of society: the fascist and the revolutionary. In social terms, the contrast is between authoritarian and libertarian organizations: on the one hand there are states with their insistence on centralized power; on the other hand looser organizations of smaller groups – imagine a society of nomads – without territorial limits or a system of hierarchy. The authors assert that there are two poles to *délire*: the real *délire* of schizophrenia, centred on flight, and the reactionary *délire* of paranoia based on the authoritarian structure of the hierarchical state.

Politically Deleuze and Guattari are against the process of generalization by which a class is elevated into an abstraction above its members and the party becomes representative of a class. In contrast they believe that revolutionary desire flows through small groups and produces collective action. In other words, it is not enough to fight fascism in the street; we must also fight it in our own heads, setting our revolutionary schizophrenia against our own fascist paranoia. Influenced by the ideas of Wilhelm Reich's *Mass Psychology of Fascism*, they believe that the unconscious is a political force and that fascism dwells in it as much as on the historical stage or in political parties.

The authors of *Anti-Oedipus* argue that Freudian psychoanalysis is an example of 'interpretation as impoverishment'. It is what happens when the lived complexity of a patient's life is 'rewritten' within the confined limits of the Freudian 'family romance'. They go on to attack the reductiveness of all schemes that seek to limit and thus impoverish a complex reality in the name of interpretation. Complex reality is always rewritten in terms of a 'mastercode' or 'master narrative' which is then given as the 'meaning' of what is interpreted. Marxism is one such 'mastercode'. In teleological Marxism there is a providential or salvational account of history as a 'master narrative'.

In a sense, Deleuze and Guattari perceive all explanation or interpretation as an expression of the Nietzschean will to power. But they insist that their attack is not directed against interpretation as such but against Marxism as a 'transcendent' interpretation. *Transcendent interpretation* is transcendent in the sense that its significance is based on going outside the text, on some extratextual set of norms. Against this notion of transcendent interpretation they counterpose their demand for *immanent interpretation*, a mode of analysis that respects the internal norms and values and the complexity as it is given of the reality to be interpreted.

Not only Deleuze and Guattari but also Foucault and the 'new philosophers' argue that traditional Marxism has been 'transcendent' in the sense that it has produced 'meaning' by allegorizing in terms of the 'mastercode' provided by Marx. They all see in Marxism a prime example of an interpretative system that inevitably transforms itself into an instrument of political and physical domination.

I mentioned just now that Deleuze and Guattari are anti-Freudian. Their arguments against the Oedipus complex are these: since the Oedipus complex is supposed to be universal, the results of any interpretation are known in advance. Freud was just a clairvoyant; he recognized the predictable character of his interpretations. Secondly, the richness of the patient's productions is reduced to ready-made explanations. Hence, Freudian interpretation is a form of repression. Thirdly, there is a patriarchal bias in the Oedipus complex (the reduction of desire to the male sexual organs). These arguments are part of a more general criticism of psychoanalysis. Psychoanalysis imposes Lack, Culture and Law on the unconscious, thus structuring, reducing and repressing desire. The unconscious, on the other hand, is productive; it produces desire and threatens to smother the body politic with it; hence its revolutionary character and the necessity for its repression by psychoanalysis, the watch-dog of the modern state.

Psychoanalysis, it is argued, is basically an interpretation-machine. It translates all the patient says into another language and thus turns the patient into a subject in both senses of the term. Moreover, psychoanalysis depends upon a form of power: the patient submits to the analyst and his flow of libido is reduced to words and interpretations. An important current within post-structuralism explores the possibilities and potentialities of *desire*. For Deleuze and Guattari desire emerges as a mysterious and disruptive, all-pervading, productive force of libido. The authors idealize Lacan's concept of the imaginary (the stage before the acquisition of language) and emphasize his theory of desire. They see the transition into the symbolic (language, structure and society) as a loss. Entrance into structure and society is seen as a tragedy. Only a return to the imaginary can spell the end of sociopolitical repression, of the dictatorship of the symbolic. For Deleuze and Guattari the really important condition is schizophrenia. Indeed, attacking classical psychoanalysis and Marxism, they develop a new theory, provocatively named schizoanalysis.

Deleuze and Guattari envisage a politics of the Lacanian imaginary. The goal of politics is to return to humankind's freedom, to a sense of being a passionate animal. They glorify the pre-symbolic stage of direct, fusional relationships, of spontaneity, of primitive, unmediated desire. They reject phallocentrism and denounce the family as the bearer of hierarchy and taboo. They look to children, primitive peoples and, most of all, to the mad as examples of people in touch with the power of the pre-symbolic. What these marginal groups are assumed to have in common is that they have not yet been fully 'Oedipalized', that is, that the symbolic has not yet entered them. The book is a diatribe against Oedipalization. Although the authors' attack on Oedipalization is also an attack on psychoanalysis, the book relies on Lacan's particular way of theorizing the Oedipus complex as the process by which society enters the individual.

Psychiatric theory is usually based on a negative concept of madness, in which madness is perceived as a deficit, a lack of rationality, a state of being less than one could be. Lacan has never supported this pejorative view. He has spoken of the analyst as someone deeply in touch with the knowledge 'that it is possible for each of us to go mad'. Man's being, he says, cannot be understood without reference to madness, nor would man be man without his carrying madness within as the limit of his freedom. Lacan, then, is sympathetic to the anti-psychiatrists who identify themselves with the mad in so far as they claim to have a message that cannot be communicated in ordinary ways. Like the schizophrenic they have to destroy ordinary language in order to communicate. In the case of anti-psychiatry Lacan's support comes from the way he demolishes the notion that there is a 'normal' self that is autonomous, coherent, its own 'centre'. The notion of the decentred subject is a crucial link between Lacan and the anti-psychiatric movement, which refuses to view madness as something alien to 'normals'.

Deleuze and Guattari are sympathetic to madness. They argue in *Anti-Oedipus* that in modern life there is an incompatibility between reason and impulse – spontaneity is being squeezed out. The authors take Lacan's ideas about the decentred subject and carry them several steps further than he does. They believe that the schizophrenic makes no separation between personal and social experience; his or her personal expressions are themselves political expressions. For the schizophrenic, word and thing are one, saying is doing. The relationship between word and action, wish and action, is direct and immediate. In a way, Deleuze and Guattari advance 'a politics of schizophrenia'. They regard schizophrenia as a privileging experience and believe that the schizophrenic is not trapped within the Oedipal prison, in which the complexity and fluidity of the unconscious are distorted, frozen and flattened, but that he or she is in touch with fundamental truths about society. In short, they exalt the schizophrenic's proximity to the imaginary, to fusional relationships and to flux. The self is all flux and fragmentation, collection of machine parts. In human relationships one whole person never relates to another whole person because there is no such thing as the 'whole person'. There are only connections between 'desiring machines'. Fragmentation is a universal of the human condition, not something specific to the schizophrenic.

It will not have escaped notice that the work of Deleuze and Guattari proceeds through conceptual dichotomies: the hierarchical state and the nomadic tribe, paranoia and schizophrenia. It is often said that desire differs from need in that it cannot attain fulfilment; it is an ever-renewed failure, a constant yearning. But there are several ways of conceiving desire. In the Lacanian psychoanalytic tradition, for example, it is a striving after a lost primary object. Deleuze and Guattari, however, reject the Lacanian definition of the real as the impossible. They invert it: 'in reality everything becomes possible'. Reality is what my desire fabricates.

Deleuze and Guattari are Nietzschean in the sense that their book is a celebration of 'the numinous energies of existence in a joyous activity of free play'. The schizo produces himself as a free man, irresponsible, solitary, and joyous, finally able to say and do something simple in his own name, without asking permission; a desire lacking nothing, a flux that overcomes barriers and codes, a name that no longer designates any ego whatever. He has simply ceased being afraid of becoming mad.[2]

In criticism of Deleuze and Guattari I would argue that their conception of desire culminates in sheer idealism. As a sympathetic commentator on *Anti-Oedipus* has remarked:

> The advice is let yourself go. Do your own thing, scream your own screams. In other words, take risks and go against the grain of common sense. This thesis offers no objective assessment of a state of affairs; it is rather a call for action.[3]

Their notion of productive desire is none other than the Nietzschean will to power. In their view there is only one class, that of the slaves, in which some dominate the others. One consequence of all this is that the class struggle is politely consigned to the museum. Though the vocabulary of *Anti-Oedipus* is sometimes Marxist, sometimes Freudian, the main critical strand is Nietzschean from start to finish.[4]

Prisoners of discourse

In one of its developments post-structuralism became a convenient way of evading political questions altogether. The work of Derrida and others had cast great doubt upon the classical notions of truth, reality, meaning and knowledge. If meaning, the signified, was a passing product of words or signifiers, always shifting and unstable, part-present and part-absent, how could there be any determinant truth or meaning at all? If reality was constructed by our discourse rather than reflected by it, how could we ever know reality itself, rather than merely knowing our own discourse? According to this dogma we can never know anything at all; we are the prisoners of our discourse.

One of Foucault's main concerns is the transition from the classical age to nineteenth-century culture. In all of his works there is a similar narrative framework: the relatively open and freewheeling world of the sixteenth century gives way to the classical age, which is superseded by the densely regulated, 'disciplined' society of today. Serious thinking about modern life has polarized into two sterile antitheses which

Marshall Berman has called 'modernolatry' and 'cultural despair'.[5] For the practitioners of the former, from Marinetti and Mayakovsky to Le Corbusier, all the personal and social dissonances of modern life can be resolved by technological and administrative means. The means are all at hand, and the only thing needful is leaders with the will to use them. For the intellectuals of cultural despair, from Eliot and Ezra Pound to Marcuse and Foucault, all of modern life seems uniformly hollow, sterile, flat, 'one-dimensional', empty of human possibilities. Anything that looks or feels like freedom or beauty is really only a screen for more profound enslavement and horror.

There is no freedom in Foucault's world, nor does he have a theory of emancipation. The more powerful the vision of some increasingly total system or logic, the more powerless the reader comes to feel. The critical capacity of Foucault's work is paralysed because the reader is made to think that the project of social transformation is vain, trivial, hopeless. I think Habermas is correct when he argues that Foucault's later work 'replaced' the model of repression and emancipation developed by Marx and Freud with a pluralism of power/discourse formations. 'These formations intersect and succeed one another and can be differentiated according to their style and intensity. They cannot, however, be judged in terms of validity.'[6]

It is largely because of the impact of Foucauldian discourse that many intellectuals feel that they cannot use general concepts any more; they are taboo. The system as a whole cannot be combated because there is in fact no 'system as a whole'. Nor is there any central power; power is everywhere.[7] The only forms of political action now felt to be acceptable are of a local, diffused, strategic kind. The worst error is to believe that such local projects should be brought together.

I want to argue that some of the Nietzschean themes in Foucault's thought are the basis of his anti-Marxist position. He insists that any general theory should be renounced and that life cannot be grasped from a single perspective. Believing that truth and power are linked, he adopts a relativist position; modern society is not necessarily better than past ones. We are not progressing from the dark to the light. Foucault attacks Marxists because they believe that they have deciphered the secret of history. For him history is discontinuous and Marxism is a global totalitarian theory which is out of date.

The celebration of intensity

One can also see the shift away from Marxism if one looks at the political trajectory of Jean-François Lyotard. He was a militant for fifteen years in a small left-wing group called *Socialisme ou Barbarie*. This group, which contained well-known theorists such as Cornelius Castoriadis and Claude Lefort, came out of Trotskyism and developed a critique of Soviet bureaucracy.[8] It argued that both the US and the Soviet Union were state capitalist countries.

Lyotard's first book was a monograph on phenomenology, and traces of this commitment are still very apparent in his work. He has never accepted all the injunctions of structuralism and has criticized aspects of the work of Lévi-Strauss. During the events of 1968 Lyotard was a professor of philosophy at Vincennes. He has written that the preoccupations of *Socialisme ou Barbarie* were expressed in '68; in many ways the student revolt was libertarian and anarchist rather than Marxist. One has only to look at the posters and the graffiti ('it is forbidden to forbid') to realize that the movement was largely a protest against bureaucratization, depersonalization, routinization, repression, and not wholly an expression of class antagonism. In Lyotard's view people began to feel that there was a discrepancy between the rhetoric of Marxism and the actual content of the students' movement. In 1968 many people turned away from Marxism.

Lyotard next wrote about the tension between the discursive and the figural (the verbal and the visual) in his book *Discours/figure*.[9] He has always been fascinated by the non-linguistic, is critical of Lacan's view that the unconscious is structured like a language and suggests that it is the Other of language. He associates the unconscious with figural representation and the preconscious with language. Language is on the side of censorship and repression; figural representation is on the side of desire and transgression. Lyotard thinks of modern art as being fragmented and believes that it is liberatory. Fragmentation and disruption are attempts to make the unconscious process visible. Art, then, involves the disruption of convention; but this raises the question, 'Can art exist for ever as a transgression of previous assumptions?'

During the time of *Discours/figure* Lyotard was still writing from within the Marxist tradition, but he was beginning to be critical of some aspects of it. He argued against the Hegelian notion that there is a coincidence between the movement of thought and the movement of reality. He also rejected the Lukácsian view that Marxism is the expression of the revolutionary consciousness of the proletariat, the 'voice of history'.[10] Lyotard argued against this view because he believed that the bureaucratic communist parties often claimed to speak in just such an authoritative (and authoritarian) way. Nevertheless, during this period he wanted to retain the concept of alienation because he was concerned with the individual, unlike Althusser, who rejected it as being an ideological remnant from the work of the young Marx.[11]

In recent years Lyotard has supported symbolic protest actions because he believes that through such actions societal veils are dropped. But it has often been noticed that this sort of activity, an interruption of routine, gradually comes to replace revolutionary political activity itself. Once a political act is severed from revolution and becomes symbolic, then all it does is produce a shock effect, which is also a stylistic device of many artists. In detaching action from political goals this sort of activity becomes a self-defeating convention.

The younger generation of post-structuralist thinkers are very concerned not only with the spontaneous but also with the subjective. Lyotard, for example, values the intensity of experience and suggests that if we are always thinking of what we are, we cannot 'let go'. If we are always theorizing about things, we cannot enjoy them for their own sake. In Lyotard's view there should be a shift from the dominance of dry, abstract thinking to a greater appreciation of the emotional. The main message seems to be that we should move from criticism of the present to hedonistic affirmation. It could be argued against Lyotard that he has forgotten that Nietzsche's affirmative view implies that we have to affirm suffering as well. The importance of Nietzsche is that he tells us to put reason *and* impulse together.

Basically, what the post-structuralists like Lyotard are saying is that there is more to life than politics. If we are totally immersed in the political, we miss what is going on here and now. Marxists are always criticizing the status quo in the name of an ideal. Militants are so inflexible that they have no time to enjoy life as it is now. Ideals cut us off from the present.

Instead of having a nostalgia for an unalienated community that may have existed in the past we should celebrate aspects of contemporary life – its anonymity, its fragmentation, its consumptionism. The post-structuralists also want to extol everything that has been left out in the totalizing theories. And so they focus on the marginal, the excluded. But for how long can a group or movement stress the marginal without becoming marginal itself? Furthermore, it could be argued that if all that matters is intensity (the quest for 'kicks'), then one can get as much intensity acting within the system as outside it.

The 'new philosophers'

Some intellectuals, though not strictly post-structuralists themselves, have been deeply influenced by the post-structuralists and have used their ideas in their attack on Marxism. Ten years after the events of 1968 a group of French intellectuals achieved notoriety by making criticisms of Marxism and the socialist societies. This group, which includes Bernard-Henri Lévy, André Glucksmann, Jean-Marie Benoist and others, made successful use of the media to propagate their views against what they call the dogmatism of Marx, of Marx's logos.

But before I give an exposition of the views of the 'new philosophers', let me enumerate briefly a few of the more common arguments – about the limits and limitations of Marxism – on which their ideas are based. The writings of Marx and Engels clearly express the idea that the economy is determinant in the final instance and that therefore the superstructures are in some sense determined. However, the superstructures are not simply reducible to the economy, they have relative autonomy. One of the most serious consequences of the lack of any precise mechanism connecting these two propositions – economic determination and the relative autonomy of the superstructures – is the absence of a theory of the political level. Additionally, the formal, abstract categories of 'base' and 'superstructure' have become an obstruction to analysis since they have displaced real human activities and historical processes as objects of study.

Moreover, Marx did not produce any coherent or comparative analysis of the political structures of bourgeois class power. There is no developed analysis in his work of the capitalist state.[12] Marx neglected changes in the international state system and did not appreciate the importance of nationalism and national cultures. And what is more, he was a positivist. The positivist conception of science within his works has had harmful consequences for the articulation of a Marxist politics. Indeed, a preoccupation with the scientificity of Marxism is said to be the source of the neglect of the centrality of human agency, experience and consciousness.[13]

There are also problems in Lenin's theory and practice. We are often told that there was a contradiction between his conceptions of workers' councils as a necessary revolutionary form of proletarian power and the subsequent reality of party authoritarianism and the development of a monolithic bureaucratic apparatus.[14] To put it simply, Lenin failed to integrate his doctrine of the party with his account of the soviets.

After Leninism, Stalinism. If it was possible for a single individual to create a personality cult around himself, there must be something wrong with the theory of historical materialism (which denies the role of 'the great individual' in history). On the other hand, if the cult arose from the Soviet system (Lenin?), then socialist society itself must bear the responsibility for the inherent potential of Stalinism.

And then there is the question of socialism. Marxism has little of substance to offer on the nature of the transition from capitalism to socialism. The nature of that which is to emerge from the ruins of bourgeois society remains problematic and relatively unformulated. One of the problems was the difference between the classical vision of Marxism and the reality of those states which became part of the Soviet bloc. Marx did not realize that the transitional period of 'socialism' might produce an authoritarian and monolithic state machine. By then it was quite clear that the power and pervasiveness of the state machine had created a situation in which, even given the abolition of capitalist private property, the producers did not exercise control over the processes of production and distribution. Rather, control was centralized, hierarchically organized, and exercised by an élite, ostensibly in the interest of the producers.

Western European countries have seen the apparent decline of a militant working class and the emergence of 'non-class' political–subject groups. During the events of May '68, for example, there arose mass movements, composed of many spontaneously organized 'group-uscles'. There were new social groupings around specific issues such as education, women's liberation, ecology and so forth. The hierarchically organized Marxist parties tended to be conservative and could not represent the interest and desires of the new groups. There were struggles that could not be conceptualized as class struggles. When are Marxists going to learn that the 'political' consists of more than class politics?

The so-called 'socialist' states did not represent a good model. The party political organization had become synonymous with the bureaucratic machine. Moreover, powerful and privileged ruling strata had come into being and there were regular violations of human rights. In short, these states testified to the limitations of Marxist theory.[15]

The 'new philosophers'' denunciation was largely based on these criticisms. They were fond of comparing the dominance of Marxism in post-war France with the dominance of Aristotle's logic in medieval times. Highly critical of Sartre, they contended that his notion of freedom was irreconcilable with his Marxist views, and leaned towards the anti-Soviet position adopted by Camus in the early 1950s. The leading publicist of the group, Bernard-Henri Lévy, in his book *La Barbarie à visage humain*, attacked the Marxist theory of power in which power is seen as maintained by varying combinations of ideological mystification and physical repression.[16] Against this model Lévy deployed a vulgarized fusion of ideas drawn from Foucault and Lacan in which power is everywhere and yet is 'nothing'. It is nothing since it cannot be located in specific mechanisms of institutions. Rather than being imposed from above it filters up from below, permeating *every* social relation. Now, in Foucault there were at least 'resistances' counterposed to power, but for Lévy there was only the impossibility of liberation: the idea of a good society was an absurd dream.

Besides power, the 'new philosophers' were critical of the concepts of reason, theory and history. The idea that the social formation is an analysable totality was rejected. They seemed to have a vision in which conflict is no longer a political conflict between social *classes* but an ethical struggle within the individual between the 'desire for submission' and the 'love of freedom'. In a way, we are all oppressors and we are all oppressed.

The 'new philosophers' saw all ideologies which envisaged an end point to history (historicism) as dangerous and wrong. In their view theories that promise an end to power relations convince people that they can justify present means by that future end and so rationalize inhumanity and suffering. Deeply rooted in the unconscious is the lust for power. The only ethical way to live is to take the goal of limiting power as the basis of one's actions without believing that power can ever be eliminated.

It is significant that when Lévy wanted to express this he chose to tell his story through Lacanian concepts. For Lévy a Freudian politics that understands constraint, contradiction and the inevitability of power is our only hope, and it is Lacan who suggests its form with his theory of knots, his new topographical image for the indissociability of the imaginary, symbolic and real.[17] Power is tied to desire and the impossibility of final resolutions just as the symbolic is tied to the imaginary and the real. There is no escape to the imaginary except

through psychosis, and for Lévy this is not a workable solution. There is
no Utopia, no 'beach underneath the cobblestones'.

The two writers highly regarded by the 'new philosophers' were
Lacan and Foucault. Lacan never claimed to be a Marxist and explicitly
mocked the idea of 'sexual liberation' in the name of traditional
Freudian pessimism. Foucault's work, ever since the beginning,
contained an implicit and explicit critique of Marxist concepts. In many
respects Foucault's early book *Madness and Civilization* is privileged
above its successors, since it is in this book that the 'new philosophers'
find inspiration for their belief in the inherent oppressiveness of reason.

Not only does the new philosophy claim inspiration from his work (as
it does from Lacan's) but Foucault himself in certain respects shared the
same intellectual and political trajectory as the militants who have
become the 'new philosophers'. On his own account it was the explosion
of May '68 and after – the development of localized struggles in the
school, the prison, the psychiatric hospital – which made it possible for
him to take up explicitly the problem of the interrelation of power and
knowledge.[18]

As I remarked earlier, Foucault rejects the traditional conception of
power as invested in a central, organizing state from which it filters down
to successive levels. To Foucault the state is merely one apparatus
among many. Both in Foucault and in the 'new philosophers' one comes
across the idea that global struggles are recuperative, leading from one
domination to another, while only local and partial struggles are truly
subversive. It is interesting that several writers have noticed a similarity
between Foucault's concept of power, with its rejection of class analysis
in favour of a vision of a complex of forces which continually
disaggregate and coalesce, and the views of American functionalists.

For the 'new philosophers' the so-called socialist countries of Eastern
Europe represented technological rationality and tyranny. Much of their
writing was about the concept of Gulag, a term denoting Soviet
oppression, derived from Solzhenitsyn. One of their leading represen-
tatives, André Glucksmann, has said:

> I reproach Marx with having traced a certain number of intellectual routes:
> the cult of the total and final Revolution; of the State that terrorizes for the
> good of the collectivity, and of social science that permits the masses to be
> guided in spite of themselves. These paths do not lead directly to the Gulag
> but to non-resistance to the Gulag.[19]

The 'new philosophers' represented, in part, an intellectual move from the 'scientific', value-free problematic to the problematic of the individual and human rights. They started to emphasize not human subjectivity but the philosophy of the person. It was argued that they should concern themselves not with abstract categories ('the masses') but with respect for the individual. Besides respect for the human, 'the otherness of others', there must also be a new respect for other cultures and religions. They believed that the question of human rights was vital and that it made the work of Kant relevant again. His *Critique of Practical Reason* provided a framework within which they could seriously think of ethical problems. Kant insisted that we should treat people not as means but as ends in themselves: 'Always act on that maxim which you can at the same time will to become a universal law.' This ultimately leads to an ethic of love – love addressed to a single person.[20]

What criticisms can be made of the 'new philosophers'? I would argue that they were so involved with their ethical concerns that they did not make any significant attempt to improve the world through political action. They never referred to the exploitation and violence of capitalism and its support of authoritarian regimes throughout the world. In short they focused on the individual and neglected the social. Most of these philosophers, who drew heavily on Nietzsche's thought, rejected both science and politics. It seems to me that they were part of an intellectual trend that stressed plurality and difference (the characteristics of postmodernism, a movement which will be discussed in a later chapter), the singular and the subjective. Many of them were seeking solace in aesthetics, metaphysics and religion.[21]

Conclusion

In this chapter it has been argued that many of the fundamental beliefs of post-structuralism have their roots in Nietzscheanism. If one looks at the work of the post-structuralists, such as Deleuze and Guattari, Derrida, Foucault, Lyotard and others, one can see the influence of Nietzsche's philosophy. They share with him an antipathy to any 'system'. Secondly, they reject the Hegelian view of history as progress. Thirdly, they are aware of the increasing pressure towards conformity and are highly critical of this tendency. Fourthly, their obsession with the subjective and the 'small story' has led them to affirm the anti-political individual.

Post-structuralism is largely 'a product of 1968'. Unable to break the structures of state power, post-structuralism found it possible to subvert the structures of language: 'The student movement was flushed off the streets and driven underground into discourse.'[22] Its enemies became coherent belief-systems of any kind, in particular all forms of political theory and organization which sought to analyse and act upon the structures of society as a whole. All total, systematic thought was now suspect: conceptual meaning itself, as opposed to libidinal gesture and anarchist spontaneity, was feared as repressive.

After briefly introducing the leading post-structuralists I turned to the work of the 'new philosophers'. It was stated that the 'new philosophy' is not just an aberration of a few intellectuals but must be seen as mirroring a widespread mood of disorientation among the generation of '68. The 'new philosophers' believe that human society is permanently and inherently oppressive; but domination is no longer conceived of in class terms. They uphold various forms of romanticism and individualism. They denounce 'science' and any totalizing beliefs in the name of the spontaneous and the particular. Most of these philosophers hold the view that science always operates within and reinforces relations of power; that Marxism was in some way responsible for the terror of the Soviet camps; that the state is the central source of social and political oppression and that therefore any politics directed towards the seizure of state power is dangerous and vain. These ideologues combine an odd idealization of rebellion with an ultimately passive pessimism and an acquiescence in the status quo. This is not surprising, as they have no conception of historical advance or permanent transformation.

Most of the theorists I have mentioned in this chapter think of Marxism as the last systematic attempt to understand the world, to find an immanent order in it. As such, they argue, it is a metaphysics. Marxism, they assert, no longer connects with the present. Indeed, it is a belief system which cuts people off from reality. Lyotard, for example, now sees Marxism as a form of religious discourse: the suffering proletariat is supposed to bring about, some time in the future, the redemption of the world.

The attitude of many post-structuralists seems to be: 'If Marxism isn't true, then nothing is.' Many thinkers feel that we are at a stage of confusion ('we don't know where we are going') and that Nietzsche best expresses that confusion. The irony is that theorists like Lyotard and others need a general theory to support their assertion as to why there cannot be a general theory. As they cannot provide any grounds for their views, they think of their viewpoint as being provisional, 'ironic'. These intellectuals focus only on the heterogeneous, the diverse, the subjective, the spontaneous, the relative and the fragmentary.

Further reading

V. Descombes, *Modern French Philosophy*, Cambridge: Cambridge University Press, 1980.
Not an introductory text but a most useful and stimulating guide which discusses Kojève, Merleau-Ponty, structuralism, Althusser, Foucault, Derrida, Deleuze and Lyotard.

R. Harland, *Superstructuralism: The Philosophy of Structuralism and Post-Structuralism*, London: Methuen, 1987.
This ambitious book, on the philosophy of structuralism and post-structuralism, covers all the major thinkers but focuses particularly on Derrida and Foucault. It is clear, comprehensive and most useful.

R. Kearney, *Modern Movements in European Philosophy*, Manchester: Manchester University Press, 1986.
A systematic overview of thinkers associated with phenomenology, critical theory and structuralism. It has useful introductions to Derrida, Foucault, Lacan and others.

V. Leitch, *Deconstructive Criticism: An Advanced Introduction*, London: Hutchinson, 1983.
The book focuses on the main theories of language, contemporary theories of literature and provides a survey of specific deconstructive readings and new forms of writing. Leitch discusses all the major post-structuralists – Derrida, Lacan, Foucault, Barthes – in a most thoughtful and helpful way. An excellent book.

J.G. Merquior, *From Prague to Paris: A Critique of Structuralist and Post-Structuralist Thought*, London: Verso, 1986.
This critical study begins with Jakobson and focuses largely on Lévi-Strauss and Barthes. The last chapter, an overview, moves on from structuralism to post-structuralism and is a polemic against Derrida and Foucault.

K. Silverman, *The Subject of Semiotics*, Oxford: Oxford University Press, 1983.
A most useful book which makes accessible the relationships between

and among structuralism, semiotics, psychoanalysis, feminism and post-structuralism. The author maintains the centrality of psycho-analysis to semiotics and gives many examples from literary and film texts. It is an excellent introduction to the work of Saussure, Freud's primary and secondary processes, metaphor and metonymy, Freudian and Lacanian models of the human subject, and the interpretive strategies of Roland Barthes.

J. Sturrock (ed.), *Structuralism and Since: From Lévi-Strauss to Derrida*, Oxford: Oxford University Press, 1979.
A useful book; it contains helpful discussions of the work of Lévi-Strauss, Barthes, Foucault, Lacan and Derrida.

C. Weedon, *Feminist Practice and Poststructuralist Theory*, Oxford: Basil Blackwell, 1987.
A clear introduction to post-structuralism. The author argues its political usefulness to feminism, and considers its implications for feminist critical practice. It includes chapters on psychoanalysis (Lacan), language and subjectivity, discourse and power (Foucault).

Chapter 5

□

Cixous, Irigaray, Kristeva: French feminist theories

Introduction

In this chapter I want to provide a brief introduction to the work of three French thinkers: Hélène Cixous, Luce Irigaray and Julia Kristeva. Of course, there are many similarities and differences between them. One characteristic that they have in common is that they have all been influenced, in different ways, by Lacanian psychoanalysis. Another common feature is that they all have something interesting to say about subjectivity, sexuality, language and desire.

Hélène Cixous

Introduction

Besides being a novelist, Hélène Cixous is a critic and commentator. In my presentation I will focus on only two aspects of her work: her antagonism to all forms of dualistic thinking based on oppositions and hierarchies, and her espousal of a feminine practice of writing related to the body. She sees feminine sexuality as rich and plural and she draws a parallel between feminine libido and writing. She believes that the patriarchal order can be challenged by feminine writing.

In the essay 'Sorties' Cixous describes the set of hierarchical oppositions which, she argues, have structured Western thought and governed its political practice.[1] She cites oppositions such as 'culture/ nature', 'head/heart', 'form/matter', 'speaking/writing', and relates them to the opposition between 'man' and 'woman'. She notes that one term of the opposition is always privileged. Each couple is based on the repression of one of its terms, yet both terms are locked together in violent conflict. Without nature, culture is meaningless; yet culture continually struggles to negate nature. Another example of a dualist structure of unequal power is colonialism; she remarks how the Arab population was both necessary to, and despised by, the French.

Such dialectical structures, Cixous argues, also dominate the formation of subjectivity, and thus of sexual difference. She uses Hegel's Master/Slave relation to illustrate this.[2] In this story the subject requires the recognition of an Other from whom the individual differentiates him- or herself. Yet this recognition is experienced as threatening, and the Other is immediately repressed, so that the subject can return to the security and certainty of self-knowledge. Now, consider the opposition man/woman. Within a patriarchal society, woman becomes represented as the Other, necessary to the constitution and recognition of identity, but always threatening to it. Sexual difference is thus locked into a structure of power, where difference, or otherness, is tolerated only when repressed. The movement of the Hegelian dialectic depends on an inequality of power between the two oppositional terms. The well-known story of Sleeping Beauty exemplifies this. The woman is represented as sleeping, as possessed of negative subjectivity until she is kissed by a male. The kiss gives her existence, but only within a process that immediately subordinates her to the desire of 'the prince'.

In her early work Cixous focuses attention on the space in which women are placed by culture. She questions the naturalness or inevitability of structural hierarchies. Wanting to overcome these hierarchies, her strategy, as we shall see, is to explore the subversive possibilities of a 'feminine' writing practice.

An important part of Cixous's project is to unearth the myths that sustain the logic of patriarchy, undoing their 'naturalness'. Let us take as an example her interesting interpretation of the *Oresteia* myth. She reads it as a narrative of the origins of patriarchy. Seeing Orestes as placed at a turning point in history, Cixous focuses on the debate in the *Eumenides* over the relative claims of revenge for murder of a husband (Agamemnon by Clytemnestra) and murder of a mother (Clytemnestra by Orestes). She draws attention to Apollo's ruling that 'the woman you call the mother of the child is not the parent, just a nurse to the seed . . . the *man* is the source of life' – an account of reproduction that diminishes the gravity of matricide, and thus seems to license the development of patriarchal social relations. She notes that it is Electra's voice that is the loudest in the demand for the death of her mother; she is the leader of the phallocrats.

Cixous rejects both the Freudian and Lacanian models of sexual difference, which she sees as condemning women to negativity in their privileging of the phallus. Instead, she argues for the possibility of sustaining a bisexuality: not as a denial of sexual difference, but as a lived recognition of plurality, of the simultaneous presence of masculinity and femininity within an individual subject.

Writing and the body

For Cixous, writing is a privileged space for the exploration of such non-hierarchically arranged bisexuality. Writing, she believes, can be the site of alternative economies; it is not obliged simply to reproduce the system. This argument is developed in the context of close readings of a series of texts by Kleist, Shakespeare, Poe, Genet and others. It is clear that she favours texts that are excessive in some way, texts that undermine fixed categories.

Cixous, then, is committed to the production of a form of writing that would embody bisexuality, and operate in the interests of women.[3] In her view women's relations to their bodies are culturally inscribed. She believes that the cultural is organized differently for men and women, and that a writing practice that reformulates the cultural is of particular importance for women.

Cixous then goes on to theorize an alternative economy of femininity in relation to the concept of 'the gift'. She describes two possible attitudes to giving: one, which is described as 'masculine', is caught up in the mechanisms of exchange, and will give only with a certainty of immediate return. Cixous suggests an alternative, or feminine, economy of giving which derives from the work of Georges Bataille. He was very interested in those aspects of human culture that are not reducible to the classical economic balance between production and consumption. These aspects include art, games, spectacles, war and perverse sexuality. In his view such activities show the futility of a mechanical systematization of human existence. His favourite example is the radiation of the sun, which dispenses energy (wealth) without any return. The sun gives without ever receiving.

Taking up this theme Cixous writes:

Can one speak of another spending? Really, there is no 'free' gift. You never give something for nothing. But the difference lies in the why and how of the gift, in the values that the gesture of giving affirms, causes to circulate; in the type of profit the giver draws from the gift and the use to which he or she puts it.[4]

This different relation to giving is what Cixous sees as characteristic of an alternative, feminine, practice of writing. Such writing would reject the security of fixed categories of stable identity; moreover, it would not be afraid to create subjectivities that are plural and shifting.

Feminine writing, asserts Cixous, cannot be defined. Nevertheless, she does ascribe one characteristic to it: its proximity to voice. Speech is privileged because of its closeness to song and thus to the unconscious. Cixous wants to explore the associative logic of music over the linear logic of philosophical and literary discourse. For Cixous, speaking is a powerfully transgressive act for women, and writing is a privileged space for transformation.

Cixous believes that writing is produced and understood in relation to the body. She believes that we often separate mind and body. Most of us have an illusion of intellectual control but it is at the cost of erasing, censoring and hystericizing the body. This interest in the relation between language and the body leads her to an engagement with the unconscious. Cixous often uses both myth and dream in her texts as ways of exploring the archaic and the repressed, and as ways of unsettling the illusion of subjective autonomy and conscious control. It should, perhaps, be added that Cixous's commitment to moving beyond the categories of the rational and the knowable, towards the site of creation, multiple subjectivity and the bodily roots of human culture derives from a close study of Nietzsche.[5]

This focus on writing as a political strategy has a biographical significance for Cixous. As both woman and Jew she has experienced loss and exclusion. She has been closely identified with the group *Psychoanalyse et Politique* (*Psych et Po*) who struggled to develop revolutionary theories of the oppression of women on the basis of psychoanalytic theory. Wanting to challenge the unconscious structures of patriarchal oppression, the group worked 'like moles' to disturb the dominant order. They were hostile towards groups that described themselves as 'feminist', seeing such groups as reformist, and as working simply to gain access to, and to reproduce, the structures of masculine power.

Cixous's comments on writers are always linked to her desire to theorize the power of language, to evade the habitual, to move beyond the hierarchies of dual opposition. From her studies of authors like James Joyce, E.T.A. Hoffmann, Heinrich von Kleist, Edgar Allan Poe, Sigmund Freud and others she derives an understanding of the relations between subjectivity, textuality and sexual difference which is crucial to her own writing practice.

One of Cixous's main interests is in forms of writing that disturb the notion of individual subjectivity as unified and stable, and explode the boundaries of the self. Many critics are interested in Poe because his writings explore structures of subjectivity and because he seems to foreshadow many of the concerns of modernism. Cixous believes that Poe's writing, in its very excess and perversity, represents a challenge to existing forms of subjectivity, desire and sexual difference. She admires Poe's writing because it removes the illusion of subjective autonomy and of a unified homogeneous identity. It is the power of Poe's writing to move beyond the rigid categories of love/death or conscious/unconscious which Cixous values.

What I find impressive is that, besides her theoretical works, Cixous has also produced a large number of *fictional* texts.[6] These fictions stretch the limits of the novelistic: character is uncertain, the narrative point of view is unstable, the apparent transparency of language is challenged, and linear temporality is unsettled. In these texts she explores many of the issues that also dominate her theoretical and critical works: subjectivity, the corporeal roots of language, femininity, relations to the Other, and the possibilities of social and subjective transformation.

Having established the political importance of feminine writing for women, Cixous found a woman practising such a writing. This is really quite remarkable. Having theorized the limitations and dangers of dualist thought, of subjectivity based on the obliteration of the Other, Cixous discovered another woman writer who was exploring *the same issues* in fictional form: Clarice Lispector.

To understand this fully, one has to remember that Cixous's theorization of feminine writing had taken place almost entirely in terms of the texts of canonical male writers such as Joyce, Kleist or Hoffmann. And her theoretical vocabulary had been largely derived from male theorists such as Lacan and Derrida. And then, suddenly, she came across a writer who was largely unknown in France, who was Jewish, who was a woman and who shared many of her philosophical and stylistic preoccupations.[7]

Cixous found in Lispector, the Brazilian novelist and short-story writer, a sustained exploration of the relations between subjectivity and writing. Lispector embodies many of the ideas which Cixous had propagated. Cixous greatly appreciates Lispector's exploration of subjectivity, her positing of alternative relations to otherness, her stylistic minimalism, and the audacity of the ethical issues with which she engages. And so these writers have much in common; both explore the possibility of an alternative economy of representation to the bodily, the overturning of hierarchies, and the recognition of the multiplicity of subjectivity. Like Lispector, Cixous wants to reject the constraining masks of social identity in favour of a Heideggerian notion of the multiple and temporal experience of Being.

Writing and the theatre

Much of Cixous's recent writing has been for the theatre. Theatre has provided Cixous with a space in which to develop her analyses of subjectivity, and to explore further the bodily roots of meaning. She has been able to challenge what she sees as the dominant forms of thought and reason, and to posit new structures of historical explanation. She feels that the theatre is a space where the poetic can still survive within the forms of a public and accessible ritual.

Cixous stresses the importance in drama of moments of crisis, of personal or historical turning points which carry within them the possibility of change. In the theatre (unlike a novel) time cannot be re-run; the ending cannot be read first. The audience is locked into a bodily experience of time. Cixous is keenly aware of the thought of Heidegger, who stressed the ways in which a recognition of the temporal aspects of Being lead to the confrontation of our own mortality, and thus to the necessity of choice.

To put it concisely, Cixous uses the theatre as a space in which to develop her critique of the forms of subjectivity and representation that dominate contemporary life. She believes that the theatre, in the past, consistently objectified women. Referring to the ultimate fate of Electra, Ophelia and Cordelia, Cixous concludes that theatre functions as specular fantasy, where women characters function as mirrors of male heroism. Women in such theatre are silenced and repressed, their bodies both negated and elevated to the level of display.

As I mentioned earlier, Cixous has a great interest in forms of thought that do not rely on hierarchical oppositions, but are instead open to the possibility of multiple differences. Such forms of thought have been theorized by Jacques Derrida, with his concept of difference, the process of differing and deferring.[8] These philosophical concepts are important because they are attempts to avoid categorical oppositions in favour of a never completely finished process of production of meaning.

Cixous's early plays are principally concerned with women's relation to patriarchical culture. I am thinking of *Portrait of Dora* and *Le Nom d'Oedipus*. Her two most recent plays have involved the analysis of historical change and political structures. Both plays have been located in Asian countries. *The Terrible but Unfinished Story of Norodnom Sihanouk* deals with the history of Cambodia from 1955 to the Vietnamese invasion of 1979. Cixous's shift in this play from sexual politics to national struggle disconcerted many of her readers but it could be said on her behalf that she seems to have had an intuitive understanding about the increasing importance of ethnic and national struggles.

In *L'Indiade* (*The Indiad, or the India of their Dreams*) Cixous dramatizes the history of India from 1937 to 1948, a period which saw the culmination of the Indian struggle for independence from British rule, the partition of India into India and Pakistan, and the assassination of Gandhi. It dramatizes the different conceptions of national identity which lay behind the policies of the politicians. The partition of India becomes a metaphor for the competition between different conceptions of personal and social relations.

Cixous displays an increasing interest in the concept of resistance, and in the need to preserve and protect vulnerable peoples and cultures against the forces of homogenization and oppression. She believes in the possibility of an alliance between different forms of otherness, which would protect and respect difference, but would be strong enough to represent significant resistance. Cixous sees a political and ethical role for the theatre in terms of a capacity for openness to the Other.

Writing for the theatre has both extended and transformed Cixous's project. It has allowed her to explore different relations to otherness, to develop her theorization of the bodily dimensions of language, to posit the existence of alternative social and subjective economies, and to tie her theoretical work to the mechanisms of historical change.

These developments have led Cixous's work away from the intense focus on feminine subjectivity and its relations to the female body that were so important to her work in the 1970s. Instead, she is now committed to understanding women's struggle as part of a broader political and ethical movement: to realize the subjective and collective dimensions of a feminine economy, to preserve cultural diversity in the face of homogenization, and to resist the different forms of social domination.

Luce Irigaray

Introduction

Luce Irigaray, a feminist philosopher, uses psychoanalysis in her examination of philosophy and its presuppositions. She is difficult to read partly because of her many references to German philosophy, and because a large number of her terms derive from Lacan and Derrida which she often reworks or redefines. In my selective account of Irigaray's work I will focus on her critique of patriarchy especially in philosophy, her critique of psychoanalysis, and her claim that women need a language of their own.

One of Irigaray's main aims is to expose the foundations of patriarchy and, in particular, to show it at work in philosophy.[9] Secondly, Irigaray wants to define female identity. But one of the problems she faces is: how does one define female specificity without getting locked once again inside the patriarchal framework one is trying to escape from?

Irigaray does not have much time for the attempt to reverse the order of things, simply to reverse the balance of power between men and women. What she is concerned with is to promote and encourage the development of a social form specific to women. She believes that an *entre-femmes* (a sociality among and between women) is a necessary condition for the creation of female identity and subjectivity.

The danger is always that in accepting the terms of the system currently in force, women will become 'men'. Whatever equality means, it does not mean becoming like men. Fighting for equal wages and equal rights is, in the end, subordinate for her to the more important struggle which is to challenge the foundation of the social and cultural order.

On reason and rationality

Western feminism in all its forms is an inheritor of the Enlightenment and its contradictions. It is clear to Irigaray that Enlightenment values have not been applied to women. Moreover, the faith in reason underestimated the non-rational elements in the human mind and its will to power, to control, manipulate and destroy in the name of the rational. She sees this reason as peculiarly male. For Irigaray the culture of the West is monosexual; the status of women is that of 'lesser men', inferior or defective men. She insists that there is no neutral or universal in this culture. What is taken to be neutral, for example, science or philosophy, is in fact gendered: it is the discourse of the male subject.

Irigaray's critique of rationality is not a prescription for female irrationality; when she argues that rationality is male she implies that it has a certain structure. In her view Western rationality is characterized by the principle of identity; the principle of non-contradiction (A is A, A is not B), in which ambiguity/ambivalence has been reduced to a minimum; and binarism, for example, the opposition of nature/reason, subject/object, which assumes that everything has to be either one thing or another.

Many writers have used male–female symbolism to describe rationality as male and the female as unconscious. But, one wonders, is it not dangerous to regard women as irrational, or as the unconscious of culture? What is important is that rationality is categorized by Irigaray as male, not in order to oppose it, but in order to suggest a more adequate conceptualization in which the male does not repress or split off the female/unconscious, but acknowledges and integrates it.[10]

Irigaray is also critical of Marxist categories and believes that the emphasis on production and economic relations obscures the domain of symbolic relations. She argues that women need to interpret their present situation and status not only in economic terms but also in symbolic terms. The only way in which the status of women could be fundamentally altered is by the creation of a powerful female symbolic.

On psychoanalysis

Irigaray's relation to psychoanalysis is complex; it is characterized by indebtedness and by critical distance. The strength of her analysis is that she uses the theories of both Freud and Lacan against them to put forward a psychoanalytic explanation for theoretical bias. Her criticisms of psychoanalysis can be summarized as follows:

1. Psychoanalysis, like other disciplines, is historically determined. This means that its attitude to women is historically determined as well. As psychoanalysis does not recognize this, its phallocentric bias is elevated into a universal value.
2. The social order which determines psychoanalysis rests on the unacknowledged and incorporated mother.
3. Psychoanalytic theory is governed by unacknowledged and uninterpreted fantasies. It purports to analyse the fantasies of others, but meanwhile its own discourse perpetuates the dominant cultural fantasies.[11]

Despite her critique, Irigaray is convinced of the powerful potential of psychoanalysis. With language as the instrument, real and profound change can take place in the life of the analysand. It is essential, however, to rethink psychoanalysis from women's point of view.

This is what Irigaray has begun to do. Her work can be seen as a sort of psychoanalysis of Western culture, seeking what underpins its fragile rationality, looking for the 'repressed' or unconscious of culture. Irigaray's method is to look for the fantasies that haunt philosophical discourse. She argues that the male projects his own ego on to the world, which then becomes a mirror which enables him to see his own reflection wherever he looks.

Her second step is to look for the mother. The mother supports the processes of the male imaginary but is not herself represented, a neglect equivalent to matricide. Irigaray's strategy is to look for the resistances and defences which conceal the original crime of matricide. These two principles, to look for the specular relationship and to uncover the buried mother, underlie all her analyses of the philosophers. She is seeking the varied fantasies which persist in discourse as symptoms of the patriarchal unconscious. Western culture, in short, is a monologic, monosexual culture in which men speak to men. What Irigaray wants to do is to work out the conditions of women's subjectivity. How can women assume the I of discourse in their own right and not as a derivative male 'I'?

Let us now turn to the question, how does the female function within the Western imaginary? (By 'imaginary' I am referring to unconscious fantasy.) Irigaray aims to show that Western philosophical and psychoanalytic discourse sees sexual differences as though there were only one sex, and that sex were male (that is to say, women are defective men). She writes that we need to look at the fantasies underlying the propositional statements of male thinkers. In her own work she has analysed the unconscious fantasies underlying the Freudian and Lacanian systems. She argues that Freud's model of sexuality is male. In his fantasy the role of women in childbirth is not recognized and women inevitably appear in his scenario as defective males. To reiterate: Western culture, identity, logic and rationality are symbolically male, and the female is either the outside, the hole or the unsymbolizable residue. The feminine always finds itself defined as deficiency, imitation or lack.

It is not surprising, then, that women face immense problems. These problems do not arise from immutable characteristics of women's 'nature' but are an effect of women's position relative to the symbolic order. Hate, envy or rivalry are often operative between women because a way of symbolic negotiation is not available.

Irigaray is very concerned with the unsymbolized mother–daughter relationship. By this she means that there is an absence of linguistic, social, cultural representation of that relationship. We can readily think of examples of the mother–son relationship, but we have to go back to Greek mythology to find culturally embodied representations of the mother–daughter relationship.[12] In short, the mother–daughter relationship has been by-passed.

An unsymbolized mother–daughter relationship makes it very difficult, if not impossible, for women to have an identity in the symbolic order that is distinct from the maternal function. Irigaray accepts the clinical view that women have difficulty in separating from their mothers, that they tend to relationships in which identity is merged and in which the boundaries between self and other are not clear. She represents this psychoanalytic diagnosis as a symptom or result of women's position in the symbolic order. If women do not have access to society and to culture, they remain in a state of abandonment, of dereliction.

Reinterpreting classical myths

For Irigaray the gesture which excludes women from philosophy and the gesture which excludes women from the polis are one and the same. There is a connection between the status of woman in Western thought and the status of women in Western society. Irigaray has interpreted many classical myths. She believes, like Cixous, that in mythology we can see a struggle taking place between the maternal and paternal genealogies, eventually ending in the installation of patriarchy.

The final section of Irigaray's book *Speculum* consists of a remarkable reading of the myth of the cavern in Plato's *Republic*.[13] In Irigaray's reinterpretation, the roles of the imaginary mother and father are attributed to the cavern (the womb) and the Idea respectively. In progressively moving away from the shadows towards the light, the prisoner is moving away from the mother. She argues that truth has come to mean leaving behind the Mother (the cavern) and her role in reproduction. Irigaray demonstrates that Plato's ideal republic, despite appearances, is not at all egalitarian; his city is monosexual, his women are all 'men' – they accede to all the civic functions in so far as they resemble men and renounce their specificity.

Like Cixous, Irigaray is fascinated by Greek myth. Irigaray has written about the myth of Athena, daughter of Zeus. It is on Athena's advice that Apollo, against the chorus of women, instals patriarchy by decreeing that Orestes's matricide was justifiable. In Irigaray's account of the myth, patriarchy covers its tracks by attributing the justification of matricide to a woman. Athena, the father's daughter, was an alibi for patriarchy.

Athena carried the head of Medusa on her shield. Any man who looked on Medusa was turned to stone. Freud comments that Athena is thus also the sexually unapproachable woman; being turned to stone is equated with castration. And castration is linked with death; man turns away from his fears and projects them on to 'woman'.

Another myth that fascinates Irigaray is that of Antigone. The myth represents a moment of transition from the genealogy of the maternal to that of the paternal. Antigone and her brother have the same mother; they are linked by the blood tie which Antigone puts before the claims of the polis. Walled up alive in the tomb, Antigone is an image of woman in patriarchy, unable to be heard, but also a guilt-producing fantasy.

Irigaray points out that whereas the brother acts, using the sister as a 'living-mirror' for his actions, and leaving her to be the guardian of his burial rites, the action is not reciprocated; there is no one to recognize Antigone's act. The law of the polis is founded over her suppression; she is confined to family relations and to burying the dead; she does not, like her brother, act in the universal. She signifies the limited ethical sphere of the family.

For Irigaray, the polis, from Plato's ideal republic to Hegel's universal sphere, is founded upon an act of exclusion; what is left outside is *nature*. The *social* is constructed against men's fears of death and mortality. In the process it is women, the living reminders of birth, and therefore of transience and death, to whom the sign of 'nature' has been attached.[14]

A house of language

Irigaray claims that women need a language of their own. Men continually seek and construct houses for themselves everywhere: grottoes, huts, women, towns, theory, concepts, language. Women too need a house of language; they need a house of habitation that does not imprison them, instead of an invisible prison which keeps them captive; a habitation in which they can grow is the condition of becoming. Irigaray's analysis of language indicates the immense cultural transformations that will be needed. Hence she makes a vital distinction between speaking *like* a woman and speaking *as* a woman, since the latter implies not simply psychological positioning but also social positioning.

It is often said that to speak or write like a man is to assert mastery, to be in control of meaning, to claim truth, objectivity, knowledge, whereas to speak like a woman is to refuse mastery, to allow meaning to be elusive or shifting, not to be in control, or in possession of truth or knowledge. In other words, to be assertive, to make claims, to be 'dogmatic', which means to have a thesis, a meaning, a political position, is to take up a 'male' stance, whatever one's sex.

When Cixous or Kristeva want to give examples of a different kind of writing, they instance the 'feminine' writing of certain male authors: Mallarmé, Lautréamont, Joyce. And Irigaray has stated that philosophers like Nietzsche, Hegel, Levinas, Derrida are all interested in feminine identity, and in their identity as feminine or women. It is well known that male and female identifications can be made by either sex. But, as Irigaray points out, one should not confuse identification with identity. According to the above scenario we are left in a rather odd position; men, the writers and philosophers who want to write like women, are better at being women than women are!

Irigaray sees the 'feminine' of the philosophers as an attempt at colonization which once more pushes out women from the cultural space. It is for this reason that Irigaray emphasizes woman-as-subject; she says that occupying the subject position is not simply a question of the position of enunciation, it must be rooted in social practices too. A part of the definition of woman-as-subject is that women must be involved in the making of cultural and political reality.

Julia Kristeva

Introduction

Julia Kristeva arrived in Paris from Bulgaria in 1966. She started out as a linguist in the late 1960s and first wrote about topics related to women and feminism in 1974, around the time she was beginning her training as a psychoanalyst. From the late 1970s onwards her work has been increasingly concerned with psychoanalytic issues, sexuality and femininity. Overall, her main interests are language, truth, ethics and love. Recently she has written on the 'stranger', the outsider and the notion of 'strangeness' within the self – a person's own deep sense of being.

Let me begin by asking: what do Kristeva and Irigaray have in common? Well, first of all, Kristeva and Irigaray share a familiarity with Freud's work, and a knowledge of Lacanian theory. Secondly, they share Lacan's anti-humanism, his commitment to the primacy of language in psychic life, and his understanding of the necessarily sexualized position assumed by the subject in the symbolic. Thirdly, both focus on the relation obscured in Freud's and Lacan's work: the mother–child relation (Kristeva) and the mother–daughter relation (Irigaray). Fourthly, both affirm the archaic force of the pre-Oedipal, which although repressed is also permanently preserved. Finally, both assert the fluid, polymorphous perverse status of libidinal drives.

There is no doubt that Lacanian psychoanalysis remains the fundamental conceptual and methodological grid for Kristeva's work. Her earliest writings are based on Lacan's notions of the mirror stage and the castration complex.[15] These two moments provide the necessary conditions for the subject's acquisition of a speaking position. Though Kristeva has taken Lacan's conceptual apparatus as the starting point for developing her own methods and objects of investigation, nevertheless, she is critical of certain aspects of his work.

Unlike Lacan, Kristeva is always aware of the historical and social aspects of signification and subjectivity. She thinks that Lacan rarely includes concrete determinations in his work. For Kristeva, however, the social and historical determination of individuals and signifying practices is always essential.

Secondly, in contrast to Lacan, for whom the imaginary order functions only in a visual register, Kristeva stresses all the sensory registers. The imaginary is not only a visual order, it is also, Kristeva claims, organized by voice, touch, taste and smell. Kristeva believes that Lacan concentrates too heavily or exclusively on verbal language at the expense of other models of signification. Moreover, while Lacan insists on a definitive break between the imaginary and the symbolic, Kristeva posits more of a continuity. Kristeva's concepts testify to the pre-Oedipal and pre-mirror stage processes and relations generally neglected in psychoanalysis. Indeed, her work on pre-Oedipal, narcissistic identificatory relations and maternal dependencies provides an orientation that is underemphasized in Freud and Lacan, and which owes a debt to the work of Melanie Klein and D.W. Winnicott.

In spite of these theoretical differences Kristeva uses the Lacanian concepts of the symbolic order and the subject to form the basis of a theory of signifying practice. In brief, Kristeva sees the ideological and philosophical basis for modern linguistics as fundamentally authoritarian and oppressive. She wants to shift away from the Saussurian concept of *langue* towards a re-establishment of the *speaking subject* as an object for linguistics. Kristeva has a notion of a speaking subject that is divided and decentred. Language, for her, is not a monolithic system but a complex, heterogeneous, signifying process located in and between subjects. Language is *productive* as opposed to a mere reflection of social relations.

There seems to be some agreement that Kristeva, as opposed to Cixous and Irigaray, cannot strictly speaking be considered a purely feminist theorist. Kristeva's views lead her to reject any idea of an *écriture féminine* or a *parler femme* that would be inherently feminine or female. Though Kristeva does not have a theory of 'femininity', and even less of 'femaleness', what she does have is a theory of marginality, subversion and dissidence. She believes in the potentially revolutionary force of the marginal and repressed aspects of language. Like Cixous, Kristeva argues that there are feminine forms of signification which cannot be contained by the rational structure of the symbolic order and which therefore threaten its sovereignty and have been relegated to the margins of discourse.

However, unlike Cixous, Kristeva does not locate feminine aspects of language in women's female libido. The feminine is a mode of language open to male and female writers. In the section that follows I will outline Kristeva's views on how the semiotic and the symbolic are aligned with feminine and masculine libidinal energy, and how the return of the repressed feminine (the semiotic) is manifest, for example, in the 'marginal' discourse of the literary avant-garde.

The semiotic and the symbolic

Kristeva's general model of signifying practice is derived from Lacan's integration of Freudian analysis and structural semiology. Her conception of the semiotic and the symbolic functions operating in psychical, textual and social life is based on the distinction Freud developed between pre-Oedipal and Oedipal sexual drives.

The *semiotic*, as Kristeva uses the term, can be correlated with the anarchic, pre-Oedipal component drives, and polymorphous erotogenic zones, orifices and organs. The semiotic is the 'raw material' of signification, the corporeal, libidinal matter that must be harnessed and appropriately channelled for social cohesion and regulation. These infantile drives are indeterminate, capable of many aims, sources and objects. Kristeva describes the semiotic as 'feminine', a phase dominated by the space of the mother's body.

Kristeva defines this space, following Plato's *Timaeus*, as the semiotic *chora*.[16] It is a space or receptacle, an undecidably enveloped and enveloping locus from which the subject is both produced and threatened with annihilation. The *chora* defines and structures the limits of the child's body and its ego or identity as a subject. It is the space of the subversion of the subject, the space in which the death drive emerges and threatens to engulf the subject, to reduce it to the inertia of non-existence.

Now, though this is a 'feminine' phase dominated by the mother, the mother is always considered phallic. She is the consequence of a masculine fantasy of maternity, rather than women's lived experience of maternity.

If the semiotic is pre-Oedipal, based on primary processes and is maternally oriented, by contrast the *symbolic* is an Oedipalized system, regulated by secondary processes and the Law of the Father. The symbolic is the domain of positions and propositions. The symbolic is an order superimposed on the semiotic. The symbolic control of the various semiotic processes is, however, tenuous and liable to break down or lapse at certain historically, linguistically and psychically significant moments. It results in an upheaval in the norms of the smooth, understandable text. The semiotic overflows its boundaries in those privileged 'moments' Kristeva specifies in her triad of subversive forces: madness, holiness and poetry.

Let me try to make clearer the link between the semiotic and the avant-garde. The semiotic is the rhythmic, energetic, dispersed bodily series of forces which strive to proliferate pleasures, sounds, colours or movements experienced in the child's body. Like the repressed, the semiotic can return in/as disruptions within the symbolic. The semiotic is both the precondition of symbolic functioning and its uncontrollable excess. It is used by discourses but cannot be articulated by them.

Kristeva is fascinated with the avant-garde 'texts' of Mallarmé, Lautréamont, Artaud, Joyce, Schoenberg, Cage, Stockhausen and even Giotto and Bellini.[17] These texts, whether they are written, dramatic, musical, visual or auditory, are disturbing because they provide a more direct expression of the semiotic than is usually possible in more conventional symbolic representational systems. These semiotic eruptions represent transgressive breaches of symbolic coherence. In short, the symbolic/Oedipal/social mode owes a debt of existence to an unspeakable and unrepresentable semiotic/maternal/ feminine.

I mentioned the pre-Oedipal phase just now. Kristeva's theory is mostly concerned with developments in the pre-Oedipal phase where sexual difference does not exist. The question of difference only becomes relevant at the point of entry into the symbolic order. In discussing this situation for little girls, Kristeva points out that since the semiotic is pre-Oedipal, it is linked to the mother, whereas the symbolic is dominated by the Law of the Father. Faced with this situation, the little girl has to make a choice: 'either she identifies with her mother, or she raises herself to the symbolic stature of her father. In the first case, the pre-oedipal phases (oral and anal eroticism) are intensified.'[18] If, on the other hand, the little girl identifies with the father, 'the access she gains to the symbolic dominance will censor the pre-oedipal phase and wipe out the last trace of dependence on the body of mother'.

Kristeva thus delineates two different options for women: mother identification which will intensify the pre-Oedipal components of the woman's psyche and render her marginal to the symbolic, or father identification which will create a woman who will derive her identity from the same symbolic order. Now, though the fluid mobility of the semiotic is associated with the pre-Oedipal phase, and therefore with the pre-Oedipal mother, Kristeva makes it quite clear that, like Freud and Klein, she sees the pre-Oedipal mother as a figure that encompasses both masculinity and femininity. In her view men can also be constructed as marginal by the symbolic order, as her analyses of male avant-garde artists – Artaud, Céline, Joyce, Lautréamont, Mallarmé – have shown.

Kristeva seems to regard only men as writers or producers of the avant-garde. Although exclusively male in Kristeva's terms, the avant-garde is nevertheless the best representative of the repressed, feminine semiotic order. An important part of Kristeva's argument is that any strengthening of the semiotic, which knows no sexual difference, must lead to a weakening of traditional gender divisions.

But what about women writers? In Kristeva's view, women are not inside the symbolic in the same way as men. Women tend to write in one of two ways. They may either produce books that are largely compensatory substitutes for a family, that simulate a family structure – novels of autobiography, romance or family history – they produce stories, images or fantasies in place of an actual family; or else, women write as hysterical subjects, bound to the body and its rhythms.

To conclude, let me recapitulate the interplay of the semiotic and symbolic processes. On Kristeva's model all texts and all cultural products are the result of a dialectical process: the interaction between two mutually modifying historical forces. One is the setting in place, the establishment of a regulated system, or 'unity' – which is the symbolic. Underlying and subverting this is the semiotic, a movement of 'cutting through', breaking down unities. In times of rupture, renovation and revolution (which Kristeva identifies with the symptomatic eruptions of the avant-garde) the symbolic is no longer capable of directing the semiotic energies into already coded social outlets. Its subversive, dispersing energies transgress the boundaries or tolerable limits of the symbolic. Sooner or later, depending on the extent of the threat it poses, the semiotic is recodified, reconstituted into a new symbolic system. The semiotic, like the return of the repressed, challenges the borders of the symbolic through the work of the avant-garde, which poses a new transgression and a new recodification of the symbolic.[19]

By transgressing the boundaries of the symbolic order, the avant-garde creates upheavals and ruptures which may enable what is usually unspoken to be articulated. Of course, the avant-garde text risks co-option or recuperation in functioning as a 'safety valve' or outlet for what may otherwise have become a more disruptive political practice. In reconverting the semiotic back into a new symbolic, its energy is dissipated in the conservation and stabilization of the symbolic. It also risks the opposite extreme, fascism, in which the disruptive semiotic processes are rechannelled into both a (narcissistic) love relation with the charismatic leader, and a rigidified organization hierarchized in even tighter form through this identification.

Further reading

R. Braidotti, *Patterns of Dissonance: A Study of Women and Contemporary Philosophy*, Cambridge: Polity Press, 1990.

T. Brennan (ed.), *Between Feminism and Psychoanalysis*, London: Routledge, 1989.
The main debates covered in this important book are: essentialism, the kind of symbolic law culture requires, sexual difference, how far knowledge is inherently patriarchal and the practical and political use of Lacanian psychoanalysis. There are fourteen papers including the following: Morag Shiach on Cixous, Margaret Whitford on Irigaray, Elizabeth Wright on Kristeva. For advanced work.

E. Grosz, *Sexual Subversions: Three French Feminists*, London: Allen & Unwin, 1989.

E. Marks and Isabelle de Courtivron (eds), *New French Feminisms*, Brighton: Harvester Press, 1980.

T. Moi, *Sexual/Textual Politics: Feminist Literary Theory*, London: Methuen, 1985.
One of the best introductions to Anglo-American and French feminist literary theory. The second part is a most useful discussion of three representative French figures: Cixous, Irigaray and Kristeva.

J. Rose, *Sexuality in the Field of Vision*, London: Verso, 1986.
A brilliant collection of ten essays that explore the encounter between feminism, psychoanalysis, semiotics and film theory. There are scholarly discussions about femininity, feminine sexuality, the imaginary, Dora, Kristeva and many helpful sections on Lacan.

M. Shiach, *Hélène Cixous: A Politics of Writing*, London: Routledge, 1991.
An accessible book which deals with all aspects of Cixous's work and puts them in their historical and philosophical contexts. The author looks at her theoretical writings, her work as a critic, the fictional writings and, finally, her work for the theatre. A very useful book.

M. Whitford, *Luce Irigaray: Philosophy in the Feminine*, London: Routledge, 1991.
This book is a thoughtful and scholarly discussion of Irigaray's work and

argues that she is a philosopher who is redefining the terrain of philosophy. The author usefully outlines Irigaray's method of 'psycho-analysing the philosophers' and her use of psychoanalysis as a dynamic model. The second part discusses the marginalization of women in the social order. For advanced work.

Chapter 6

□

Lyotard and
postmodernism

Introduction: meanings and characteristics

In this chapter I want to explore the many meanings and characteristics of the term postmodernism. After giving an outline of Lyotard's main theses about the postmodern condition, focusing especially on his views about scientific knowledge and aesthetics, I make some criticisms of his work. I conclude with a discussion on some aspects of the relationship between feminism and postmodernism.

Postmodernism is being talked and written about everywhere in contemporary Western societies. The term postmodernism is being used in many artistic, intellectual and academic fields. The figures usually associated with postmodernism include: Rauschenberg, Baselitz, Schnabel, Kiefer, Warhol and, perhaps, Bacon, in art; Jencks and Venturi in architecture; Artaud in drama; Barth, Barthelme and Pynchon in fiction; Lynch in film (*Blue Velvet*); Sherman in photography; Derrida, Lyotard, Baudrillard in philosophy. There are, of course, other subjects that should be mentioned: anthropology, geography, sociology . . . the list is endless, and the names of those included and excluded lead to vigorous debates and bitter controversies. But one thing is clear: postmodernism is of great interest to a wide range of people because it directs our attention to the changes, the major transformations, taking place in contemporary society and culture. The term is at once fashionable and elusive.

Let us begin by looking briefly at the following 'family' of terms: modernity and postmodernity, modernization, modernism and postmodernism, words which are often used in confusing and interchangeable ways. We should be aware that many writers in this field change register from one term to the next and often switch usages.

Modernity

Modernity is generally held to have come into being with the Renaissance and was defined in relation to Antiquity. From the point of view of German sociological theory, which is very influential, modernity implies the progressive economic and administrative rationalization and differentiation of the social world. (By differentiation is meant, for example, the separation of fact from value, of the ethical from the theoretical spheres.) For Weber, Tönnies and Simmel these were the processes which brought into being the modern capitalist industrial state. In short, modernity can be taken as a summary term, referring to that cluster of social, economic and political systems brought into being in the West from somewhere around the eighteenth century onwards.

Postmodernity

Postmodernity suggests what came after modernity; it refers to the incipient or actual dissolution of those social forms associated with modernity. Some thinkers assume that it is a movement towards a post-industrial age, but there are many ambiguities: should the postmodern be regarded a part of the modern? Is it a continuity or a radical break? Is it a material change or does it indicate a mood, a state of mind?

I know there are dangers in thinking in terms of binary oppositions but for teaching purposes I often polarize modernism and postmodernism, modernity and postmodernity. I think that postmodernity emphasizes diverse forms of individual and social identity. It is now widely held that the autonomous subject has been dispersed into a range of plural, polymorphous subject-positions inscribed within language. Instead of a coercive totality and a totalizing politics, postmodernity stresses a pluralistic and open democracy. Instead of the certainty of progress, associated with 'the Enlightenment project' (of which Marxism is a part), there is now an awareness of contingency and ambivalence. The productiveness of industrial technology which Marx so much admired, and which he hoped to tame by means of communism, has ceded place to universal consumerism. Puritan asceticism has given way to the pleasure principle.

Modernization

This term is often used to refer to the stages of social development which are based upon industrialization. Modernization is a diverse unity of socio-economic changes generated by scientific and technological discoveries and innovations, industrial upheavals, population movements, urbanization, the formation of national states and mass political movements, all driven by the expanding capitalist world market.

Modernism

Modernism concerns a particular set of cultural or aesthetic styles associated with the artistic movement which originated around the turn of the century and have dominated the various arts until recently. Modernism developed in conscious opposition to classicism; it emphasized experimentation and the aim of finding an inner truth behind surface appearance. The figures usually categorized as modernists include: Joyce, Yeats, Proust, Kafka in literature; Eliot and Pound in poetry; Strindberg and Pirandello in drama; Cézanne, Picasso, Matisse, the Expressionist, Futurist, Dadaist and Surrealist movements in painting; Schoenberg and Berg in music.

The basic features of modernism can be summarized as: an aesthetic self-consciousness and reflexiveness; a rejection of narrative structure in favour of simultaneity and montage; an exploration of the paradoxical, ambiguous and uncertain, open-ended nature of reality; and the rejection of the notion of an integrated personality in favour of an emphasis upon the Freudian 'split' subject. One of the problems with trying to understand modernism is that many of these features appear in definitions of postmodernism as well. Another problem with defining modernism is the question of how far back into the nineteenth century should one go?

Postmodernism

Postmodernism is the name for a movement in advanced capitalist culture, particularly in the arts. There is a sense in which if one sees modernism as the culture of modernity, postmodernism is the culture of postmodernity. The term postmodernism originated among artists and critics in New York in the 1960s and was taken up by European theorists in the 1970s. One of them, Jean-François Lyotard, in a famous book entitled *The Postmodern Condition*, attacked the legitimating myths of the modern age ('the grand narratives'), the progressive liberation of humanity through science, and the idea that philosophy can restore unity to learning and develop universally valid knowledge for humanity. Postmodern theory became identified with the critique of universal knowledge and foundationalism. Lyotard believes that we can no longer talk about a totalizing idea of reason for there is no reason, only reasons.

Among the central features associated with postmodernism in the arts are: the deletion of the boundary between art and everyday life; the collapse of the hierarchical distinction between élite and popular culture; a stylistic eclecticism and the mixing of codes. There is parody, pastiche, irony and playfulness. Many commentators stress that postmodernists espouse a model which emphasizes not depth but surface. They are highly critical of structuralism and Marxism and are antagonistic to any theory that 'goes beyond' the manifest to the latent. The decline of the originality and genius view of the artistic producer has been replaced by the assumption that art can only be repetitious. It is also said that in postmodernism there is: a shift of emphasis from content to form or style; a transformation of reality into images; the fragmentation of time into a series of perpetual presents. There are continual references to eclecticism, reflexivity, self-referentiality, quotation, artifice, randomness, anarchy, fragmentation, pastiche and allegory. Moreover, with the development of postmodernism in recent years, there has been a move to 'textualize' everything: history, philosophy, jurisprudence, sociology and other disciplines are treated as so many optional 'kinds of writing' or discourses.

The postmodern condition

I now want to discuss the question of social change in contemporary societies by drawing on the recent work of the French thinker Jean-François Lyotard whom I briefly introduced in Chapter 4. I think that an examination of his thesis can help us to understand some of the main concerns of postmodernism.

I will focus on Lyotard's reflections on science, the changing nature of knowledge in computerized societies, the differences between narrative knowledge and scientific knowledge, the ways in which knowledge is legitimated and sold, and the social changes that may take place in the future.

Many people are aware that Western societies since the Second World War have radically changed their nature in some way. To describe these changes social theorists have used various terms: media society, the society of the spectacle, consumer society, the bureaucratic society of controlled consumption, post-industrial society. A fashionable description of such societies is that they are postmodern. Lyotard is a post-structuralist who adopts a postmodernist stance. Postmodernism is in part a description of a new type of society but also, in part, a new term for post-structuralism in the arts. (In this chapter I will use postmodernism and post-structuralism synonymously.)

In *The Postmodern Condition* Lyotard argues that during the last forty years the leading sciences and technologies have become increasingly concerned with language: theories of linguistics, problems of communication and cybernetics, computers and their languages, problems of translation, information storage and data banks.[1]

The technological transformations are having a considerable impact on knowledge. The miniaturization and commercialization of machines are already changing the way in which learning is acquired, classified, made available and exploited.

Lyotard believes that the nature of knowledge cannot survive unchanged within this context of general transformation. The status of knowledge is altered as societies enter what is known as the postmodern age. He predicts that anything in the constituted body of knowledge that is not translatable into quantities of information will be abandoned and the direction of new research will be dictated by the possibility of its eventual results being translatable into computer language. The old principle that the acquisition of knowledge is indissociable from the training of minds, or even of individuals, is becoming obsolete. Knowledge is already ceasing to be an end in itself. It is and will be produced in order to be sold.

It is widely accepted that computerized knowledge has become the principal *force of production* over the last few decades. This has already had a noticeable effect on the composition of the work-force of the most highly developed countries. (There is a decrease in the number of factory and agricultural workers and an increase in professional, technical and white-collar workers.)[2] Knowledge will be the major component in the world-wide competition for power and it is conceivable that nation-states will one day fight for control of information, just as they battled for control over territories in the past. In the postmodern age science will probably strengthen its pre-eminence in the arsenal of productive capacities of the nation-states and the gap between developed and developing countries will grow even wider.

But already in multinational corporations, which are really new forms of the circulation of capital, investment decisions have passed beyond the control of nation-states. Lyotard suggests that power and knowledge are simply two aspects of the same question: who decides what knowledge is? Who knows what needs to be decided?[3]

In the computer age the question of knowledge is now more than ever a question of government. It is suggested that the functions of regulation, and therefore of reproduction, are being and will be further withdrawn from administrators and entrusted to machines. Increasingly the central question is: who will have access to the information these machines must have in storage to guarantee that the right decisions are made?

For Lyotard knowledge is a question of competence that goes beyond the simple determination and application of the criterion of truth, extending to the determination of criteria of efficiency (technical qualification), of justice and/or happiness (ethical wisdom), of beauty (auditory or visual sensibility), etc. Knowledge is what makes someone capable of forming not only 'good' denotative utterances but also 'good' prescriptive and 'good' evaluative utterances. But how are they to be assessed? They are judged to be good if they conform to the relevant criteria (of justice, beauty, truth and efficiency) accepted in the social circle of the 'knower's' interlocutors.

It is important to mention here that Lyotard, who has been greatly influenced by Wittgenstein's notion of language games, makes the following observations.[4] Each of the various categories of utterance can be defined in terms of rules specifying their properties and the uses to which they can be put. The rules of language games do not carry within themselves their own legitimation, but are objects of a contract, explicit or not, between players; if there are no rules, there is no game. Every utterance is thought of as a 'move' in a game. Messages have quite different forms and effects depending on whether they are, for example, denotatives, prescriptions, evaluatives, performatives, etc.[5]

Lyotard believes that language games are incommensurable. He distinguishes the denotative game (in which what is relevant is the true/false distinction) from the prescriptive game (in which the just/unjust distinction pertains) and from the technical game (in which the criterion is the efficient/inefficient distinction). It seems to me that Lyotard sees language games as essentially embodying a conflictual relationship between tricksters. I said earlier that we always tend to act according to the way in which we conceive of things. One pervasive metaphor in our arguments in war. We say some positions are indefensible, we talk of attacking, demolishing, shooting down other people's arguments. We can win or lose arguments. I maintained in Chapter 4 that we could always use other metaphorical concepts than that of war. For Lyotard, however, to speak is to fight:

> In a discussion between two friends the interlocutors use any available ammunition . . . questions, requests, assertions, and narratives are launched pell-mell into battle. The war is not without rules, but the rules allow and encourage the greatest possible flexibility of utterance.[6]

Narrative knowledge and scientific knowledge

Scientific knowledge does not represent the totality of knowledge; it has always existed in competition and conflict with another kind of knowledge which Lyotard calls narrative. In traditional societies there is a pre-eminence of the narrative form. Narratives (popular stories, myths, legends and tales) bestow legitimacy upon social institutions, or represent positive or negative models of integration into established institutions. Narratives determine criteria of competence and/or illustrate how they are to be applied. They thus define what has the right to be said and done in the culture in question.

In traditional societies a narrative tradition is also the tradition of the criterion defining a threefold competence – 'know-how', 'knowing how to speak' and 'knowing how to hear' – through which the community's relationship to itself and its environment is played out. In the narrative form statements about truth, justice and beauty are often woven together. What is transmitted through these narratives is the set of rules that constitute the social bond.

Lyotard discusses the retreat of the claims of narrative or story-telling knowledge in the face of those of the abstract, denotative or logical and cognitive procedures generally associated with science. In the science language game the sender is supposed to be able to provide proof of what s/he says, and on the other hand s/he is supposed to be able to refute any opposing or contradictory statements concerning the same referent. Scientific rules underlie what nineteenth-century science calls verification, and twentieth-century science falsification.[7] They allow a horizon of consensus to be brought to the debate between partners (the sender and the addressee). Not every consensus is a sign of truth, but it is presumed that the truth of a statement necessarily draws a consensus. Now, scientists need an addressee, a partner who can verify their statements and in turn become the sender. Equals are needed and must be created.

Didactics is what ensures that this reproduction takes place. Its first presupposition is that the student does not know what the sender knows; obviously this is why s/he has something to learn. Its second presupposition is that the student can learn what the sender knows and become an expert whose competence is equal to that of the teacher. As the students improve their skills, experts can confide in them what they do not know but are trying to learn. In this way students are introduced to the game of producing scientific knowledge. In scientific knowledge any already accepted statement can always be challenged. Any new statement that contradicts a previously approved statement regarding the same referent can be accepted as valid only if it refutes the previous statement.

The main difference between scientific knowledge and narrative knowledge is that scientific knowledge requires that one language game, denotation, be retained and all others be excluded. Both science and non-scientific (narrative) knowledge are equally necessary. Both are composed of sets of statements; the statements are 'moves' made by the players within the framework of generally applicable rules. These rules are specific to each particular kind of knowledge, and the 'moves' judged to be 'good' in one cannot be the same as those judged 'good' in another (unless it happens that way by chance). It is therefore impossible to judge the existence or validity of narrative knowledge on the basis of scientific knowledge or vice versa: the relevant criteria are different.

Lyotard argues that narrative knowledge certifies itself without having recourse to argumentation and proof. Scientists, however, question the validity of narrative statements and conclude that they are never subject to argumentation or proof. Narratives are classified by the scientist as belonging to a different mentality: savage, primitive, underdeveloped, backward, alienated, composed of opinions, customs, authority, prejudice, ignorance, ideology. Narratives are fables, myths, legends fit only for women and children.

Here there is an interesting twist in Lyotard's argument. He says that scientific knowledge cannot know and make known that it is the true knowledge without resorting to the other, narrative kind of knowledge, which from its point of view is no knowledge at all. In short, there is a recurrence of the narrative in the scientific.[8]

The state spends large amounts of money to enable science to pass itself off as an epic. The state's own credibility is based on that epic, which it uses to obtain the public consent its decision-makers need. Science, in other words, is governed by the demand of legitimation. The two myths which have acted as justifications for institutional scientific research – that of the liberation of humanity and that of the speculative unity of all knowledge – are also national myths. The first, political, militant, activist, is the tradition of the French eighteenth century and the French Revolution. The second is the German Hegelian tradition organized around the concept of totality. Lyotard examines these two myths as versions of the narrative of legitimation of knowledge. The subject of the first of these versions is humanity as the 'hero' of liberty. Lyotard writes: 'All peoples have a right to science. If the social subject is not already the subject of scientific knowledge, it is because that has been forbidden by priests and tyrants. The right to science must be reconquered.' The state resorts to the narrative of freedom every time it assumes direct control over the training of 'the people' under the name of the 'nation', in order to point the people down the path of progress.

Lyotard remarks:

> In Stalinism, the sciences only figure as citations from the metanarrative of the march towards socialism, which is the equivalent of the life of the spirit. But on the other hand Marxism can . . . develop into a form of critical knowledge by declaring that socialism is nothing other than the constitution of the autonomous subject and that the only justification for the sciences is if they give the empirical subject (the proletariat) the means to emancipate itself from alienation and repression.[9]

According to Lyotard these (older) master narratives no longer function in contemporary society. He argues that the grand narrative has lost its credibility, regardless of whether it is a speculative narrative or a narrative of emancipation. The decline of the unifying and legitimating power of the grand narratives of speculation and emancipation can be seen as an effect of the blossoming of techniques and technologies since the Second World War, which has shifted emphasis from the *ends* of action to its *means*.

The mercantilization of knowledge

With the Industrial Revolution it was found that a technical apparatus requires an investment; but since it optimizes the efficiency with which the task to which it is applied is carried out, it also optimizes the surplus-value from this improved performance. It is at this moment that science becomes a force of production, a moment in the circulation of capital.

An important aspect of research is the production of proof. Proof needs to be proven. A scientific observation depends on facts being registered by sense organs. But the range and powers of discrimination are limited. This is where technology comes in. Technical devices follow the principle of optimal performance, maximizing output and minimizing input. Technology is, therefore, a game pertaining not to the true, the just or the beautiful, but to efficiency. A technical 'move' is 'good' when it does better and/or expends less energy than another. Devices that optimize the performance of the human body for the purpose of producing proof require additional money. The game of science becomes the game of the rich, in which whoever is wealthiest has the best chance of being right.[10] It is thus that an equation between wealth, efficiency and truth is established.

To put it in another way, the goal in science is no longer truth, but performativity – that is, the best possible input/output equation. Scientists, technicians and instruments are bought not to find truth, but to augment power. Since performativity increases the ability to produce proof, it also increases the ability to be right; the technical criterion cannot fail to influence the truth criterion.

The shift of attention from ends of action to its means, from truth to performativity, is reflected in present-day educational policy. It has been clear for some time that educational institutions are becoming more functional; the emphasis is on skills rather than ideals. It is probable that in the near future knowledge will no longer be transmitted *en bloc* to young people, once and for all; rather it will be served 'à la carte' to adults as a part of their job retraining and continuing education.

To the extent that learning is translatable into computer language and the traditional teacher is replaceable by memory banks, didactics (teaching) will be entrusted to machines linking traditional memory banks (libraries, etc.) and computer data banks to terminals placed at the students' disposal. Lyotard argues that pedagogy would not necessarily suffer. The students would have to learn to use the terminals and the new languages; they would have to be taught what is the relevant memory bank for what needs to be known.

It is only in the context of the grand narratives of legitimation – the life of the spirit and/or the emancipation of humanity – that the partial replacement of teachers by machines may seem inadequate or even intolerable. Lyotard remarks that it is probable that these narratives are already no longer the principal driving force behind interest in acquiring knowledge. The question now being asked by the student, the state or the university is no longer 'Is it true?' but 'What use is it?' In the context of the mercantilization of knowledge, more often than not this question is equivalent to: 'Is it saleable?' And in the context of power-growth: 'Is it efficient?'

It is clear that education must provide not only for the reproduction of skills but also for their progress. Therefore training must be given in all the procedures that can increase one's ability to connect the fields jealously guarded from one another by the traditional organization of knowledge. What is vitally important for students to have is the capacity to actualize the relevant data for solving a problem here and now, and to organize that data into an efficient strategy. Data banks are the encyclopaedia of tomorrow; they are 'nature' for postmodern men and women. What is important is arranging the data in a new way. This capacity to articulate what used to be separate can be called imagination. It is imagination which allows one either to make a new move (a new argument) within the established rules or to invent new rules, that is to say, a new game.

Lyotard writes that countless scientists have seen their invention of new rules ignored or repressed, sometimes for decades, because that invention too abruptly destabilized the accepted positions, not only in the university and scientific hierarchy but also in the discipline. The more striking the invention, the more likely it is to be denied the minimum consensus, precisely because it changes the rules of the game upon which consensus had been based.[11] Lyotard argues that such behaviour is terrorist. By terror he means the efficiency gained by eliminating, or threatening to eliminate, a player from one's language game. He is silenced or consents, not because he has been refuted but because the other players' ability to participate has been threatened: 'Adapt your aspirations to our ends – or else. . . .'

Bourgeois art and its function in society

Having given an exposition of Lyotard's book, I want to place his thesis in the context of the controversy about modernism and postmodernism. But before I do that I want to contextualize the controversy. The debate about postmodernism is partly about the arts and so in this section I will say something about the institution of art in bourgeois society and the bitter struggle waged against it in the 1920s by the avant-garde.

The best way I can think of understanding the recent development of art is by a glance at Peter Bürger's *Theory of the Avant-Garde*.[12] Distinguishing between sacral, courtly and bourgeois art, Bürger suggests the following historical typology:

Sacral Art (for example, the art of the High Middle Ages) served as a cult object. It was wholly integrated into the social institution 'religion', and was produced collectively as a craft.

Courtly Art (for example, the art of the court of Louis XIV) served the glory of the prince. It was part of the life-praxis of courtly society, just as sacral art was part of the life-praxis of the faithful. Courtly art is different from sacral art in that the artist produced as an individual and developed a consciousness of the uniqueness of his individuality.

Bourgeois Art. Whereas in different ways both sacral and courtly art are integral to the life-praxis of the recipient, bourgeois art forms a sphere which lies outside the praxis of life.

The tension between art as an institution and the content of individual works tends to disappear in the second half of the nineteenth century. All that which is dissociated from the praxis of life now becomes the content of works of art. The terminal point is reached in aestheticism, a movement in which art becomes the content of art.

Aestheticism, Bürger writes, must be seen in connection with the tendency towards the division of labour in bourgeois society. Gradually the artist also turns into a specialist. As the social subsystem 'art' defines itself as a distinct sphere, the positive aspect is aesthetic experience. Its negative side is the artist's loss of any social function.

What, then, is the function of art in bourgeois society? Herbert Marcuse has argued that works of art are not received as single entities, but within institutional frameworks and conditions that largely determine the function of the works.[13] In his seminal essay 'The Affirmative Character of Culture' Marcuse has described art's function in bourgeois society as a contradictory one: on the one hand it shows 'forgotten truths' (thus it protests against a reality in which these truths have no validity), on the other, such truths are detached from reality.

The term 'affirmative' therefore characterizes the contradictory function of a culture that retains 'remembrance of what could be', but is simultaneously a justification of the established form of existence. Through the enjoyment of art the atrophied bourgeois individual can experience the self as personality. But because art is detached from daily life, this experience remains without tangible effect – it cannot be integrated into that life.

Let me recapitulate Marcuse's argument. All those needs that cannot be satisfied in everyday life, because the principle of competition pervades all spheres, can find a home in art, because art is removed from the praxis of life. Values such as humanity, joy, truth, solidarity are excluded from life and preserved in art. In bourgeois society art has a contradictory role, it projects the image of a better life and to that extent protests against the bad order that prevails. But by realizing the image of a better order in *fiction*, which is semblance only, it neutralizes those forces that make for change. Marcuse demonstrates that bourgeois culture exiles humane values to the realm of the imagination and thus precludes their potential realization. Art thus stabilizes the very social conditions against which it protests.

As long as art interprets reality or provides satisfaction of residual needs only in the imagination it is, though detached from the praxis of life, still related to it. It is only in aestheticism that the tie to society, still existent up to this moment, is severed. The term 'the autonomy of art' is used to describe *the detachment of art* as a special sphere of human activity from the praxis of life. But somehow this concept blocks recognition of the social determinacy of the process. The idea of the relative dissociation of the work of art from the praxis of life in bourgeois society has become transformed into the erroneous idea that the work of art is totally independent of society. We should remember that this detachment of art from practical contexts is a historical process; it is socially conditioned. Perhaps the reason that the artist's product could acquire importance as something special, 'autonomous', lies in the continuation of the handicraft mode of production after the division of labour – and the separation of workers from their means of production – had become the norm.

The main features of the avant-garde

Only after art has detached itself completely from the praxis of life can two things be seen: the progressive separation of art from real life contexts and the crystallization of a distinctive sphere of experience – the aesthetic.

Let us now turn to the historic avant-garde and its attempt to negate the autonomy of art.[14] The production of the autonomous work of art is generally seen as the act of an individual – who is often a genius. The avant-garde's response to this is *the negation of the category of individual creation*. For example, Marcel Duchamp, by signing mass-produced objects, mocked a society in which the signature meant more than the quality of the work.

The avant-garde did not develop a style; there is no such thing as a Dadaist or Surrealist style. One of the characteristics of the avant-garde is the availability to it of and its mastery over artistic techniques of past epochs. It is through the efforts of the avant-garde that the historical *succession* of techniques and styles has been replaced by a *simultaneity* of the radically disparate. For the Surrealists a general openness to impressions is not enough. They attempt to bring the extraordinary about. In the avant-garde movements *shocking the recipient* becomes the dominant principle of artistic intent. Moreover, the Surrealists emphasize the role of *chance*. Starting from the experience that a society organized on the basis of a means–ends rationality increasingly restricts the individual's scope, the Surrealists attempted to discover elements of the unpredictable in daily life.

The avant-garde is totally opposed to society as it is. Bürger writes:

> Since the Surrealists do not see that a given degree of control over nature requires social organization, they run the risk of expressing their protest against bourgeois society at a level where it becomes protest against sociality as such. It is not the specific object, profit as the governing principle of bourgeois-capitalist society, that is being criticized but means–ends rationality as such. Paradoxically, chance, which subjects man to the totally heteronomous, can thus seem a symbol of freedom.[15]

It is with the avant-garde movements that self-criticism begins. The main point is that they no longer criticized schools that preceded them, but criticized *art as an institution*. The avant-garde turns against both the distribution apparatus on which the work of art depends and the status of art in bourgeois society as defined by the concept of autonomy. This protest, whose aim it is to reintegrate art into the praxis of life, reveals the nexus between autonomy and the absence of any consequences – art's lack of social impact.

Of course, we now know that the attack of the historic avant-garde on art as an institution failed.[16] Art as an institution continues to survive. Ironically, the procedures invented by the avant-garde with anti-artistic intent are now being used for artistic ends by the postmodernists.

Modernism and postmodernism

As I said at the beginning of the chapter, there is a general feeling among many thinkers that at some point after the Second World War a new kind of society began to emerge. The society is labelled in various ways depending on the way it is analysed: consumer society, post-industrial society, society of the spectacle, postmodernist society, etc. Post-structuralists, on the whole, argue that this new society is post-Marxist. They assert that Marxist theory is now outmoded; it does not and cannot apply to the new social developments. This argument often overlaps with another one concerning modernism and postmodernism. The crucial question in these debates is: has the Enlightenment project failed? Should we, like the post-structuralists and postmodernists, declare the entire project of modernity a lost cause? Or should we try to hold on to the intentions and aims of the Enlightenment and of cultural modernism?

The project of modernity formulated in the eighteenth century by the philosophers of the Enlightenment consisted in their efforts to develop objective science, universal morality and law and autonomous art. Philosophers like Condorcet wanted to use this accumulation of specialized culture for the enrichment of everyday life. They hoped that the arts and sciences would promote not only the control of natural forces but also understanding of the world and of the self, moral progress, the justice of institutions and even the happiness of human beings.

But what has happened is in marked contrast to the hopes and ideals of the Enlightenment. Gradually each domain has been institutional-ized; science, morality and art have become autonomous domains separated from the life-world. The structures of cognitive–instrumental, of moral–practical and of aesthetic–expressive rationality have come under the control of special experts.[17]

In America, France and elsewhere, cultural modernism is now under attack from many different quarters. An American neo-conservative, Daniel Bell, made a powerful critique some years ago of modernity.[18]

According to Bell modernist culture had infected the values of everyday life. Because of the forces of modernism the principle of unlimited self-realization, the demand for authentic self-experience and the subjectivism of a hyperstimulated sensitivity have come to be dominant. This unleashes hedonistic motives irreconcilable with the discipline of professional life in society. Neo-conservatives like Bell see hedonism, the lack of social identification, the lack of obedience, narcissism, the withdrawal from status and achievement competition as the result not of successful capitalist modernization of the economy but of cultural modernism.

More recently, the Enlightenment project has been denounced by the French 'new philosophers' and their contemporary English and American counterparts. It has also been attacked, less stridently but with more intellectual sharpness, by the post-structuralists. I believe that their work should be included among the manifestations of postmodernism.

The concept of postmodernism is ambiguous and is not yet widely understood. It has probably emerged as a specific reaction against the established forms of high modernism. For some thinkers postmodernism is a periodizing concept whose function is to correlate the emergence of new features in culture. The concept seems to be connected with the appearance, between the 1950s and the 1960s, of a new social and economic order. Sometimes a useful distinction is made between premodernists, those who want to withdraw to a position anterior to modernity, antimodernists and postmodernists. In my opinion post-structuralists like Foucault, Derrida and Lyotard are postmodernists. There are so many similarities between post-structuralist theories and postmodernist practices that it is difficult to make a clear distinction between them.

The main features of postmodernism

We may be able to understand postmodernism better by returning to Lyotard and seeing what he means by 'modern'. Lyotard uses the term 'modern'

> to designate any science that legitimates itself with reference to a metadiscourse ... making an explicit appeal to some grand narrative, such as the dialectics of the Spirit, the hermeneutics of meaning, the emancipation of the rational or working subject or the creation of wealth.[19]

To put it another way:

> Societies which anchor the discourses of truth and justice in the great
> historical and scientific narratives (récits) can be called modern. The French
> Jacobins don't speak like Hegel but the just and the good are always found
> caught up in a great progressive odyssey.[20]

Postmodernists distrust metanarratives; there is a deep suspicion of
Hegel, Marx and any form of universal philosophy.

For Lyotard, then, the postmodern condition is one in which the
grands récits of modernity – the dialectic of Spirit, the emancipation of
the worker, the accumulation of wealth, the classless society – have all
lost credibility.[21] He goes on to define a discourse as modern when it
appeals to one or another of these *grands récits* for its legitimacy. The
grands récits are master narratives – narratives of mastery, of man seeking
his *telos* in the conquest of nature. The Marxist master narrative ('the
collective struggle to wrest a realm of Freedom from a realm of
Necessity') is only one version among many of a modern narrative of
mastery. The advent of postmodernity signals a crisis in a narrative's
legitimizing function, its ability to compel consensus.

Lyotard is critical of Marxism because he holds that it wishes to create
a homogeneous society which can only be brought about through the
use of coercion. He believes that the individualistic, fragmented society
that we have today is here to stay. Yet, oddly enough, he seems to be
nostalgic for a premodern (traditional) society. As I said earlier,
traditional societies stress narrative, that is to say, myth, magic, folk
wisdom and other attempts at explanation.[22] Lyotard believes that there
is a conflict between narrative and science (theoretical knowledge).
Narrative is disappearing and there is nothing to replace it. He seems to
want the flexibility of narrative knowledge – in which the aesthetic,
cognitive and moral are interwoven – and yet want also to retain the
individualism which developed with capitalism.

Lyotard argues that art, morality and science (the beautiful, the good
and the true) have become separated and autonomous. A characteristic
of our times is the fragmentation of language games. There is no
metalanguage. No one can grasp what is going on in society as a whole.
He seems to be saying that there is no one system of domination. There
are parallels between these ideas and some right-wing theorists (like
Hayek) who argue that society works much better in terms of micro-
events; a society that is left to market forces is better than a consciously
planned society.

In short, the argument of Lyotard (and some other post-structuralists) is this: big stories are bad, little stories are good. Instead of a truth/falsity distinction Lyotard adopts a small/grand narrative criterion. Narratives are bad when they become philosophies of history. Grand narratives have become associated with a political programme or party, while little narratives are associated with localized creativity. (The stress on the local has often been associated with the conservative tradition, with the thinking of Edmund Burke and others.) These ideas are similar to those held by Foucault, who is also against grand narratives and supports the idea of local struggles. But what puzzles me is this: why are the post-structuralists so frightened of the universal? And why is Lyotard telling us yet another grand narrative at the end of grand narrative?

Two significant features of postmodernism, as described by the American critic Fredric Jameson, are 'pastiche' and 'schizophrenia'.[23] Jameson begins by explaining that the great modernisms were predicated on the invention of a personal, private style. The modernist aesthetic was organically linked to the conception of an authentic self and a private identity which can be expected to generate its own unique vision of the world and to forge its own unmistakable style. The post-structuralists argue against this; in their view the concept of the unique individual and the theoretical basis of individualism are ideological. Not only is the bourgeois individual subject a thing of the past, it is also a myth, it never really existed in the first place; it was just a mystification. And so, in a world in which stylistic innovation is no longer possible all that is left, Jameson suggests, is pastiche. The practice of pastiche, the imitation of dead styles, can be seen in the 'nostalgia film'. It seems that we are unable to focus on our present. We have lost our ability to locate ourselves historically. As a society we have become incapable of dealing with time.

Postmodernism has a peculiar notion of time. Jameson explains what he means in terms of Lacan's theory of schizophrenia. The originality of Lacan's thought in this area is to have considered schizophrenia as a language disorder. Schizophrenia emerges from the failure of the infant to enter fully into the realm of speech and language. For Lacan the experience of temporality, human time, past, present, memory, the persistence of personal identity is an effect of language. It is because language has a past and a future, because the sentence moves in time, that we can have what seems to us a concrete or lived experience of time. But since the schizophrenic does not know language articulation in that way, he or she does not have our experience of temporal continuity either, but is condemned to live in a perpetual present with which the various moments of his or her past have little connection and for which there is no future on the horizon. In other words, schizophrenic experience is an experience of isolated, disconnected material signifiers which fail to link up into a coherent sequence.

On the one hand, then, the schizophrenic does have a more intense experience of any given present of the world than we do, since our own present is always part of some larger set of projects which includes the past and the future. On the other hand, the schizophrenic is 'no one', has no personal identity. Moreover, he or she does nothing since to have a project means to be able to commit oneself to a certain continuity over time. The schizophrenic, in short, experiences a fragmentation of time, a series of perpetual presents. Jameson contends that experiences of temporal discontinuity, similar to those described above, are evoked in postmodernist works such as the compositions of John Cage and the texts of Samuel Beckett.

Totality or fragmentation

You may have noticed that I have made several references to totality and fragmentation. I have said that Lyotard repudiates the big stories, the metanarratives of Hegel and Marx; he believes that no one can grasp what is going on in a society as a *whole*. It seems fashionable nowadays to say that there is no single theoretical discourse which is going to offer an explanation for all forms of social relations or for every mode of political practice. Postmodernists and others are always making this point against Marxism: they insist that it has totalizing ambitions and resent its claim to provide explanations for all aspects of social experience.

Rejecting totality, Lyotard and other postmodernists stress fragmentation – of language games, of time, of the human subject, of society itself. One of the fascinating things about the rejection of organic unity and the espousal of the fragmentary is that this belief was also held by the historic avant-garde movements. They too wanted the dissolution of unity. In their activities the coherence and autonomy of the work was deliberately called into question or even methodically destroyed.

Walter Benjamin's concept of allegory has been used as an aid to understanding avant-gardiste (non-organic) works of art.[24] Benjamin described how the allegorist pulls an element out of the totality of the life context, isolating it, depriving it of its function. (Allegory is thus essentially a fragment, the opposite of the organic symbol.) Then the allegorist joins several isolated fragments and thereby creates meaning. This is posited meaning and does not derive from the original context of the fragments.

These elements of Benjamin's concept of allegory accord with what is called montage, the fundamental principle of avant-garde art. Montage presupposes fragmentation of reality; it breaks through the appearance of totality and calls attention to the fact that it is made up of reality fragments. The avant-gardiste work proclaims itself an artificial construct, an artefact. The opposite holds true for the organic work: it seeks to make unrecognizable the fact that it has been made. In the organic work of art the material is treated as a whole, while in the avant-gardiste work the material is torn out of the life totality and isolated. The aesthetic avant-gardist fragment *challenges* people to make it an integrated part of their reality and to relate it to their experience. The best example of this principle is probably the Brechtian play. A play by Brecht does not aim at organic unity but consists of interruptions and juxtapositions which disrupt conventional expectations and force the audience into critical speculation.

The question as to whether a work of art should be an organic unity or consist of fragments is perhaps best understood by having a look at the debate between Georg Lukács and Theodor Adorno.[25] The contrast between organic and non-organic work underlies both Lukács's and Adorno's theories of the avant-garde. Whereas Lukács holds on to the organic work of art ('realism') as an aesthetic norm and from that perspective rejects avant-gardiste works as decadent, Adorno elevates avant-gardiste, non-organic work to a historical norm and condemns all efforts to create a realistic art in our time.

While Lukács adopted Hegel's view that the organic work of art (for example, the realistic novels of Goethe, Balzac, Stendhal) constitutes a type of perfection, Adorno believed that the avant-garde work is the only possible authentic expression of the contemporary state of the world, the historically necessary expression of alienation in late capitalist society. Like Adorno, Lukács believed that the work of the avant-garde is the expression of alienation in capitalist society, but he was very scathing about the blindness of bourgeois intellectuals who could not see the real historical counterforces working towards a structural transformation of society.

Adorno, however, did not have this political perspective. He believed that instead of baring the contradictions of society in our time, the organic work promotes, by its very form, the illusion of a world that is whole.[26] For him avant-gardiste art is a radical protest that rejects all false reconciliation with what exists and is therefore the only art form that has historical legitimacy. Lukács, on the other hand, acknowledges its character as protest but condemns avant-gardiste art because that protest remains abstract, without historical perspective and blind to the real counterforces that are striving to overcome capitalism. He rejects the idea that avant-gardiste work allows ruptures and 'gaps' of reality to show through the fragmentary nature of the work itself.

But an important similarity between Lukács and Adorno should be noted: they both argue within the institution of art and are unable to criticize it as an institution for that very reason. I hope that I have said enough to signal that the Lukács–Adorno debate really consists of two antagonistic theories of culture. Adorno not only sees late capitalism as definitely stabilized but also feels that historical experience has shown the hopes placed in socialism to be ill-founded. In this respect he is very much like most of the postmodernists.

It could be said that there are two main traditions or modes of understanding the avant-garde. The first mode of thought is associated with Adorno, Artaud, Barthes, Breton and Derrida. (Many writers have pointed out that the philosophies of Derrida and Adorno display interesting similarities.) The other mode of thought is associated with Benjamin and Brecht.

It is largely from the work of Benjamin that we have learnt that the social effect of a work of art cannot simply be gauged by considering the work itself but that it is decisively determined by the institution within which the work functions. It is art as an institution which determines the measure of political effect avant-garde works can have and which determines that art in bourgeois society continues to be a realm distinct from the praxis of life. Art as an institution neutralizes the political content of the individual work. It prevents the contents of works that press for radical change in a society – the abolition of alienation – from having any practical effect. Received in the context of artefacts whose shared characteristic is their apartness from the praxis of life, 'organic' works of art tend to be perceived as 'mere' art products.

It should be remembered that had there never been any avant-garde movements, Brecht's and Benjamin's reflections regarding a restruc-turing of the production apparatus would not have been possible. Brecht never shared the intention of the historic avant-garde artists to destroy art as an institution. Though he despised the theatre of the educated bourgeoisie, he did not conclude that the theatre should be abolished altogether: instead he proposed radically to change it.[27]

I believe that there are so many difficulties with the positions of Lukács and Adorno that they are both unsatisfactory. I want to suggest that one possible way out of the situation may be through the use of the materialist theories inspired by Benjamin and Brecht.

In the next section I will discuss Lyotard's view of language games and his interpretation of 'the sublime'. After that, there are some criticisms of Lyotard, and the chapter ends with a discussion on the relationship between feminism and postmodernism.

On language games and the sublime

I want to draw attention to three features of postmodernist thought. Firstly, there is a tendency to reduce all truth-claims to the level of rhetorics, narrative strategies or Foucauldian discourses conceived as existing solely by virtue of the differences or rivalries between them, so that no single claimant can assert itself at the expense of any other.

Secondly, a related point, there is often an appeal, especially in Lyotard, to the Wittgensteinian notion of 'language games' (sometimes called 'forms of life'). A belief in heterogeneous language games, each involving a different set of cognitive, historical or ethico-political criteria, implies that it is not possible to decide between rival interpretations.

Thirdly, there is a turn towards the Kantian sublime as a means of devaluing cognitive truth-claims and elevating the notion of the *unrepresentable* (that is to say, intuitions that cannot be 'brought under' adequate concepts) to absolute pride of place in the ethical realm. In other words there has been a move to aestheticize politics by removing ethical and political questions as far as possible from the realm of truth and falsehood.[28] I will discuss some of these points by focusing on Lyotard's views on language games and the sublime.

Precursors of the postmodern critique of philosophy were found in Nietzsche, Heidegger and Wittgenstein (and the more 'deviant' authors like Artaud, Bataille and Sade). As I have just mentioned, Lyotard adopts a Wittgensteinian language games approach to knowledge proposing that we conceive of various discourses as language games with their own rules, structure and moves. Different language games are thus governed by different criteria and rules, and none is privileged.

Language games for Lyotard are indeed the social bond which holds society together, and he characterizes social interaction primarily in terms of making a move in a game, playing a role and taking a part in various discrete language games. In these terms he characterizes the self as the interaction of all the language games in which it participates. Lyotard's model of a postmodern society is thus one in which one struggles within various language games in an agonistic environment characterized by diversity and conflict.

While the post-structuralist historian Foucault drew on Nietzsche, Lyotard, the postmodernist philosopher, draws on Wittgenstein and Kant. Kant wanted to prevent any confusion between the realms of cognitive understanding and practical reason (ethics). He was also careful to distinguish between truth-claims entailing the existence of adequate grounds and those 'ideas of reason' which could never be confirmed or falsified by any such standard. For some recent commentators, Lyotard among them, this has opened the way to a postmodern reading of Kant that stresses the absolute heterogeneity, the lack of any common ground for judgement between the various 'phrase-regimes', 'discourses' or 'language games' involved.

Lyotard adopts a pluralist outlook wherein each litigant respects the other's difference of viewpoint, even to the extent of suspending his or her own truth-claims. In his view we fail to respect the diversity of language games if we take just one (for example, the cognitive) and treat it as enjoying a privileged status vis-à-vis questions of historical truth and ethical accountability. Lyotard believes that if things belong to heterogeneous language games then any attempt to convince the other party would amount to a form of speech-act coercion, an injustice or infraction of the conversational ground-rules. In short, Lyotard argues that issues of fact have absolutely no bearing on issues of ethical judgement.

Let us now consider Lyotard's treatment of the Kantian sublime, a topic whose significance extends far beyond the realm of the aesthetic. For Kant, the sublime is that which exceeds all our powers of representation, an experience for which we can find no adequate sensuous or conceptual mode of apprehension, and which differs from the beautiful in so far as it affords no sense of harmonious balance or agreement between these faculties.[29] The sublime figures for Kant as a means of expressing (by analogy) what would otherwise be strictly inexpressible.

The Kantian sublime serves as a reminder of the gulf that opens up – the 'differend', as Lyotard terms it – between truth-claims lacking any common measure of justice by which to resolve their dispute.[30] Lyotard remarks that applying a single rule of judgement to both in order to settle their differend (an irreducible conflict of interests) would wrong at least one of them, and both of them if neither side admits the rule.

In other words the sublime comes to figure, for Lyotard, as an index of the radical heterogeneity that inhabits our discourses of truth and value, or the kinds of injustice that inevitably result when one such 'phrase-regime' – most often the cognitive – seeks to monopolize the whole conversation. Lyotard argues that we are confronted with issues that cannot be resolved within the 'phrase-regime' of cognitive judgement and whose character is much better grasped by analogy with the Kantian discourse on aesthetics, especially where that discourse invokes the sublime as a figure for modes of experience or feeling that exceed all the powers of sensuous (phenomenal) cognition on the one hand, and conceptual understanding on the other. For Lyotard, the sublime brings us up against that limit point of thought where judgement has to recognize its own lack of resources, or the absence of agreed-upon criteria, for dealing with cases that exceed all the bounds of rule-governed, 'rational' adjudication.

Critics of Lyotard, like Christopher Norris, argue that there is a widespread tendency to exploit Kant's notion of the sublime to a point far beyond anything licensed by Kant. Where Lyotard parts company with Kant is in promoting the aesthetic sublime to a position of transcendent authority.

Lyotard's version of the Kantian sublime mystifies issues of social and ethico-political judgement by treating them, in effect, as modalities of aesthetic understanding, questions that cannot be settled except by suspending all reference to matters of empirical truth and falsehood. This reading of the sublime offers a pretext for aestheticizing politics by imposing the maximum possible distance between issues of actual or historical truth and issues of ethico-political justice. In Norris's view, what results from Lyotard's postmodernist reading of the sublime is an outlook of extreme cognitive scepticism, along with a politics completely cut off from questions of real-world relevance and accountability.[31]

Some criticisms of Lyotard's work

Lyotard's book *The Postmodern Condition* is on one level about the status of science and technology, about technocracy and the control of information. But on another level it is a thinly veiled polemic against Jürgen Habermas, who stands for a 'totalizing' and dialectical tradition. Habermas thinks that the totality of life has become splintered and argues that the cognitive, ethical and political discourses should come closer together. He wants, in short, to defend modernity against the neo-conservative postmodernists.

In contrast, Lyotard's main target is the Hegelian-Marxist concept of totality. He is scornful of Habermas's vision of a transparent, fully communicational society and sees language situations as an unstable exchange between speakers, as the 'taking of tricks', the trumping of an adversary. He repudiates, in short, Habermas's notion of a consensus community. Lyotard's view of science and knowledge is that of a search not for consensus but for 'instabilities'; the point is not to reach agreement but to undermine from within the very framework in which the previous 'normal science' had been conducted.

Lyotard thinks that Habermas makes the assumption that it is possible for all speakers to come to agreement on which rules are universally valid for language games, when it is clear that language games are incommensurable, subject to heterogeneous sets of pragmatic rules. He argues that the principle of consensus as a criterion of validation, as elaborated by Habermas, is inadequate: it is a conception based on the validity of the narrative of emancipation.[32] Lyotard writes, 'We no longer have recourse to the grand narrative – we can resort neither to the dialectic of Spirit nor even to the emancipation of humanity as a validation for postmodern scientific discourse'.[33] In his view the little narrative remains the quintessential form of imaginative invention.

Lyotard assumes the breaking up of the narratives without describing how and why this theoretical collapse has taken place and why he is himself polemicizing against these discourses. There are many sorts of grand narratives, but Lyotard tends to lump all of them together. Even if some of the narratives of legitimation are dubious, why should we reject all grand narratives?

Many postmodernists fail to specify what causes the rupture in society and history that produces the postmodern condition. Theorists who reject master narratives, or historical, periodizing social theory, are naturally going to have difficulty producing such a narrative, and thus find themselves in an aporetic situation.

Lyotard rejects totalizing social theories, the master narratives, because he believes they are reductionist and simplistic. Yet he himself is offering a theory of the postmodern condition which presupposes a dramatic break from modernity. But surely the concept of postmodernism presupposes a master narrative, a totalizing perspective? While Lyotard resists grand narratives, it is impossible to discern how one can have a theory of postmodernism without one.

Some critics of Lyotard believe that he goes too quickly from the premise that philosophy cannot ground social criticism to the conclusion that criticism itself must be local, ad hoc and non-theoretical.

Lyotard insists that the field of the social is heterogeneous and non-totalizable. As a result he rules out the sort of critical social theory which employs general categories like gender, race and class. From his perspective, such categories are too reductive of the complexity of social identities to be useful. In short, there is no place in Lyotard's universe for critiques of relations of dominance and subordination along lines like gender, race and class.

In Lyotard's view there is nothing to be gained in the critical analysis of large-scale institutions and social structures. He contends that sociological synthesis must be abandoned for playful deconstruction and the privileging of the aesthetic mode.

Influenced by Nietzsche, post-structuralists like Lyotard attack philosophy as an imposition of truth. (Nietzsche is famous for his attack on truth; all perspectives, he said, are illusory.) At one time Lyotard supported Marxism but he now sees it as one of the 'grand narratives' he is against. He writes about the force of language beyond truth and wants to develop a theory of philosophical fiction – a discourse that tries to persuade without the traditional notion of 'argument'. In Lyotard's work problems of power are put to one side, and his views have led him to a form of relativism.

There is an ambiguity throughout Lyotard's work and that of other post-structuralists who have been influenced by Nietzsche's critique of systems. Lyotard argues that all theoretical conceptualizations, such as history, are coercive; in his view any interpretation of history is dogmatic. He does not make a distinction between large-scale theories and dogmatism; it is taken for granted that any large-scale theory is dogmatic. Now, it could be argued that some Marxist theories are dogmatic but that, given time and effort, the dogmatism could be dissolved. However, the post-structuralists never consider this possibility.

Why is this? Richard Rorty has suggested an explanation. He has criticized writers like Foucault and Lyotard for their extraordinary *dryness*:

> It is a dryness produced by a lack of identification with any social context, any communication. Foucault once said that he would like to write 'so as to have no face'. He forbids himself the tone of the liberal sort of thinker who says to his fellow citizens: '*We* know that there must be a better way to do things than this; let us look for it together.' There is no 'we' to be found in Foucault's writing, nor in those of many of his French contemporaries . . . It is as if thinkers like Foucault and Lyotard are so afraid of being caught up in one more metanarrative about the fortunes of 'the subject' that they cannot bring themselves to say 'we' long enough to identify with the culture of the generation to which they belong.[34]

Politically, it is clear that thinkers like Lyotard and Foucault are neo-conservatives. They take away the dynamic upon which liberal social thought has traditionally relied. They offer us no theoretical reason to move in one social direction rather than another. On the whole, post-structuralists think of rationality as a limiting framework. They are against what they call the imperialism of reason. Lyotard's intellectual trajectory has brought him to the position where he now wants to abstain from anything that is connected with the 'metanarrative of emancipation'.

Feminism and postmodernism

In a number of recent discussions it has been said that few women have engaged in the modernism/postmodernism debate and that feminists have little or nothing to say about postmodernism. Meagan Morris believes that this curious *doxa* emerges from texts by male critics referring primarily to each other commenting on the rarity of women's speech. She feels strongly about the continued, repeated, basic exclusion of women's work from a highly invested field of intellectual and political endeavour. Morris is scathing about those male critics who construct bibliographies that do not mention the work of Catherine Clément, Hélène Cixous, Luce Irigaray, Shosana Felman, Jane Gallop, Sarah Kofman, Alice Jardine, Michele Le Doueff, Gayatri Chakravorty Spivak, Jacqueline Rose – and many others. As Morris has argued, since feminism has acted as one of the enabling conditions of discourse *about* postmodernism, it is therefore appropriate to use feminist work to frame discussions of postmodernism.[35]

Feminism and postmodernism have emerged as two of the most important political–cultural currents of the last decade. First, let us note the similarities: both have offered deep and far-reaching criticisms of philosophy, and of the relation of philosophy to the larger culture. Both have tried to develop new paradigms of social criticism which do not rely on traditional philosophical underpinnings. But there are differences as well. Postmodernists offer sophisticated criticisms of foundationalism and essentialism but their conceptions of social criticism tend to be anaemic. Feminists offer robust conceptions of social criticism, but they tend to lapse into foundationalism and essentialism. Nancy Fraser and Linda Nicholson have suggested that each of these tendencies has much to learn from the other; each is in possession of valuable resources which can help remedy the deficiencies of the other.

I will give a brief précis of their article 'Social Criticism without Philosophy'.[36] I think this will be useful because it provides a brief recapitulation of Lyotard's thesis, gives examples of some feminist theories which are now considered (reductive and) essentialist and, finally, makes a few suggestions about the integration of feminism and postmodernism.

Lyotard and other postmodernists begin by arguing that Philosophy with a capital 'P' is no longer a viable or credible enterprise. With the demise of foundationalism, philosophy (or theory) can no longer function to ground politics and social criticism. The modern conception must give way to a new postmodern one in which criticism floats free of any universalist theoretical ground. No longer anchored philosophically, the character of social criticism becomes more pragmatic, ad hoc, contextual and local.

Lyotard offers a 'postmodern' conception of what he calls the 'social bond'. What holds the social bond is a weave of criss-crossing threads of discursive practices, no single one of which runs continuously throughout the whole. Individuals are the nodes where such practices intersect and, so, they participate in many simultaneously. It follows that social identities are complex and heterogeneous. They cannot be mapped on to one another nor on to the social totality. Indeed, strictly speaking, there is no social totality and there is no possibility of a totalizing social theory.

Feminists, like postmodernists, have sought to develop new paradigms of social criticism which do not rely on traditional philosophical underpinnings. Practical imperatives, however, have led some feminists to adopt modes of theorizing which resemble the sorts of philosophical metanarrative criticized by postmodernists. In some early feminist writings theory was often understood as the search for the one key factor which would explain sexism cross-culturally and illuminate all of social life. Many of the social theories feminists have used share some of the essentialist and ahistorical features of metanarratives; they are insufficiently attentive to historical and cultural diversity, and they falsely universalize features of the theorist's own era, society, culture, class, 'race' or gender.

Fraser and Nicholson give three examples of such feminist theorizing. The first example: in the late 1960s many Marxist men argued that gender issues were secondary because they could be subsumed under class. Against this view, a radical feminist, Shulamith Firestone, resorted to an ingenious tactical manoeuvre: she invoked biological differences between men and women to explain sexism.[37] This enabled her to turn the tables on the Marxists by claiming that gender conflict was the most basic form of human conflict and the source of all other forms, including class conflicts. Now, from a postmodernist perspective appeals to biology to explain social phenomena are essentialist and monocausal. They are essentialist in so far as they project on to all women and men qualities which develop under historically specific social conditions. They are monocausal in so far as they look to one set of characteristics (such as women's physiology or men's hormones) to explain women's oppression in all cultures.

The second example draws on anthropology. In the 1970s anthropologists began to argue that appeals to biology do not allow us to understand the enormous diversity of forms which both gender and sexism assume in different cultures. One promising approach, that of Michelle Rosaldo, was based on the argument that common to all societies was some sort of separation between a 'domestic sphere' and a 'public sphere', the former associated with women and the latter with men.[38] Although the theory focused on differences between men's and women's spheres of activity rather than on differences between men's and women's biology, it was essentialist and monocausal none the less. It posited the existence of a domestic sphere in all societies and thereby assumed that women's activities were basically similar in content and significance across cultures.

The third example is the theory developed by Nancy Chodorow, who posited a cross-cultural activity, mothering, as the relevant object of investigation.[39] She asked the question: how does mothering produce a new generation of women with the psychological inclination to mother and a new generation of men not so inclined? The answer she gave was in terms of 'gender identity': female mothering produces women whose deep sense of self is 'relational' and men whose deep sense of self is not.

A criticism of this theory is that it posits the existence of a single activity, mothering, and stipulates that this basically unitary activity gives rise to two distinct sorts of deep selves, one relatively common across cultures to women, the other relatively common across cultures to men. From a postmodernist perspective Chodorow's thesis is essentialist because she states that women everywhere differ from men in their greater concern with 'relational interaction'. The idea of a cross-cultural, deep sense of self, specified differently for women and men, is deeply problematic. Moreover, while her concept of 'gender identity' gives substance to the idea of sisterhood, it does so at the cost of repressing differences among women.

By these and other examples Fraser and Nicholson lucidly demonstrate that many feminists have used categories to construct a universalistic social theory which projects the socially dominant views of their own society on to others, thereby distorting important features of both.

Fraser and Nicholson's main argument is that feminist theory must become postmodernist. They assert, contra Lyotard, that postmodern feminist theory could include large-scale narratives and analyses of macrostructures. Such a theory would be comparativist rather than universalizing. It would dispense with the idea of a subject of history, and would replace unitary notions of 'woman' with plural complexly constructed conceptions of social identity, treating gender as one relevant strand among others such as class, 'race', ethnicity, age and sexual orientation. In short, postmodern feminist theory would be pragmatic, and tailor its methods and categories to the specific task at hand.

Fraser and Nicholson believe that, on the one hand, there is decreasing interest in grand social theories; on the other hand, essentialist vestiges persist in the continued use of ahistorical categories without reflection as to how, when and why such categories originated and were modified over time. They suggest that this tension is symptomatically expressed in the work of French psychoanalytic feminists and believe that Cixous, Irigaray and Kristeva propositionally deny essentialism even as they performatively enact it.

Further reading

T. Eagleton, *Literary Theory: An Introduction*, Oxford: Basil Blackwell, 1983.
A lively, comprehensive account of modern literary theory. There is a clear explanation of structuralism, semiotics, post-structuralism, psychoanalysis and the need for political criticism. A brilliant and successful popularization.

H. Foster, *Postmodern Culture*, London: Pluto Press, 1985.
A famous collection of nine key essays on postmodernism by Baudrillard, Said, Habermas and others. An excellent introduction to the main debates.

D. Harvey, *The Condition of Postmodernity: An Enquiry into the Origins of Cultural Change*, Oxford: Basil Blackwell, 1989.
An ambitious materialist study of postmodernity. Harvey is interested not only in political and social ideas but in art, literature and architecture. He begins with an analysis of modernity, modernism, modernization. After looking at the political–economic transformation of late-twentieth-century capitalism, he considers postmodernity. The most stimulating argument concerns the nature of 'time–space compression' and how we experience it.

F. Jameson, *Postmodernism, or, The Cultural Logic of Late Capitalism*, London: Verso, 1991.
A fundamental text which covers culture, ideology, video, architecture, theory, economics, film. It deals with not just the cultural but the political and social implications of postmodernism. A big book in every sense, it is both demanding and rewarding.

M. Morris, *The Pirate's Fiancée: Feminism, Reading, Postmodernism*, London: Verso, 1988.
A book of twelve essays on Baudrillard, Daly, Le Doeuff, Foucault, Lyotard, photography, postmodernity, politics and the film *Crocodile Dundee*. It contains a comprehensive bibliography of women's writing on feminism, theories of reading and postmodernism.

R. Young (ed.), *Untying the Text: A Post-Structuralist Reader*, London: Routledge, 1981.
A most useful anthology of contemporary criticism, it gives examples of the work of various critics who have absorbed and developed the ideas of

Lacan, Derrida and Foucault. Among the texts discussed in this informative book are works by Wordsworth, Poe, Joyce, Nietzsche and Freud.

The following writings are from a feminist point of view:

N. Fraser and L. Nicholson, 'Social Criticism without Philosophy: An Encounter between Feminism and Postmodernism', in Andrew Ross (ed.), *Universal Abandon? The Politics of Postmodernism*, Edinburgh: Edinburgh University Press, 1988.

D. Haraway, *Simians, Cyborgs and Women*, London: Free Association Books, 1990.

S. Hekman, *Gender and Knowledge: Elements of a Postmodern Feminism*, Cambridge: Polity Press, 1990.

L. Kipnis, 'Feminism: The Political Conscience of Postmodernism?', in Andrew Ross (ed.), *Universal Abandon? The Politics of Postmodernism*, Edinburgh: Edinburgh University Press, 1988.

S. Lovibond, 'Feminism and Postmodernism', *New Left Review*, 178, November–December 1989.

L. Nicholson (ed.), *Feminism/Postmodernism*, London: Routledge, 1990.

P. Waugh, *Feminine Fictions: Revisiting the Postmodern*, London: Routledge, 1989.

Chapter 7

□

Baudrillard and some cultural practices

Baudrillard

Jean Baudrillard's provocative and controversial works have recently become very fashionable. He is a sociologist who obviously loves *ideas* (he has so many of them) and his writings contain many stimulating insights. His work is valuable because he has evolved a theory that tries to comprehend the nature and impact of mass communications.

Baudrillard began his writings as an effort to extend the Marxist critique of capitalism to areas that were beyond the scope of the theory of the mode of production. He found that the productivist metaphor in Marxism was inappropriate for comprehending the status of commodities in the post-war era. Later, as we shall see, he gradually abandoned Marxism and adopted the tenets of postmodernism.

The early work: commodity as sign

In *The System of Objects* (1968) Baudrillard explores, from a neo-Marxist perspective, the possibility that consumption has become the chief basis of the social order.[1] He argues that consumer objects constitute a classification system and that they have their effect in structuring behaviour. Advertising codes products through symbols that differentiate them from other products, thereby fitting the object into a series. The object has its effect when it is consumed by transferring its 'meaning' to the individual consumer. A potentially infinite play of signs is thus instituted which orders society while providing the individual with an illusory sense of freedom.

In *Consumer Society* (1970) Baudrillard, still a Marxist, continues to develop the argument that consumer objects constitute a *system of signs* that differentiate the population.[2] Consumer objects are best understood not as a response to a specific need or problem but as a network of floating signifiers that are inexhaustible in their ability to incite desire.

There has been a movement away from regarding goods merely as utilities having a use-value and an exchange-value which can be related to some fixed system of human needs. Baudrillard has been particularly important in this context, especially his theorization of the commodity-sign. He argues that the commodity has now become a sign in the Saussurian sense, with its meaning arbitrarily determined by its position in a self-referential system of signifiers. Consumption, then, must not be understood as the consumption of use-values, but primarily as the consumption of signs.

Baudrillard believes that it is through objects that each individual searches out his or her place in an order. The function of commodities, then, is not just to meet individual needs, but also to relate the individual to the social order. Consumption is not just the end point of the economic chain that began with production, but a system of exchange, a language in which commodities are goods to think with in a semiotic system that precedes the individual, as does any language. For Baudrillard there is no self-contained individual, there are only ways of using social systems, particularly those of language, goods and kinship, to relate people differently to the social order and thus to construct the sense of the individual.

Baudrillard's critique of Marx culminated in *The Mirror of Production* (1975).[3] It is symptomatic of his desire to distance himself from Marx's alleged economic reductionism, and the alleged inability of Marxist theory to conceptualize language, signs and communication. Each of Marx's major positions (the concept of labour, the dialectic, the theory of the mode of production, the critique of capital) is in turn revealed as a mirror image of capitalist society. Marxism emerges in this book not as a radical critique of capitalism but as its highest form of justification. In his early work Baudrillard emphasized symbolic exchange in opposition to consumption, to production and to all the values of bourgeois society. Borrowing from the ideas of Marcel Mauss and Georges Bataille, Baudrillard's symbolic exchange is a positive antithesis to 'productive' activity, it is beyond exchange and use, beyond value and equivalence. Connected with festival, prodigality, potlatch (a public distribution of goods; the holder of a potlatch makes a claim to status on the basis of his or her power *to give*), it is a form of interaction that lies outside of modern Western society and therefore haunts it like its own death.

As the politics of the 1960s receded so did Baudrillard's radicalism: political economy was no longer the foundation, the social determinant, or even a structural reality in which other phenomena could be interpreted and explained. From a radical position on the Left, he gradually moved towards a right-wing post-structuralism and post-modernism.

Theories like Marxism, psychoanalysis and structuralism now come under attack.[4] *On Seduction* (1979) is about these theories that deny the surface appearance of things in favour of a hidden structure or essence. These interpretive strategies, these 'depth' models, all privilege forms of rationality. Against them Baudrillard celebrates the Nietzschean critique of the 'truth' and favours a model which plays on the surface, thereby challenging theories that 'go beyond' the manifest to the latent.

From modernity to postmodernity

Baudrillard grounds his thought in a historical sketch of the transition from modernity to postmodernity. He writes about a world constructed out of models or simulacra which have no referent or ground in any 'reality' except their own. The first order of simulacrum can be called 'early modernity', the second period 'modernity', and the third 'postmodernity'. (These orders, by the way, are not to be read as a universal history.)

Early modernity   This is the period from the Renaissance to the beginning of the Industrial Revolution. Before the Renaissance, in feudal society, things function unequivocally. Everyone is assigned to a specific social space and the mobility of social class is impossible. The unquestioned positioning of each individual in a social space guarantees a total transparency and clarity. A ferocious hierarchy prevents disorder; any confusion of signs is punished. With the rise of the bourgeoisie, the caste order breaks down.

Modernity   The advent of the Industrial Revolution moves us into the second order of simulacrum. Modernity is the era of the bourgeoisie, of the primacy of industrial production. Later, with the technological revolution, social reproduction replaces production as the organizing principle of society. The dominant image of the first order, theatre and the stucco angel, is replaced in this period by photography and the cinema.[5]

Postmodernity   We are now in the third order of simulacrum, the order of models. In our current system, formed after the Second World War, the theoretical basis of the system of power has been transferred from Marxist political economy to structuralist semiology. What Marx considered as the non-essential part of capital, such as advertising, media, information and communication networks, has become the 'essential' sphere.

The use-values of commodities, the imperatives of production, have been replaced by models, codes, simulacra, spectacles and the hyper-realism of 'simulation'. In the media and consumer society people are caught up in the play of images, simulacra, that have less and less relationship to an outside, to an external 'reality'. In fact we live in a world of simulacra where the image or signifier of an event has replaced direct experience and knowledge of its referent or signified.

The new postmodern universe tends to make everything a simulacrum. By this Baudrillard means a world in which all we have are *simulations*, there being no 'real' external to them, no 'original' that is being copied. There is no longer a realm of the 'real' versus that of 'imitation' or 'mimicry' but rather a level in which there are only simulations.[6]

The media and the masses

Baudrillard suggests that the mass media symbolize a new era in which the old forms of production and consumption have given way to a new universe of communication. This new universe, unlike the old one (which he argued involved striving ambition, and the struggles of the Son against the patriarchal Father), relies on connections, feedback and interface; its processes are narcissistic and involve constant surface change.

Baudrillard writes that today the scene and the mirror no longer exist; instead there is screen and network; the period of production and consumption has given way to the era of connections and feedback. We live in the ecstasy of communication.[7] And this ecstasy is obscene. Advertising invades everything as public space disappears. In a subtle way this loss of public space occurs contemporaneously with the loss of private space. The one is no longer a spectacle, the other no longer a secret. At one time there was a clear difference between an exterior and an interior. Now this opposition is effaced in a sort of obscenity where the most intimate processes of our lives become the virtual feeding ground of the media.

Media practices have rearranged our senses of space and time. What is real is no longer our direct contact with the world, but what we are given on the TV screen: TV is the world. TV is dissolved into life, and life is dissolved into TV. The fiction is 'realized' and the 'real' becomes fictitious. Simulation has replaced production.

There are interesting parallels between Marshall McLuhan and Baudrillard's later writings. Baudrillard believes that McLuhan was right: the medium is the message; that is to say, not content but *the form* of the media is of importance.[8] In Baudrillard's increasingly pessimistic view, the function of TV and mass media is to prevent response, to privatize individuals; to place them into a universe of simulacra where it is impossible to distinguish between the spectacle and the real.

Baudrillard states that we are in a universe where there is more and more information and less and less meaning. He suggests that the refusal of meaning is the only form of resistance possible in a society like ours which suffers from information overload.[9] We are just bombarded with information-rich images every moment of our lives, and the only way we can cope with this, the only way we can resist the power of this information to take over our lives, is to accept the images only as signifiers, only as surfaces, and to reject their meanings, their signifieds.

Consider television news. It is simply a succession of surface images, of signifiers, for the viewers to experience. People cannot recall last night's news because there is nothing to recall, there are only images, only signifiers to experience. The news is a collage of fragmented images, and each image spawns more, calls up more, each image is a simulacrum – a perfect copy that has no original. The news is images of images of images, the final hyper-reality. In the news there is a postmodernist denial of historicity, the past is treated simply as a resource bank of images for casual reuse, a collapse of everything into the present. The postmodern experience is one of synchronicity; it plunders the past for its images and in using them denies their historicity and makes them into a kind of eternal present.

I have just used the term hyper-reality. What does 'hyper-reality' mean? Hyper-reality is a new condition in which the old tension between reality and illusion, between reality as it is and reality as it should be, has been dissipated. In Baudrillard's world everything is 'hyper' – in excess of itself. Being hyper means dissolving the old oppositions, not transcending or resolving them. When the borderline between the real and imaginary is eroded, reality is no longer checked, called to justify itself. It is 'more real than real' as it has become the only existence.

What is the relationship between the media and the masses? Without the media, there are no masses; without the masses, there are no 'mass' media. It should be noted that Baudrillard's formulation of the masses goes beyond 'mass society' theory which denounces the masses as destroying authentic bourgeois culture, and the Frankfurt School which sees the masses as stupefied by a capitalist 'culture industry'.

In 'The Beaubourg-Effect' (1982) Baudrillard reads an art centre as a miniaturized model of our current system.[10] In traditional critical thought artworks, museums, cultural centres (such as the Pompidou Centre, Beaubourg, Paris) are the devices by which the bourgeois culture produces cultural dupes, narcotizing the masses. Or, to follow the argument of cultural élitism, artworks elevate the masses to a higher cultural level, and invoke critical consciousness. But Baudrillard tells a different story. When the masses enter into the Beaubourg, they do not conform to the official culture, they transgress and destroy the myth of the system. They simulate and play with the models. They do not make sense of the cultural objects, for they know there is no meaning but only simulation.

In the essay 'The Masses: The Implosion of the Social in the Media' Baudrillard recapitulates some of the main themes of his work in the 1980s. One, the media generate a world of simulations which is immune to rationalist critique.[11] Two, the media represent an excess of information and they do so in a manner that excludes response by the recipients. Three, this simulated reality has no referent, no ground, no source. It operates outside the logic of representation. The masses, however, have found a way of subverting it with the strategy of silence or passivity. By absorbing the simulations of the media, by failing to respond, the masses undermine the code.

In Baudrillard's writings, the masses, the silent majorities, passively consume commodities, television, sports, politics, mass-produced simulations to such an extent that traditional politics and class struggle become obsolete. This is the era of consumer culture, and consumer culture, for Baudrillard, is effectively a postmodern culture: traditional distinctions and hierarchies have collapsed, polyculturalism is acknowledged; kitsch, the popular and difference are celebrated.

Before I conclude this section with some criticisms of Baudrillard's work I must first briefly mention the work of the Canadian writer Arthur Kroker because he has emerged, next to Baudrillard himself, as the leading proponent of a radical postmodernism. His book *The Postmodern Scene* is in many ways an attempt to out-Baudrillard Baudrillard.[12] He believes that there has been a radical rupture between modernity and postmodernity, and that Marxism should be rejected as a relic of antiquated modernism. The Enlightenment project of human liberation has been annulled. We are now living in an era of *implosion*, of the collapse of previous differences, distinctions and hierarchies. There has been a transformation from stable referents to 'floating signs'.

The old modern order rooted in industrial production, the exchange of objects, relations of physical force, direct communication has been replaced by the new postmodern order of media, information, communications and signs. Signs are incredibly important. The dominant principle of postmodernity is not production but *semiurgy*, the proliferation of interpellative signs, a quantitative development which leads to a qualitative break. Using Baudrillard's major concepts (implosion, semiurgy, simulation and hyper-reality) Kroker argues that Subject, Meaning, Truth, Nature, Society, Power and Reality have all been abolished in the transformation of industrial–commodity society into a post-industrial mediascape.

Some criticisms of Baudrillard

I want to make the following criticisms of Baudrillard's work. He seems to have a conservative nostalgia for face-to-face communication, which implies that face-to-face communication is superior to other forms. He would like dissimilar modes of communication to conform to the features of this privileged mode but he fails to take account of *differences* between media. Baudrillard's theory is close to being a sort of technological or semiotic determinism. He abstracts media from the social system and fails to see that media in contemporary society are a contested terrain, an arena of struggle, in which social conflicts are worked out. In Baudrillard's world there is no notion of project, a design which can be chosen and justified in its choice, to which society aims and struggles.

The most trenchant criticism of Baudrillard's views on truth and falsehood has been made by Christopher Norris.[13] He argues that Baudrillard has been deeply influenced by contemporary French thought, particularly post-structuralism. Post-structuralism promoted the idea that 'reality' is a purely discursive phenomenon, a product of the various codes, conventions, language games or signifying systems which provide the only means of interpreting experience from some given socio-cultural perspective. For Baudrillard, and for some other postmodernists, there is simply no appeal beyond the structures of representation, the discourses, that determine what shall count as knowledge or truth within a given interpretive context.

This is part of a widespread drift towards varieties of relativist thinking in matters of historical, political and ethical judgement. Baudrillard now takes the view that there is ultimately no difference between fictive and other, truth-telling forms of discourse; truth and falsity are wholly indistinguishable. Truth and critique are hopelessly outmoded concepts. Baudrillard rejects any defence of truth-claims in philosophy or critical theory as a hopeless appeal to obsolete 'Enlightenment' habits of thought. For Norris the result of postmodernist thought is firstly to undermine the *epistemological* distinction between truth and falsehood, and secondly to place *ethical* issues beyond reach of argued, responsible debate. Baudrillard's position leads to moral and political nihilism.[14]

Some postmodernist cultural practices

The discursive and the figural

Having given a (compressed) account of Baudrillard's main ideas, I now want to consider some postmodernist cultural *practices*. Many social thinkers have argued that modernist culture signifies in a largely discursive way while postmodernist signification is importantly figural. The discursive gives priority to words over images, it is a sensibility of the ego rather than of the id. The figural is a visual rather than a literary sensibility; it contests rationalist and/or 'didactic' views of culture; it asks not what a cultural text 'means' but what it 'does'.

When Lyotard writes of the discursive he is referring to the Freudian secondary process, the ego operating in terms of the reality principle.[15] The figural, by contrast, is the primary process of the unconscious which operates according to the pleasure principle. The figural is connected with the extension of the primary process into the cultural realm.

Lyotard has asserted the existence of two alternative economies of desire. In the first, the discursive, the secondary process makes inroads into the primary process. For example, Lyotard considers Freud's 'talking cure' itself to promote a discursive economy of desire through the colonization of the unconscious by discourse, through a subversion of the primary process by language and the transference. Lyotard clearly prefers the figural economy of desire (the image-based signification of the unconscious); he wants a sensibility, a culture and a politics in which the primary process 'erupts' into the secondary process.

Lyotard is sympathetic to the idea of the colonization of the secondary process by the primary process in art and in psychoanalysis. He rejects the concept of the psyche rigidly hierarchized into levels for one in which desire is no longer an underlying 'essence'. Instead, desire is present on the surface of social and cultural practices.

I turn now to examine some cultural practices which are figural: architecture, painting, TV, video and film.

Architecture

Modernism in architecture had its beginnings in the Bauhaus school founded in Germany in 1919. The ideas of architectural modernism were expressed in the work and writings of Walter Gropius, Le Corbusier and Mies van der Rohe. Despite their differences the work of these three architects has much in common. They believed that architecture was to be *new*; it was to use new materials and new construction techniques. Line, space and form were to be pared to their essentials. They stressed the unity and the self-sufficient functionality of every building: the exterior was to be the result of the interior. These architects had a faith in the rational. Architecture was to be the visible expression of a new unity of art, science and industry.

Architectural modernism became the dominant sign of the new. By the 1950s everyone in the industrialized nations was familiar with the simple forms, the glass and steel boxes, the 'International Style' of Mies van der Rohe and his followers. The characteristics of this style are its simplicity of form and its self-sufficiency. The modernist building does not refer to anything outside itself by quotation or allusion.

The postmodernist building is very different. Charles Jencks, one of the most influential proponents of architectural postmodernism, holds a semiotic view of the way architecture functions that derives from Saussurian theories of language.[16] Firstly, he argues that the language of architecture is not, as modernist architects would have it, a language of archetypal or absolute forms; rather its structural elements derive their meanings from their relationships of similarity and contrast with other elements. Secondly, Jencks argues that the codes which are used to understand or interpret the abstract forms of architecture are not fixed or unchanging since they always derive from and reflect the multiple contexts in which any work of architecture is experienced and 'read'.

What, then, are the main differences between modernist and postmodernist architecture? While modernist architects stress absolute unity of intention and execution in a building, postmodernist architects explore the incompatibilities of style, form and texture. Architects such as Robert Venturi like complexity and contradiction, they admire the display of architectural differences. Secondly, modernist architects reject the decorative, the superfluous, the inessential; postmodernist architects, on the other hand, are very fond of ornamentation. Thirdly, in place of the unified city, planned according to consistent principles (for example, the work of Le Corbusier in Chandigarh, Punjab), Venturi would have architects learn from the urban sprawl of Las Vegas.[17] In this view incompatible elements are laid side by side and work in juxtaposition.

Modernist architecture is associated with the functional, the impersonal, with heroic individual vision and expression. In contrast, postmodernists want an architecture which is more responsive to its contexts and more relative in style. Postmodern buildings are in many styles. There is straight revivalism; a famous example is the Paul Getty Museum in Malibu, California, which is an exact re-creation of the Villa of the Papyri at Herculaneum. Other postmodernist buildings depend on a disparity of the codes, the contemporary and the antique, the functional and the decorative, the domestic and the public, and their harmonization. Some critics want to resist the tendency to flatten out cultural differences into the uniformity of a universal architectural grammar. They therefore support the assertion of local particularities within and against modern building forms.[18]

In some contemporary buildings, like the Lloyd's Insurance building in London and the Beaubourg, the Pompidou Centre, in Paris, all the 'plumbing' is on the outside; this reminds me of Derrida's inside/outside paradox where the 'pure' inside must be protected from the impure surplus or excess of the outside. But is the Pompidou Centre modernist or postmodernist? Jencks argues that it is 'Late Modern', that is to say, it no longer has a clear commitment to modernist ideals of pure functionality. But surely one could say that the pipes and ducts are signs of functionality? A consideration of this example shows that it is never a simple matter to define the difference between modernism and postmodernism.

Let us take another example. There is a fascinating account by Jameson which focuses on a postmodern building, a house built (or rebuilt) by Frank Gehry in Santa Monica, California.[19] The architect bought an old house and built a high wall of corrugated metal around it. Between the old house and the wall he built the new glassed living space. The old house remains totally intact from the outside; you can look at it through the new house as though it was now packaged in this new skin. The old house is the core and the new house is the wrapper. The architect's own term 'wrapping' is rather like talking about text and context: the wrapped can be used as the wrapper; the wrapper can also be wrapped in its turn.

The house, then, consists of a corrugated metal shell wrapped around an existing pretty 1920s' house in a way that creates new spaces. The new areas, between the old house and the wrapper, are mostly glassed in and therefore visually open to and indistinguishable from the former outside. In the glassed areas there are numerous contradictory perspective lines, going to numerous vanishing points. Gehry's distorted perspective planes and illusionistic use of framing members confronts us with paradoxical impossibilities.

Some of the features of postmodern hyperspace (as Jameson terms it) are: the effacement of the categories of inside/outside; the bewilderment and loss of spatial orientation; the messiness of an environment in which things and people no longer find their 'place'.

As you go up the old-fashioned stairs of the old house, you reach an old-fashioned door, through which you enter an old-fashioned room. The door is a time-travel device; when you close it, you are in an old-fashioned room with its privacy, its kitsch, its chintzes. Jameson points out that the time-travel evocation is misleading because the room is not a reconstruction of the past at all, since this enclave space is our present and replicates the real dwelling spaces of the other houses on this street today. Yet it is a present reality that has been transformed into a simulacrum by the process of wrapping, or quotation.

Gehry has produced new kinds of space, space that includes old and new, inside and outside. Jameson goes on to suggest that architectural space is a way of thinking, a way of doing philosophy. We are caught within complex global networks, yet we have no way of thinking about them. He observes two features about contemporary America: the corrugated metal wall is the junk or Third World side of American life today, the production of poverty and misery, people not only out of work but without a place to live, bag people. . . . And then there is the other side, the postmodern United States of extraordinary technological and scientific achievement, the abstract wealth and real power, things which most of us will never know. These are the two antithetical and incommensurable features of America today. Gehry's house is a meditation on this problem.

Art

The American art theorist Clement Greenberg is often credited with having provided modernism in art with its most influential form of legitimation. His main thesis is that, while painting in the nineteenth century fell under the sway of the other arts, especially literature, the painting of the twentieth century set itself to rediscover what was specific and proper to painting alone. According to Greenberg, the prime characteristic of painting, unlike any of the other arts, is that paint is applied to a flat, two-dimensional surface. Painting is reducible, in the end, to this one characteristic. Art's absorption in itself is the essential principle of modernism. It should be added that in modernism there is often a desire for absolute originality. The artistic products of modernism are supposed to be pure signs of nothing but themselves.

One of the main characteristics of postmodernism in art is the multiplication of stylistic norms and methods. This emphasis on stylistic diversity is part of a larger mistrust of the modernist aesthetic of exclusion. While Greenberg and others tried to argue for a modernism that becomes what it is by purging itself of what it is not, theories of postmodernism in art stress the deep connectedness between what it acknowledges as its own and what it excludes.

Some critics have suggested that the postmodern sensibility involves a shift of emphasis from epistemology to ontology. There has been a shift from knowledge to experience, from theory to practice, from mind to body. Some critics wish to describe those contemporary works that tend towards the body and away from the intellect as postmodern. For example, one critic has written that the postmodern sensibility and the art of Francis Bacon, which focuses on the body as meat and bone, have a certain affinity.[20] The postmodernist painting of Francis Bacon breaks with the principle of formal rationality and shows desire on the canvas's surface.

In postmodernism there is often the deliberate exploration of what lies between, rather than within, art forms. The bringing together of heterogeneous images and technologies seems to throw into question the idea of pure origin or authorship. There is the well-known example of the American artist Robert Rauschenberg who has produced silk-screen canvases which use reproductions of Velázquez's *Rokeby Venus* and Rubens's *Venus at her Toilet* with painted and other images.[21] To put it briefly, Rauschenberg has moved from techniques of production to techniques of reproduction. It is this move that makes Rauschenberg's work postmodernist. Through reproductive technology postmodernist art dispenses with the aura. The fiction of the creating subject gives way to the frank confiscation, quotation, accumulation and repetition of already existing images. Works such as these which bring together heterogeneous images and technologies not only undermine many modernist assumptions but also raise questions about originality and authenticity.

Theories of postmodernism in art encompass two main strands. The first is exemplified by the work of Charles Jencks, and those associated with him, which can be called conservative-pluralist. The second strand, exemplified in the work of Rosalind Krauss, Douglas Crimp, Craig Owens, Hal Foster and other writers for the journal *October*, can be called critical-pluralist. The latter attempt to go beyond modernism by revealing the instabilities within it. The critical-pluralists aim, however, to preserve some of the oppositional exploratory ethic of suspicion which characterized many forms of modernism.

Charles Jencks believes that art can now acknowledge itself as what it always was, thoroughly bourgeois, and return itself to the forms and subjects tabooed by modernism. In place of the uncompromisingly universal horizons of modernism, he believes that we must adopt an attitude of amused, agnostic pragmatism. In contrast, Rosalind Krauss and the other writers, who embody the oppositional or critical-pluralist strand of postmodernist theory, believe in a postmodernism that challenges traditional and institutional power.[22]

TV, video and film

It has often been said that every age is dominated by a privileged form or genre. There is no doubt in Jameson's mind that in the present period it is video. He believes that experimental video is coterminous with postmodernism itself. In discussions of culture the older language of the 'work' (the work of art) has largely been displaced by the language of 'texts' and textuality. Everything can now be read as a text – the body, daily life, even the state. The videotext itself is at all moments a process of ceaseless, apparently random, interaction between elements. It may seem that one such element (or sign) somehow 'comments' on the other, or serves as its 'interpretant', but this is not the case. The main characteristic of postmodern experimental video is a ceaseless rotation of elements such that they change place at every moment, with the result that no single element can occupy the position of interpretant (or that of primary sign) for any length of time but must be dislodged in turn in the following instant.

Jameson suggests that a videotext is a structure, or sign flow, which *resists meaning*, whose fundamental inner logic is the exclusion of the emergence of themes. To put it in another way, whatever a good videotext may be, it will be bad or flawed whenever an interpretation proves possible. Jameson concludes with a fable: at one time, long ago, the sign seemed to have unproblematical relations with its referent. But now

> reification penetrates the sign itself and disjoins the signifier from the signified. Now reference and reality disappear altogether, and even meaning – the signified – is problematized. We are left with that pure and random play of signifiers that we call postmodernism, which no longer produces monumental works of the modernist type but ceaselessly reshuffles the fragments of preexistent texts, the building blocks of older cultural and social production, in some new and heightened bricolage.[23]

There are some critics who say that video exemplifies in a particularly intense way the postmodern dichotomy between avant-garde disruptive strategies and the processes whereby such strategies are absorbed and neutralized. For Jameson, TV and video represent in their forms challenges not only to the hegemony of modernist aesthetic models but also to the contemporary dominance of language. He argues that, whereas representational media like novels and/or films are committed to produce the effects of 'real time' while actually distorting it (by foreshortening, telescoping, etc.), non-narrative avant-garde video locks the viewer into the time of the video.[24]

Now let me turn to film. First of all, I would like to make some general points about the cinema before making some remarks about postmodernist films. Cinema has always given primacy to *images*. It has been stated by Christian Metz and others that the experience of viewing a film in the cinema – the dark, the succession of images, the wish fulfilment – has a great deal in common with the experience of dreaming.[25]

Many people have noted a new phenomenon: we are now learning to 'read' all the arts as we read books. Video cassette recorders, for example, allow us to watch movies as we have always read books. We often interrupt our reading to deal with other things and then we return, and start reading a few pages before we finished reading. Sometimes we read the same page again and again. We are no longer compelled to submit to the jurisdiction of an authoritarian author or *auteur*. We may play-back, or freeze the frame. There is a subjection of the work of art to one's natural or domestic rhythms. The compact disc recorder gives us similar freedoms. The principal consequence of this reproductive boom is that culture is something which 'happens' to us increasingly at home, and correspondingly less in the venues erected in the past.

The dominant form of cinema as mass cultural entertainment is what has been called the 'classical-realist' text of the Hollywood cinema, which derives from the adoption of the realist techniques and assumptions of the nineteenth-century novel and drama. What are the alternative practices in the cinema which need to be defined against the dominating model of Hollywood? Some of the variant practices are: the 'art' film, the 'avant-garde' film and the 'modernist' film.

The 'art' film is typified by the exploration of psychological complexity. The 'avant-garde' film is characterized by various forms of rejection of narrative causality. The modernist film emphasizes the film's formal exploration of its own medium (as against its domination by the mode of narrative). The modernist film is often associated with the influential *auteur* theory of the 1970s where the unique personality and individuality of the director was expected to generate his or her unique vision of the world.

Some writers have drawn attention to the fact that the cinema has been structured around sexuality, or rather around the objectification of male desire in screen images of women. In this context an important distinction has been made between 'narrative' and 'spectacle' by Laura Mulvey.[26] She argues that mass-market cinema has been structured around the 'spectacle' of women's images. She identifies film 'narrative' with Freud's ego and 'spectacle' with the sexual drives of the id.

There has been a move from realist to postmodernist cinema, and in the latter there has been a shift from narrative to spectacle. In other words, there is a contemporary trend towards a figural cinema. Postmodernist films (*Blade Runner, Diva, The Draughtsman's Contract*) are, of course, in different styles. Some of them (*American Graffiti, Star Wars, Chinatown, Body Heat*) are 'retro' films based on nostalgia. While in modernist art attention is drawn to the picture surface and to the signifying process, in postmodernist work it is not the signifying process but the fixed nature of *reality* that is questioned.

What, then, are the characteristics of postmodernist films? It has been said that these films bring the viewer into the film with a rather startling immediacy, but, having done so, the 'real' that the spectator has been drawn into is revealed as artifice. A figural cinema which privileges spectacle over narrative (or discourse) operates largely on the model of and through the primary process. Some critics believe that these films suggest the instability of subjectivity. If subjectivity is less fixed, then space is left for the construction of identities which deviate from the norm. That is, space is left for 'difference'. This is one way, perhaps, in which postmodernism can be seen as supportive of a left politics rooted in principles of pluralism and difference.

One account suggests that many contemporary Hollywood films may be read as cultural statements which locate within small-town America all the terrors and simulated realities that Lyotard and Baudrillard see operating in the postmodern period. A reading of such films could provide a deeper understanding of the kinds of experiences the postmodern period makes available. Sometimes, of course, critics are unable to agree on what genre a film belongs to, and some films resist classification; hence they are read in multiple ways.

There are a number of popular films which could be categorized as postmodern, and I will mention a few. They take up, in one way or another, the controversial topics of race, gender, class, ethnicity, Japan (Asian) and American relations, and the media in the postmodern age. The films are *Blue Velvet, Do the Right Thing, I've Heard the Mermaids Singing, Chan is Missing, Thelma and Louise, Black Rain* and *Broadcast News*.

Norman Denzin has observed that films like David Lynch's *Blue Velvet* simultaneously display the two features of postmodernist texts that Jameson has identified: namely, an effacement of the boundaries between the past and the present (typically given in the forms of parody and pastiche), and a treatment of time which locates the viewing subject in a perpetual present.[27] These films bring the unpresentable (sexual violence, sado-masochistic rituals, for example) to the viewer and challenge the boundaries that ordinarily separate private and public life.

Denzin's argument, then, is that postmodern films echo and reproduce the tensions and contradictions that define our time. These films awaken desires and fears that expose the limits of the real and the unreal in contemporary, everyday life. He shows how *Blue Velvet*, for example, is pastiche and parody, an effacement of the boundaries between the past and the present, and a presentation of the unpresentable. Postmodern cultural texts locate strange, eclectic, violent, timeless worlds in the present. As Lyotard has remarked: 'The Postmodern would be that . . . which searches for new presentations . . . in order to impart a stronger sense of the unpresentable.'[28] And yet, at the same time, these films often attempt to find safe regions of escape in the fantasies and nostalgia of the past. They search for new ways to present the unpresentable so as to break down the barriers that keep the profane out of the everyday. However, they take conservative political stances, while they valorize and exploit the radical social margins of society. Denzin concludes that as the world political system turns ever more violent and conservative, the need for cultural texts which sustain the key elements of conservative political economy increases.

Further reading

S. Connor, *Postmodernist Culture: An Introduction to Theories of the Contemporary*, Oxford: Basil Blackwell, 1989.
In this introduction to postmodernist debates, the author clearly out-lines the philosophical positions of Lyotard, Jameson and Baudrillard. Most of the book is then devoted to a discussion of postmodernism in architecture, the visual arts, literature, TV, video, film and popular culture. The book contains a useful bibliography.

M. Gane, *Baudrillard: Critical and Fatal Theory*, London: Routledge, 1991.

M. Gane, *Baudrillard's Bestiary: Baudrillard and Culture*, London: Routledge, 1991.

D. Kellner, *Jean Baudrillard: From Marxism to Postmodernism and Beyond*, Cambridge: Polity Press, 1989.
In this interesting study Kellner analyses the development of Baudrillard's ideas over twenty years. A scholarly and critical work.

□

Conclusion

Taking history seriously

Lyotard is only one of many post-structuralists, 'new philosophers' and others who attack Marxism for being a 'grand narrative' and mock its belief in the emancipation of humanity. As they assert that Marx's story under Hegel's inspiration clearly exhibits a providential plot, it is important to ask, 'What is "narrative"?' One of the insights of recent literary theory is that narrative or story is not specifically a literary form. Fredric Jameson believes that narrative is really not so much a literary form or structure as an epistemological category.[1] Like the Kantian concepts of space and time, narrative may be taken not as a feature of our experience but as one of the abstract or 'empty' co-ordinates within which we come to know the world, a contentless form that our perception imposes on the raw flux of reality. This is not to say that we make up stories about the world to understand it; Jameson is making the much more radical claim that the world comes to us in the shape of stories.

Jameson argues that it is hard to think of the world as it would exist outside narrative. Anything we try to substitute for a story is, on closer examination, likely to be another sort of story. Physicists, for example, 'tell stories' about subatomic particles. Anything that presents itself as existing outside the boundaries of some story (a structure, a form, a category) can only do so through a kind of fiction. In Jameson's view structures may be abundantly useful as conceptual fictions, but reality comes to us in the form of its stories. Narrative, just by being narrative, always demands interpretation, and so we must always be aware of the distinction between manifest meaning and latent content. Moreover, we should remember that every narrative simultaneously presents and represents a world, that is, simultaneously creates or makes up a reality and asserts that it stands independent of that same reality. In other words, narrative seems at once to reveal or illuminate a world and to hide or distort it.

Narrative, the contentless form of our most basic experience of reality, has a function: it is a specific mechanism through which the collective consciousness represses historical contradictions. This is what is meant by 'the political unconscious'. Ironically, it was Freud who actually discovered the political unconscious but who, imprisoned through ideological circumstance within such illusory categories as 'the individual psyche' and the like, was in no position to understand the consequences of his discovery.

It is obvious that Jameson has been much influenced by structuralist thinking: there is the idea, for example, that the notion of 'individual consciousness' is incoherent. (This notion, he would say, implies some idea of a 'collective consciousness' or total social system.) For Jameson Marxism is the story of a fall out of collective life and consciousness into a world of estrangement and alienation where 'individual identity' becomes a primary category within thought. He would say that separation or individuality at the level of consciousness is itself a symptom of estrangement from the life of the collective. To treat the 'I', the feeling or experience of individual identity, as the main ontological category is to repress history itself.

Jameson is antagonistic to those post-structuralists who reject the idea of a master code or master narrative. He finds the notion of master code a valuable one and uses it in his own work. He argues that formalism, whose claims are based on immanent interpretation, is really a form of transcendent interpretation in disguise. Formalist criticism simply rewrites literary works in terms of an ethical master code that is a product of its historical moment. Another example is structuralism, a form of transcendent interpretation that uses the master code language.

Jameson argues that the 'master code' of any interpretative method is the ideology it works to perpetuate. Ideology is the repression of those underlying contradictions that have their source in history. Jameson conceives of ideologies as strategies of containment, and of literature as an ideological production mirroring such strategies at the level of individual works.[2] He tries to subject literature to symptomatic analysis, a mode of interpretation that reveals the specific ways in which works deny or repress history. Symptomatic analysis is also able to show that critical approaches usually assumed to be in competition with one another (the Freudian, the formalist, the structuralist, etc.) share at the deep level an identical set of assumptions, they deny history in an identical way.[3] This method has some similarities with Foucauldian or Nietzschean 'genealogy', which elicits from the structure of a cultural text that unexpressed subtext or *hors texte* it cannot acknowledge. What Jameson tries to do is to find certain patterns which represent strategies of containment; he looks at gaps or absences as specific signs of the way the text denies or represses history.

In Jameson's view taking history seriously means accepting some story as the means of knowing anything at all. (Indeed, I would argue that the more people believe that history should be moving towards the establishment of a rational society, the more likely history will be moving towards it. By making this link between theory and practice we make history conform to our notion of it.) Jameson defends the concept of 'mode of production'; the 'story' of the successive modes of production is heuristic and the value of the concept lies in its use as an instrument of social analysis. What the concept 'mode of production' is really concerned with is not some story of successive economic stages but the possibility of seeing all the social phenomena within a given historical framework as related to one another as to a totality.

Jameson conceives the social totality as something always constituted by a class struggle between a dominant and a labouring class, and he wants us to think of the social order at the cultural level in the form of a dialogue between *antagonistic class discourses*. This dialogue is always made possible by what he calls the unity of a shared code. (It is easy to forget that disagreement is made possible only by a shared language and a common set of assumptions.) The example Jameson provides is that of England in the 1640s when religion operated as the shared code within which was fought out the antagonism between opposing discourses. Historically speaking, we 'hear' only one voice because a hegemonic ideology suppresses all antagonistic class voices, and yet the hegemonic discourse remains locked into a dialogue with the discourse it has suppressed.

Towards a pedagogical political culture

The controversy over postmodernism is one example of class struggle at the cultural and political level. On the political level postmodernism is an attack on Marxism. On the cultural level it is a repudiation of the modern movement: abstract expressionism in painting, the international style in architecture, existentialism in philosophy. Most postmodernists reject the following models: the existential model of authenticity and inauthenticity, the semiotic opposition between signifier and signified, the Freudian model of latent and manifest, and the Marxist one of appearance and essence (the view that the empirical world, 'appearance', is causally connected to deeper levels, the structures and processes of the real, 'the essence'). These 'depth' models have been replaced by a conception of practices, discourses and textual play.

Jameson suggests that with postmodernism there has emerged a new kind of flatness or depthlessness, a new kind of superficiality.[4] The shift from the period of modernism to the world of the postmodern can be characterized as one in which the alienation of the subject is displaced by *the fragmentation of the subject*. The disappearance of the individual subject and the unavailability of unique and personal style has brought about a new practice: pastiche. To recapitulate, pastiche has become a ubiquitous mode (in film, especially) which suggests that we wish to be recalled to times less problematic than our own. There seems to be a refusal to engage with the present or to think historically, a refusal that Jameson regards as characteristic of the 'schizophrenia' of consumer society. He believes that there has been a disappearance of a sense of history. Our entire contemporary social system has little by little begun to lose its capacity to retain its own past; it has begun to live in a perpetual present.

There seems to be a random cannibalization of all the styles of the past. At the same time we seem increasingly incapable of fashioning representations of our current experiences. For Jameson postmodernism replicates, reinforces the logic of consumer capitalism. The emergence of postmodernism is closely related to the emergence of present-day multinational capitalism.

Jameson has usefully periodized the stages of realism, modernism and postmodernism by drawing on the work of the economist Ernest Mandel. Mandel, who argues that technology is the result of the development of capital rather than some primal cause in its own right, outlines three fundamental leaps in the evolution of machinery under capital: machine production of steam-driven motors since 1848, machine production of electric and combustion motors since the 1890s, and machine production of electronic and nuclear-powered apparatuses since the 1940s. This periodization underlines the general thesis of

Mandel's book *Late Capitalism*, namely that there have been three fundamental moments in capitalism: market capitalism, monopoly capitalism (or imperialism) and multinational capitalism.[5]

Among the theorists of the New Right the assertion is fashionable that we are living in a type of society that no longer obeys the laws of classical capitalism (namely the primacy of industrial production and the omnipresence of class struggle) and that therefore Marxism is outmoded. In contrast with this postmodernist/post-structuralist view Mandel argues that the contemporary form of capitalism represents the purest form of capitalism to have emerged. There has been a prodigious expansion of capitalism into hitherto uncommodified areas: for example the penetration and colonization of Nature and the Unconscious, that is to say, the destruction of the pre-capitalist agriculture and the rise of the media and the advertising industry.

Jameson's main political concepts, inherited from Lukács and the Frankfurt School, are those of reification and commodification. He contends that aesthetic production has become integrated into commodity production:

> This whole global, yet American postmodern culture is the internal and superstructural expression of a whole new wave of American military and economic domination throughout the world: in this sense, as throughout class history, the underside of culture is blood, death and horror.[6]

Jameson is deeply concerned about the incapacity of our minds (at least at present) to map the great global multinational and decentred communicational network in which we find ourselves caught as individual subjects. He describes how we all, in one way or another, dimly feel that not only local forms of cultural resistance but also even overtly political interventions are somehow secretly disarmed and reabsorbed by a system of which they themselves might well be considered a part, since they can achieve no distance from it.

While the high modernists were very interested in time and memory it seems that now our daily life, our cultural languages, are dominated by the category of space rather than time. Jameson uses the metaphor of an alienated city to refer to a space in which people are unable to map in their minds either their own positions or the urban totality in which they find themselves. He argues that we should map our individual social relationship to local, national and international class realities, a process that requires us to co-ordinate existential data, the empirical position of the subject, with theoretical conceptions of the totality. We need to develop an aesthetic of cognitive mapping, a pedagogical political culture which seeks to endow the individual subject with some new heightened sense of its place in the global system.

While reading this you may have been asking, 'What has all this to do with me?' I agree with Antonio Gramsci's remark that 'everything is political, even philosophy and philosophies'. Texts, philosophies and so forth acquire power through what Gramsci describes as diffusion, dissemination into and hegemony over the world of 'common sense': 'In the realm of culture and of thought each production exists not only to earn a place for itself but to displace, win out over, others.'[7] I suggest that the controversy about modernism and postmodernism should be seen in the context of ideological struggle. This debate is, implicitly, about the status, the validity of Marxism. The project of modernity is one with that of the Enlightenment. And Marxism is a child of the Enlightenment. But the postmodernists declare that progress is myth. Obviously each position on or within postmodernism is marked by our political interests and values.[8] How we conceive of postmodernism is central to how we re-present the past, the present, and the future to ourselves and others.

A characteristic of human beings is that they make a distinction between 'the real' and 'the ideal'. By the real I mean an awareness of the present situation, and by the ideal, some notion of what life, the world, could be like. Human beings have a sense of what is possible in the future and they have the hope that tomorrow will be better than today. Marxists not only have this hope, this orientation towards the future, but they try to understand the world, to develop a critical consciousness of it, and try to develop strategies for changing it. Of course, they realize that progress is uneven, not unilinear; because of the nature of contradiction there are inevitably negative aspects, sad reversals and painful losses. Marxists struggle for a better future for all, but they know that this does not mean that progress is guaranteed or that the processes of the dialectic will lead to the Perfect. I believe that it is important for people to support the Enlightenment project because education is closely connected with the notion of a change of consciousness; gaining a wider, deeper understanding of the world represents a change for the better. And this, in turn, implies some belief in a worthwhile future. Without this presupposition the education of people would be pointless.

Re-vision

Before I conclude I would like to give a brief 'précis' of the ground covered in the foregoing chapters. Its main purpose is not to tell you 'to read the chapters in a certain way' but to encourage you to reflect – and comment – on the issues raised. I began by discussing the three most influential post-structuralists: Lacan, Derrida and Foucault. Chapter 1, a general introduction to Lacan and his theory of psychoanalysis, suggested that Lacanian theory offered a way of thinking about the social and the linguistic construction of the self. We urgently need a model that overcomes the opposition between the individual and the social, because no political revolution can be completed until the 'character structures' inherited from prerevolutionary society are transformed. I think that a (revised) Lacanian model of the subject could perhaps help us to conceive of a different signification, a different subjectivity, and a different symbolic order.

There was an account of Derrida's thought in Chapter 2. I outlined his arguments against Lacan and other thinkers and then described his views on Freud, who influenced Derrida's thinking on reading texts, and Nietzsche, who influenced his understanding of the nature and function of metaphor. I argued that metaphors determine to a large extent what we can think in any field and that they shape what we do. Finally, after situating metaphor in the context of political and ideological struggle, I discussed the relationship between deconstruction and Marxism.

Chapter 3 focused on Foucault, a writer whose works are based on a vision of history derived from Nietzsche. I gave an exposition of Foucault's work, which is largely concerned with the growth of the modern sciences and the process of modernization. The relationship between knowledge and power, another Nietzschean theme, was also discussed. For Foucault knowledge is not neutral or objective but is a product of power relations. Power in modern times is productive, it operates through the construction of new capacities and modes of activity. After describing some of the similarities and differences between Foucault and Althusser, I presented Foucault's arguments against Marxism. I stressed the point that Foucault believed that Marxism was authoritarian and outmoded, a view that has been vigorously propagated by his many followers, both in France and internationally. Nietzsche's thought influenced Foucault so deeply that it is not surprising that he rejected Marx's view of economics, history, politics and method. For Foucault it was no longer feasible to conceptualize relations of power in terms of the state, class struggle, relations of production and capitalist exploitation.

In Chapter 4 I outlined some of the important differences between the philosophies of Nietzsche and Hegel and stressed the fact that Nietzsche's thought – his antipathy to any system, his rejection of the Hegelian view of history as progress, his preoccupation with the subjective – is central to the post-structuralists' anti-Marxist stance. I introduced some of the ideas of writers like Deleuze and Guattari (who see in Marxism an instrument of domination and who glorify spontaneity, subjectivity and intensity), Foucault, Lyotard and others who always emphasize the local, the heterogeneous and the fragmentary. I then discussed the 'new philosophers' who also draw heavily on Nietzsche's thought and combine certain elements and themes from the work of post-structuralist writers.

In Chapter 5 I widened the issues discussed in the book by introducing the work of Cixous, Irigaray and Kristeva. These thinkers all write about psychoanalytic issues, sexuality and femininity and, despite their many differences, they have much in common: all of them reject the notion of individual subjectivity as unified and stable. They all draw heavily on Lacanian and Derridean concepts. And they are all deeply concerned about language, reading texts, writing, justice. It was pointed out that Cixous's strategy is to explore the subversive possibilities of 'feminine' writing. I then focused on Irigaray's critique of patriarchy and her claim that women need a language of their own. I argued that though Kristeva rejects the idea of an *écriture féminine* that would be inherently feminine or female, she does have a belief in the potentially revolutionary force of the repressed aspects of language. It seems to me that these thinkers, unlike some social theorists, are ethically and politically concerned about marginalized groups. In their different ways they seem to have a project that involves psychic, linguistic and social transformation.

I began Chapter 6 with an exposition of Lyotard's thesis: as knowledge is now becoming the principal force of production, we should seriously consider the changing nature of knowledge as computerized societies enter what is known as the postmodern age. It was explained that the debate about modernism and postmodernism is (partly) about the arts, and so there was a discussion about the role of art in bourgeois society. Postmodernists/post-structuralists believe that the modern narratives of the emancipation of the working class, the classless society, have lost credibility. Marxism is outmoded.

This is also the view of Baudrillard, whom I discussed in Chapter 7. As we saw, he has gradually abandoned Marxism and espoused postmodernism. Personally, I find many of his insights stimulating and provocative but, generally, his position is deplorable. In Baudrillard's world truth and falsity are wholly indistinguishable, a position which I believe leads to moral and political nihilism.

Post-structuralists, I maintained, are antagonistic to the concept of totality and in its stead emphasize fragmentation. Everything consists of fragments; and as they do not recognize a unity against which the fragments can be measured they tend towards relativism. The post-structuralists also emphasize the local and the contingent and have a hatred of all overarching theories. With some thinkers, such as Derrida and Foucault, this has led to a conceptual relativism so strong as to seem self-defeating. It is not surprising, then, that Lyotard believes that power is increasingly becoming the criterion of truth.

Derrida, Foucault and other post-structuralists challenge the idea that knowledge 'grows' or 'progresses' in any more than a purely quantitative sense. (One paradox of their work is that although they repudiate any notion of a general theory, their theory does express a general view about the nature of knowledge.) Not only do they give up humanism's belief in epistemological progress, they also give up its belief in social historical progress. Derrida, Foucault and other modern Nietzscheans see history as 'ending' in the sense of dying. Having lost faith in the progressive character of history, they are reacting against the thinkers of the Enlightenment. They assert that the Enlightenment project of modernity has failed. In opposition to this view it was argued that Marxism, a child of the eighteenth-century Enlightenment, is committed to education, rationality and progress.

Of course, I agree with Jameson's point that we need to recover a history of society which hitherto has been misrepresented or rendered invisible. We need to develop a pedagogical political culture which seeks to endow the individual subject with some new heightened sense of its place in local, national and international realities. This is an extremely difficult project. In contemporary societies there is a struggle for interpretative power, and the prevailing ideologies limit the means by which individuals understand their material experiences. The modern culture-industry robs individuals of 'languages' for interpreting self and world by denying them the media for organizing their own experiences.

We urgently need to provide individuals and social groups with public 'spaces', in which they can deal with subliminally felt experiences and learn to understand these experiences on a more conscious, critical level.[9] History, literature, story-telling, therefore, have important functions because they provide discourses and opportunities for dealing with experiences by discussing them. Only experiences confirmed and corroborated through discussion and coped with as collective experience can be said to be truly experienced. According to this view consciousness is the historically concrete production of meaning, and every historical situation contains ideological ruptures and offers possibilities for social transformation.

□

Notes

Introduction

1 For a good introduction to these debates see K. Soper, *Humanism and Anti-Humanism*, London: Hutchinson, 1986.
2 C. Lévi-Strauss, *The Savage Mind*, London: Weidenfeld & Nicolson, 1966. The attack, Chapter 9 of the above book, is published as 'History and Dialectic' in R. and F. DeGeorge (eds), *The Structuralists from Marx to Lévi-Strauss*, New York: Anchor Books, 1972.
3 F. de Saussure, *Course in General Linguistics*, London: Fontana/Collins, 1974.
4 J. Lacan, *Écrits: A Selection*, London: Tavistock, 1977, p. 154.
5 See J. Culler, *Structuralist Poetics*, London: Routledge & Kegan Paul, 1975, p. 247.
6 It is important to differentiate clearly structuralism, structuralist Marxism and post-structuralism. By putting these three together as theories of structure (as opposed to action) many writers fail to underline the profoundly anti-Marxist nature of post-structuralism. See, for example, I. Craib, *Modern Social Theory: From Parsons to Habermas*, Brighton: Harvester Press, 1984.

Chapter I Lacan and psychoanalysis

1 S. Turkle, *Psychoanalytic Politics: Jacques Lacan and Freud's French Revolution*, London: Burnett Books, 1979, p. 67.
2 The article 'Freud and Lacan' is in L. Althusser, *Lenin and Philosophy and Other Essays*, London: New Left Books, 1971.
3 J. Lacan, *De la psychose paranoiaque dans ses rapports avec la personnalité*, Paris: Éditions du Seuil, 1975.

4 See J. Mitchell, *Psychoanalysis and Feminism*, London: Penguin, 1974.
5 S. Freud, *Beyond the Pleasure Principle*, Standard Edition, vol. 18, London: Hogarth Press, 1955.
6 J. Lacan, *Écrits: A Selection*, London: Tavistock, 1977, pp. 1–7.
7 A. Lemaire, *Jacques Lacan*, London: Routledge & Kegan Paul, 1977, p. 92.
8 Ibid., pp. 156–60.
9 Ibid., p. 166.
10 When the psychoanalytic session begins the analysand talks of himself or herself as an object. This is what Lacan calls 'empty speech'. In contrast, 'full speech' is when the subject coincides with the object, when *who* is talking coincides with *what* is being talked about.
11 See Laplanche and Leclair, 'The Unconscious: a Psychoanalytic Study', *Yale French Studies*, 48, 1972, pp. 118–75; also Lemaire, op. cit., Chapter 9.
12 Lacan, *Écrits*, p. 12.
13 J. Gallop, *Feminism and Psychoanalysis: The Daughter's Seduction*, London: Macmillan, 1982, p. 12.
14 Lacan, *Écrits*, p. 134.
15 D.W. Winnicott, *Playing and Reality*, London: Penguin, 1974, pp. 130–8.
16 Lacan, *Écrits*, p. 2.
17 J.-P. Sartre, *Being and Nothingness*, London: Methuen, 1957.
18 Lacan, *Écrits*, p. 119.
19 D. Archard, *Consciousness and the Unconscious*, London: Hutchinson, 1984, p. 25. This useful book contains a brief outline of Freud's theory and Sartre's critique of it, a clear exposition of Lacan and, finally, Timpanaro's critique of the 'Freudian slip'.
20 Lacan, *Écrits*, p. 161.
21 Ibid., p. 281.
22 A. Kojève, *Introduction to the Reading of Hegel: Lectures on the Phenomenology of Spirit*, assembled by Raymond Queneau, New York: Basic Books, Inc., 1969. It should be noted that for Hegel human consciousness was an aspect of *Geist*. Kojève brings Hegel down to earth and stresses the elements of labour, language and struggle.
23 Ibid., p. 37.
24 Ibid., p. 228.
25 Ibid., p. 206.
26 Ibid., p. 220.
27 Ibid., p. 58.
28 Lacan makes a distinction between need (a purely organic energy) and desire, the active principle of the physical processes. Desire always lies both beyond and before demand. To say that desire is beyond demand means that it transcends it, that it is eternal because it is impossible to satisfy. It is forever insatiable since it refers back to the ineffable, to the unconscious desire and the absolute lack it conceals. Every human action, even the most

altruistic, derives from a desire for recognition by the Other, from a wish for self-recognition in some form or another. Desire is the desire for desire, the desire of the Other.

29 J. Lacan, *The Four Fundamental Concepts of Psycho-analysis*, London: Penguin, 1979, pp. 196–7, 205. A useful account of the myth is given by K. Silverman, *The Subject of Semiotics*, Oxford: Oxford University Press, 1983, p. 151.

30 For a discussion of Lacan's phallocentrism and its implications see J. Mitchell and J. Rose (eds), *Feminine Sexuality: Jacques Lacan and the École Freudienne*, London: Macmillan, 1982.

31 Jameson believes that both psychoanalysis and Marxism depend fundamentally on history and story-telling. See F. Jameson, 'Imaginary and Symbolic in Lacan: Marxism, Psychoanalytic Criticism, and the Problem of the Subject', *Yale French Studies*, nos 55–6, 1977, pp. 338–95.

32 Wilhelm Reich (1897–1957), a prophet of sexual revolution, asserted that mental health is dependent on the capacity to experience orgasm and that mental illness is the result of inhibition of the capacity to experience orgasm. See C. Rycroft, *Reich*, London: Fontana, 1971.

33 M. Whitford, *Luce Irigaray: Philosophy in the Feminine*, London: Routledge, 1991, p. 88.

34 L. Irigaray, *Speculum of the Other Woman*, Ithaca: Cornell University Press, 1985, p. 89.

35 E. Grosz, *Jacques Lacan: A Feminist Introduction*, London: Routledge, p. 144.

Chapter 2 Derrida and deconstruction

1 J. Derrida, *Of Grammatology*, Baltimore and London: Johns Hopkins University Press, 1976; *Speech and Phenomena, and Other Essays on Husserl's Theory of Signs*, Evanston: Northwestern University Press, 1973; *Writing and Difference*, London: Routledge & Kegan Paul, 1978.

2 See T. Eagleton, *Literary Theory: An Introduction*, Oxford: Basil Blackwell, 1983, p. 130. I am indebted to this study for much of what follows.

3 Derrida's arguments are largely based on the chapter 'A Writing Lesson', in Lévi-Strauss's *Tristes Tropiques*, London: Penguin, 1976, p. 385.

4 For critiques of Saussure, Rousseau, Lévi-Strauss, see Derrida, *Of Grammatology*.

5 Derrida finds the same powerful metaphors at work in Husserl's meditations on language and thought; see Derrida's *Speech and Phenomena*.

6 See Derrida's 'Freud and the Scene of Writing', in *Writing and Difference*, p. 196. Derrida traces the emergence of the metaphor of writing through three texts placed on a thirty-year span in Freud's career: 'Project for a Scientific Psychology' (1895), *The Interpretation of Dreams* (1900) and 'Note on the Mystic Writing Pad' (1925).

7 J. Habermas, *Knowledge and Human Interests*, London: Heinemann Educational Books, 1972, Chapters 10–12.

8 Readers should be reminded that proper names such as Nietzsche, Freud, Heidegger, are a convenient fiction. For Derrida the names of authors indicate neither identities nor causes. Proper names are serviceable 'metonymic contractions' that refer to problems.

9 Nietzsche faces reflexive concerns that have parallels with modern relativism, but instead of stepping back, which he regards as impossible, he endorses paradox and incorporates reflexivity into his own writing. See H. Lawson, *Reflexivity: The Post-modern Predicament*, London: Hutchinson, 1985, p. 32.

10 Nietzsche, 'On Truth and Falsity in their Ultramoral Sense', in O. Levy (ed.), *The Complete Works of Friedrich Nietzsche*, New York, 1964.

11 G. Lakoff and M. Johnson, *Metaphors We Live By*, Chicago: University of Chicago Press, 1980.

12 C. Hill, *Reformation to Industrial Revolution*, London: Penguin, 1967.

13 M. Foucault, *Power/Knowledge: Selected Interviews and Other Writings 1972–1977*, edited by C. Gordon, Brighton: Harvester Press, 1980, pp. 68–70.

14 Gayatri Chakravorty Spivak, 'Translator's Preface', Derrida, *Of Grammatology*, p. lxxv. I have found this preface lucid and most helpful.

15 Ibid., p. lxxvii.

16 But, as Rée has pointed out, Derrida is so preoccupied with metaphor that he fails to remember such literary processes as narrative, story and plot. See J. Rée, 'Metaphor and Metaphysics: The End of Philosophy and Derrida', *Radical Philosophy*, 38, Summer 1984, p. 33. For an introduction to Derrida see D.C. Woods in *Radical Philosophy*, 21, Spring 1979.

17 Eagleton, op. cit., p. 138.

18 Ibid., p. 147.

19 V. Leitch, *Deconstructive Criticism: An Advanced Introduction*, London: Hutchinson, 1983, p. 246.

20 Post-structuralists, generally, favour authors who shift the textuality of their production, the ambiguity and the plurality of meanings, to the foreground. They admire authors like Rimbaud, Lautréamont, Robbe-Grillet, Joyce.

21 E.W. Said, 'Opponents, Audiences, Constituencies and Community', in H. Foster (ed.), *Postmodern Culture*, London: Pluto Press, 1985, p. 143.

22 Eagleton, op. cit., p. 148.

23 Lawson, op. cit., pp. 113–15.

24 F. Jameson, *Marxism and Form*, Princeton: Princeton University Press, 1971. See the note on p. 409. See also M. Ryan, *Marxism and Deconstruction*, Baltimore: Johns Hopkins University Press, 1982.

25 C. Norris, *Deconstruction: Theory and Practice*, London: Methuen, 1982, p. 84.

26 T. Eagleton, *Walter Benjamin or Towards a Revolutionary Criticism*, London:

New Left Books, 1981, p. 137. Eagleton may have since changed his mind. In *Literary Theory*, 1983, he writes: 'The widespread opinion that deconstruction denies the existence of anything but discourse, or affirms a realm of pure difference in which all meaning and identity dissolves, is a travesty of Derrida's own work and of *the most productive work which has followed from it*' (p. 148, my italics).

27 C. Norris, *Uncritical Theory: Postmodernism, Intellectuals and the Gulf War*, London: Lawrence & Wishart, 1992, p. 47. But for a very different view of Derrida see Stuart Sim, for whom the less satisfactory side of Derrida's project is 'the latent authoritarianism, the periodic air of nihilism, the drive towards solipsism and silence'. S. Sim, *Beyond Aesthetics: Confrontations with Poststructuralism and Postmodernism*, Hemel Hempstead: Harvester Wheatsheaf, 1992, p. 69.

Chapter 3 Foucault and the social sciences

 1 M. Foucault, 'Nietzsche, Genealogy, History', in D.F. Bouchard (ed.), *Language, Counter-Memory, Practice: Selected Essays and Interviews*, Oxford: Basil Blackwell, 1977.

 2 M. Foucault, *Madness and Civilization*, London: Tavistock, 1967.

 3 Ibid., p. 46.

 4 Ibid., p. 48.

 5 Ibid., p. 64.

 6 Ibid., p. 247.

 7 Ibid., p. 254.

 8 Derrida criticized Foucault for still being confined within the structuralist science of investigation through oppositions. See the essay entitled 'Cogito and the History of Madness', in J. Derrida, *Writing and Difference*, London: Routledge & Kegan Paul, 1978, p. 34.

 9 M. Foucault, *The Birth of the Clinic*, London: Tavistock, 1973.

10 M. Foucault, *The Order of Things*, London: Tavistock, 1970; *The Archaeology of Knowledge*, London: Tavistock, 1972.

11 M. Foucault, *Power/Knowledge: Selected Interviews and Other Writings 1972–1977*, edited by C. Gordon, Brighton: Harvester Press, 1980, p. 115.

12 M. Foucault (ed.), *I, Pierre Rivière... A Case of Parricide in the 19th Century*, London: Penguin, 1978.

13 M. Foucault, *Discipline and Punish*, London: Penguin, 1977.

14 Foucault, *Power/Knowledge*, p. 47.

15 Instrumental reason separates fact and value; it is concerned with discovering *how* to do things, not with what should be done. And so public affairs come to be regarded not as areas of discussion and choice but as technical problems to be solved by experts employing an instrumental rationality. The concept is explored in T. Adorno and M. Horkheimer,

Dialectic of Enlightenment, New York: Herder and Herder, 1972, and M. Horkheimer, *Eclipse of Reason*, New York: Seabury Press, 1974. The latter is a popularization of the former book.

16 M. Foucault, *The History of Sexuality; Volume One: An Introduction*, London: Penguin, 1981. The second volume is called *The Use of Pleasure*, Penguin, 1987; the third volume is *Care of the Self*, Penguin, 1990. Foucault died in June 1984, aged 57.

17 Foucault, *Power/Knowledge*, p. 98.

18 F. Nietzsche, *On the Genealogy of Morals*, New York: Vintage Books, 1969.

19 P. Dews, 'Power and Subjectivity in Foucault', *New Left Review*, 144, March–April 1984, p. 72.

20 L. Althusser, 'Ideology and Ideological State Apparatuses', in *Lenin and Philosophy and Other Essays*, London: New Left Books, 1971, p. 167.

21 For an excellent introduction to this debate see K. Soper, *Humanism and Anti-Humanism*, London: Hutchinson, 1986.

22 L. Althusser, *For Marx*, London: Penguin, 1969; *Reading Capital*, London: New Left Books, 1970. The latter contains a useful glossary of Althusserian terms.

23 M. Cousins and A. Hussain, *Michel Foucault*, London: Macmillan, 1984.

24 T. Benton, *The Rise and Fall of Structural Marxism: Louis Althusser and his Influence*, London: Macmillan, 1984. Benton suggests that the cognitive claims of science and its culturally produced character can perhaps be reconciled by a realist view of science, currently being developed by Roy Bhaskar and others, a view which was unavailable to Althusser. See R. Bhaskar, *A Realist Theory of Science*, Brighton: Harvester Press, 1978; *The Possibility of Naturalism*, Brighton: Harvester Press, 1979.

25 Foucault, *The Order of Things*, pp. 261–2. And see *Power/Knowledge*, p. 76.

26 Foucault, *Power/Knowledge*, p. 142.

27 Ibid., p. 62.

28 Ibid., p. 65.

29 Ibid., p. 85.

30 See M. Philp, 'Michel Foucault', in Q. Skinner (ed.), *The Return of Grand Theory in the Human Sciences*, Cambridge: Cambridge University Press, 1985, p. 79.

31 For the view that Foucault does not interrogate, as Marx did, the conditions of his own thought see M. Poster, *Foucault, Marxism and History*, Cambridge: Polity Press, 1984, p. 155.

32 Foucault, *Power/Knowledge*, p. 62.

33 Ibid., p. 203.

34 Ibid., pp. 207–8.

35 Ibid., p. 138.

36 See B. Jessop, *Nicos Poulantzas: State, Class and Strategy*, London: Macmillan, 1985.

37 See M. Ignatieff, 'State, Civil Society and Total Institutions: A Critique of Recent Social Histories of Punishment', in S. Cohen and A. Scull (eds), *Social Control and the State*, Oxford: Basil Blackwell, 1983.

38 N. Poulantzas, *State, Power, Socialism*, London: New Left Books, 1978. It has been said that this book is possibly the best exploration to date of the implications of Foucault's work for Marxist theory and politics; see B. Smart, *Foucault, Marxism and Critique*, London: Routledge & Kegan Paul, 1984, pp. 96–107.

39 Foucault, *Power/Knowledge*, p. 193.

40 R. Braidotti, 'The Ethics of Sexual Difference: The Case of Foucault and Irigaray', *Australian Feminist Studies*, Summer 1986, pp. 1–13.

41 See the Afterword by M. Foucault, 'The Subject and Power', in H. Dreyfus and P. Rabinow's book *Michel Foucault: Beyond Structuralism and Hermeneutics*, Brighton: Harvester Press, 1982.

42 For a useful summary see M. Foucault, *The History of Sexuality; Volume One*, pp. 139–40.

43 Foucault, *Power/Knowledge*, pp. 143–4.

Chapter 4 Some currents within post-structuralism

1 G. Deleuze and F. Guattari, *Anti-Oedipus: Capitalism and Schizophrenia*, New York: Viking Press, 1977. See also G. Deleuze, *Nietzsche and Philosophy*, London: Athlone Press, 1983.

2 Deleuze and Guattari, op. cit., p. 131.

3 J.-J. Lecercle, *Philosophy through the Looking-Glass: Language, Nonsense, Desire*, London: Hutchinson, 1985, p. 199.

4 V. Descombes, *Modern French Philosophy*, Cambridge: Cambridge University Press, 1980, p. 173.

5 We should note that both these modes of thought cut across the political divisions of left and right. See the remarkable book by M. Berman, *All That Is Solid Melts Into Air: The Experience of Modernity*, London: Verso, 1983, which is a brilliant study of modernization and modernism.

6 J. Habermas, 'The Entwinement of Myth and Enlightenment: Re-reading *Dialectic of Enlightenment*', *New German Critique*, 26, 1982, p. 28.

7 M. Foucault, *The History of Sexuality*, London: Allen Lane, 1979, pp. 92–102.

8 See D. Howard, *The Marxian Legacy*, London: Macmillan, 1977. Chapter 9 is on Lefort and Chapter 10 is on Castoriadis.

9 J.-F. Lyotard, *Discours/figure*, Paris: Klincksieck, 1971.

10 G. Lukács, *History of Class Consciousness*, London: Merlin Press, 1971.

11 L. Althusser, *For Marx*, London: Penguin, 1969, pp. 230, 248.

12 See E. Laclau, 'The Specificity of the Political', in *Politics and Ideology in Marxist Theory*, London: Verso, 1979, p. 51.

13 E.P. Thompson, *The Poverty of Theory and Other Essays*, London: Merlin Press, 1978. For a critical assessment of Thompson's work see P. Anderson, *Arguments within English Marxism*, London: Verso, 1980.

14 C. Claudin-Urondo, *Lenin and the Cultural Revolution*, Brighton: Harvester Press, 1977, p. 76.

15 For an elaboration of the points in this section see B. Smart, *Foucault, Marxism and Critique*, London: Routledge & Kegan Paul, 1983.

16 B.-H. Lévy, *La barbarie à visage humain*, Paris: Grasset, 1977.

17 These Borromean knots are made of interlocking circles; when one is cut, the whole chain of circles becomes undone. They are described and illustrated in S. Turkle, *Psychoanalytic Politics: Jacques Lacan and Freud's French Revolution*, London: Burnett Books, 1979, p. 235.

18 This section is indebted to Peter Dews, 'The *Nouvelle Philosophie* and Foucault', *Economy and Society*, 8, 2, May 1979. See also P. Dews, 'The "New Philosophers" and the End of Leftism', *Radical Philosophy*, 24, Spring 1980.

19 A. Glucksmann, *Les Maîtres penseurs*, Paris: Grasset, 1977.

20 These are the views of Jean-Marie Benoist, the author of *Marx est mort; The Structural Revolution*, London: Weidenfeld & Nicolson, 1978, and other works.

21 Even among British Marxists there is an increasing interest in religion. For example, Gareth Stedman-Jones has recently argued that socialism was religious before it was secular. In a sense, socialism was a post-Christian religion. See the work of Fourier and Saint-Simon.

22 T. Eagleton, *Literary Theory, An Introduction*, Oxford: Basil Blackwell, 1983, p. 142.

Chapter 5 Cixous, Irigaray, Kristeva: French feminist theories

1 H. Cixous and C. Clément, *The Newly Born Woman*, Manchester: Manchester University Press, 1986, p. 63.

2 Cixous's account is closely related to Derrida's reading of Hegel's *Phenomenology of Spirit*. See J. Derrida, *Glas*, London: University of Nebraska Press, 1986.

3 The best-known statement of this project is the essay 'The Laugh of the Medusa', in E. Marks and I. de Courtivron (eds), *New French Feminisms*, Brighton: Harvester Press, 1980.

4 Cixous and Clément, op.cit., p. 87.

5 M. Shiach, *Hélène Cixous: A Politics of Writing*, London: Routledge, 1991, p. 81.

6 For a list of English translations see ibid., p. 149.

7 The political implications of Lispector's writing are explored by Cixous in

her novel *Vivre l'orange/To Live the Orange*, bilingual text, Paris: des femmes, 1979.

8   J. Derrida, 'Différance', in *Margins of Philosophy*, Brighton: Harvester Press, 1982. See also S. Heath, 'Difference', *Screen*, 19, 3, 1978, pp. 51–112.

9   L. Irigaray, *Speculum of the Other Woman*, Ithaca: Cornell University Press, 1985; *The Sex Which is Not One*, Ithaca: Cornell University Press, 1985.

10 In this section I am indebted to M. Whitford, *Luce Irigaray: Philosophy in the Feminine*, London: Routledge, 1991, p. 73.

11 See L. Irigaray, 'The Poverty of Psychoanalysis', in M. Whitford (ed.), *The Irigaray Reader*, Oxford: Basil Blackwell, 1991.

12 See M. Whitford, 'Rereading Irigaray', in T. Brennan (ed.), *Between Feminism and Psychoanalysis*, London: Routledge, 1989, p. 108. In this book there is also the essay by Luce Irigaray, 'The Gesture in Psychoanalysis'.

13 *Speculum of the Other Woman* is divided into three main parts: the first part is a sharp critique of Freud's theory of femininity; the second part contains readings of Western philosophers from Plato to Hegel; and the third part is a close analysis of Plato's parable of the cave.

14 For some abrasive criticisms of Irigaray see T. Moi, *Sexual/ Textual Politics: Feminist Literary Theory*, London: Methuen, 1985, pp. 146–8.

15 T. Moi (ed.), *The Kristeva Reader*, Oxford: Basil Blackwell, 1986, p. 101. A comprehensive introduction to her work, the thirteen essays are representative of the three main areas of her writing: semiotics, psychoanalysis and politics.

16 Ibid., p. 93.

17 See J. Kristeva, 'Giotto's Joy' and 'Motherhood According to Giovanni Bellini', in *Desire in Language: A Semiotic Approach to Literature and Art*, Oxford: Basil Blackwell, 1981. Kristeva has claimed that it is not woman as such who is repressed in patriarchal society but motherhood. She has made several analyses of motherhood, in the form of the Madonna, in Western painting. The book also contains analyses of writings by Barthes, Beckett, Céline and Sollers.

18 J. Kristeva, *About Chinese Women*, London: Marion Boyars, 1977, p. 28.

19 E. Grosz, *Jacques Lacan: A Feminist Introduction*, London: Routledge, 1990, p. 154.

Chapter 6 **Lyotard and postmodernism**

1   J.-F. Lyotard, *The Postmodern Condition: A Report on Knowledge*, Manchester: Manchester University Press, 1984.

2   The term 'white-collar' is perhaps no longer useful as it puts together the well-paid positions at the top of the hierarchy and the mass of proletarianized workers. See the interesting chapter on clerical workers in

H. Braverman, *Labour and Monopoly Capital*, New York: Monthly Review Press, 1974.

3 The important questions are: what is transmitted? Who does the transmission and to whom? Through what medium and in what form? With what effect? Only a coherent set of answers to these questions can form a viable educational policy.

4 L. Wittgenstein, *Philosophical Investigations*, Oxford: Basil Blackwell, 1958. I have found the following books helpful: A. Janik and S. Toulmin, *Wittgenstein's Vienna*, New York: Simon & Schuster, 1973; H. Pitkin, *Wittgenstein and Justice*, Los Angeles: University of California Press, 1972.

5 Those utterances which do not describe but 'do' something, e.g. 'naming', 'betting', 'marrying', etc., J.L. Austin calls *performatives*. For a short and clear introduction to these concepts see D. Silverman and B. Torode, *The Material Word: Some Theories of Language and its Limits*, London: Routledge & Kegan Paul, 1980, Chapters 3 and 9.

6 Lyotard, op. cit., p. 17.

7 Introductions to the philosophy of science include A.F. Chalmers, *What is This Thing Called Science?*, Milton Keynes: The Open University Press, 1978; R. Harré, *The Philosophies of Science*, London: Oxford University Press, 1972.

8 Fredric Jameson has cogently observed that Lyotard is rather unwilling to posit the disappearance of the great master narratives – they could have passed underground, as it were, and may still be influencing our thinking and acting unconsciously. This persistence of buried master narratives is what Jameson calls 'the political unconscious'.

9 Lyotard, op. cit., p. 37.

10 Ibid., p. 45. About this statement Eagleton contentiously remarks: 'It is not difficult, then, to see a relation between the philosophy of J.L. Austin and IBM, or between the various neo-Nietzscheanisms of a post-structuralist epoch and Standard Oil.' See T. Eagleton, 'Capitalism, Modernism and Postmodernism', *New Left Review*, 152, July/August 1985, p. 63.

11 But resistance to change has a use. See T. Kuhn, *The Structure of Scientific Revolutions*, Chicago: University of Chicago Press, 1970, p. 65. For a discussion of Kuhn's views see I. Lakatos and A. Musgrave (eds), *Criticism and the Growth of Knowledge*, Cambridge: Cambridge University Press, 1970.

12 P. Bürger, *Theory of the Avant-Garde*, Manchester: Manchester University Press, 1984. I would like to suggest that the 'Foreword' to this book be read after the text.

13 H. Marcuse, 'On the Affirmative Character of Culture', in *Negations: Essays in Critical Theory*, London: Penguin, 1986.

14 There may be several avant-gardes. Bürger's term 'the historic avant-garde' refers to the historical uniqueness of the avant-garde movements of the 1920s such as Dadaism and Surrealism.

15 Bürger, op. cit., p. 66.

16 Bürger feels that the avant-gardistes' attempt to reintegrate art into the life process is itself a contradictory endeavour. An art no longer distinct from the praxis of life but wholly absorbed in it will lose the capacity to criticize it, along with its distance. Perhaps the distance between art and praxis of life is a necessary free space within which alternatives to what exists can become conceivable? See Bürger, op. cit., p. 54.

17 See J. Habermas, 'Modernity versus Postmodernity', *New German Critique*, 22, Winter 1981.

18 D. Bell, *The Cultural Contradictions of Capitalism*, New York: Basic Books, 1976.

19 Lyotard, op. cit., p. xxiii.

20 Lyotard in an interview with Christian Descamps.

21 Lyotard, op. cit., p. 37.

22 See the work of the anthropologist Robin Horton, for example, 'African Traditional Thought and Western Science', in B. Wilson (ed.), *Rationality*, Oxford: Basil Blackwell, 1970.

23 F. Jameson, 'Postmodernism, or the Cultural Logic of Capital', *New Left Review*, 146, July/August 1984.

24 Bürger, op. cit., p. 69.

25 For debates between Ernst Bloch, Georg Lukács, Bertolt Brecht, Walter Benjamin and Theodor Adorno see *Aesthetics and Politics*, with an afterword by Fredric Jameson, London: New Left Books, 1977.

26 For a concise description of Adorno's position see G. Rose, *The Melancholy Science: An Introduction to the Thought of Theodor W. Adorno*, London: Macmillan, 1978. See particularly Chapter 6, 'The Dispute over Modernism'.

27 See W. Benjamin, 'What is Epic Theatre?', in *Illuminations*, edited by Hannah Arendt, London: Fontana/Collins, 1973.

28 C. Norris, *Uncritical Theory: Postmodernism, Intellectuals and the Gulf War*, London: Lawrence & Wishart, 1992, p. 85.

29 I. Kant, *Critique of Judgement*, London: Oxford University Press, 1978.

30 J.-F. Lyotard, *The Differend: Phrases in Dispute*, Manchester: Manchester University Press, 1988.

31 Norris, op. cit., p. 170.

32 The rhetoric of liberation has been denounced with passionate ambivalence by M. Foucault in *History of Sexuality; Volume One: An Introduction*, London: Allen Lane, 1979. Totality and totalization have also been rejected by many contemporary theorists; see M. Jay, *Marxism and Totality: The Adventures of a Concept from Lukács to Habermas*, Oxford: Polity Press, 1984.

33 Lyotard, op. cit., p. 60.

34 R. Rorty, 'Habermas and Lyotard on Post-modernity', *Praxis International*, 4, 1, April 1984, p. 40.

35 M. Morris, *The Pirate's Fiancée: Feminism, Reading, Postmodernism*, London: Verso, 1988, p. 16.
36 N. Fraser and L. Nicholson, 'Social Criticism without Philosophy: An Encounter between Feminism and Postmodernism', in Andrew Ross (ed.), *Universal Abandon? The Politics of Postmodernism*, Edinburgh: Edinburgh University Press, 1988.
37 S. Firestone, *The Dialectic of Sex*, New York: Bantam, 1970.
38 M. Rosaldo, 'Woman, Culture and Society: A Theoretical Overview', in M. Rosaldo and L. Lamphere (eds), *Woman, Culture and Society*, Stanford: Stanford University Press, 1974.
39 N. Chodorow, *The Reproduction of Mothering: Psychoanalysis and the Sociology of Gender*, Berkeley: University of California Press, 1978.

Chapter 7 Baudrillard and some cultural practices

1 J. Baudrillard, *Le Systeme des objets*, Paris: Denoël Gonthier, 1968. For a most useful collection of writings see J. Baudrillard, *Selected Writings*, ed. Mark Poster, Oxford: Polity Press, 1988.
2 J. Baudrillard, *La Société de consommation*, Paris: Gallimard, 1970.
3 J. Baudrillard, *The Mirror of Production*, St Louis: Telos, 1975.
4 J. Baudrillard, *De la Séduction*, Paris: Denoël Gonthier, 1979.
5 W. Benjamin, 'The Work of Art in the Age of Mechanical Reproduction', in Hannah Arendt (ed.), *Illuminations*, London: Fontana/Collins, 1973.
6 J. Baudrillard, *Simulations*, New York: Semiotext(e), 1983.
7 J. Baudrillard, 'The Ecstasy of Communication', in Hal Foster (ed.), *Postmodern Culture*, London: Pluto Press, 1985, p. 130.
8 D. Kellner, *Jean Baudrillard: From Marxism to Postmodernism and Beyond*, Cambridge: Polity Press, 1989, p. 73.
9 J. Fiske, *Reading the Popular*, Boston: Unwin Hyman, 1989, p. 180.
10 J. Baudrillard, 'The Beaubourg-Effect: Implosion and Deterrence', *October*, 20, Spring 1982.
11 J. Baudrillard, 'The Masses: The Implosion of the Social in the Media', *New Literary History*, 16, 3, 1985.
12 A. Kroker and D. Cook, *The Postmodern Scene: Excremental Culture and Hyper-Aesthetics*, New York: St Martin's Press, 1986. See also A. and M. Kroker (eds), *Body Invaders: Sexuality and the Postmodern Condition*, London: Macmillan, 1988.
13 C. Norris, *Uncritical Theory: Postmodernism, Intellectuals and the Gulf War*, London: Lawrence & Wishart, 1992.
14 Ibid., p. 194.
15 J.-F. Lyotard, *Discours/figure*, Paris: Klincksieck, 1971.

16 C. Jencks, *The Language of Post-Modern Architecture*, London: Academy Editions, 1984.
17 R. Venturi et al., *Learning from Las Vegas*, Cambridge, Mass.: MIT Press, 1977.
18 K. Frampton, 'Towards a Critical Regionalism', in H. Foster (ed.), *Postmodern Culture*, op. cit.
19 There is a photograph of the Frank Gehry House in F. Jameson, *Postmodernism, or, The Cultural Logic of Late Capitalism*, London: Verso, 1991, pp. 110–11.
20 R. Boyne, 'The Art of the Body in the Discourse of Postmodernity', *Theory, Culture and Society*, 5, 1988, p. 527.
21 This painting is discussed by Douglas Crimp in Foster (ed.), *Postmodern Culture*, op. cit., pp. 45–53.
22 S. Connor, *Postmodernist Culture: An Introduction to Theories of the Contemporary*, Oxford: Basil Blackwell, 1989, p. 92.
23 Jameson, op. cit., p. 96.
24 Ibid., p. 74.
25 C. Metz, *Psychoanalysis and Cinema*, London: Macmillan, 1982.
26 L. Mulvey, *Visual and Other Pleasures*, London: Macmillan, 1989.
27 N. Denzin, 'Blue Velvet: Postmodern Contradictions', *Theory, Culture and Society*, 5, 1988, p. 461.
28 J.-F. Lyotard, *The Postmodern Condition*, Manchester: Manchester University Press, 1984.

Conclusion

1 F. Jameson, *The Political Unconscious: Narrative as a Socially Symbolic Act*, London: Methuen, 1981. For a useful introduction to this book see W. Dowling, *Jameson, Althusser, Marx*, London: Methuen, 1984.
2 Jameson claims that political criticism is the absolute horizon of all interpretation. Literary works are to be grasped not primarily as objective structures but as *symbolic* practices.
3 It has been remarked that Jameson's typical intellectual habit is to consider two or more apparently incompatible theses, show how each is symptomatic of a real historical condition and thus try to dissolve the contradictions between them. See T. Eagleton, 'The Idealism of American Criticism', *New Left Review*, 127, May/June 1981, pp. 60–5.
4 F. Jameson, 'Postmodernism, or the Cultural Logic of Capital', *New Left Review*, 146, July/August 1984, p. 58.
5 E. Mandel, *Late Capitalism*, London: Verso, 1978, p. 184.
6 Jameson, 'Postmodernism', p. 57.

7 For a study of the genealogy of the concept of hegemony see E. Laclau and
   C. Mouffe, *Hegemony and Socialist Strategy: Towards a Radical Democratic
   Politics*, London: Verso, 1985.
8 See the articles by Habermas, Jameson and Said and others in the anthology
   edited by H. Foster, *Postmodern Culture*, London: Pluto Press, 1985.
9 O. Negt and A. Kluge, *Öffentlichkeit und Erfahrung*, Frankfurt-on-Main,
   1972.

□

Index

203

Index